Aubrey Beardsley

A foot-note. From *The Savoy*, No. 2.

Aubrey Beardsley

Imp of the Perverse

Stanley Weintraub

AN AUTHORS GUILD BACKINPRINT.COM EDITION

Aubrey Beardsley
Imp of the Perverse

AN AUTHORS GUILD BACKINPRINT.COM EDITION
Published by iUniverse.com, Inc.

For information address:
iUniverse.com, Inc.
620 North 48th Street, Suite 201
Lincoln, NE 68504-3467
www.iuniverse.com

ISBN: 0-595-00808-9

Printed in the United States of America

I have one aim - the grotesque.
If I am not grotesque I am nothing.
- AUBREY BEARDSLEY

What exquisite indecency,
Select, supreme, severe, an art!
The art of knowing how to be
Part lewd, aesthetical in part,
And *fin-de-siècle* essentially.
- ARTHUR SYMONS

Contents

Author's Note

In a front-page review in the *New York Times Book Review* in 1967, art critic John Russell wrote kindly of *Beardsley* that "as a biography—a life's story" the book "needs no successor." But it now does, and here it is.

Aubrey Beardsley: Imp of the Perverse began as an updating of the original biography but the amount of additional material at hand and the need for reinterpretation of earlier material made mere updating impractical. New letters have come to light, and the manuscripts of earlier letters not available except in garbled or expurgated printed texts have emerged. Memoirs and letters of Beardsley's contemporaries previously unavailable have now been published, or become accessible. And the climate for publishing has become far more receptive to truth in biography, however explicit.

An editor involved in the publication of the earlier life cautiously put aside certain relevant textual and pictorial material on grounds that "lady librarians" would be repelled, and sales would thus suffer. One can hope that female readers—lady librarians included—are, if not were, more sophisticated than that, and can accept as well as understand the permutations of Beardsley's complex and tragic genius, here presented in much more detail than before.

Aubrey Beardsley sets out to enrich our view of the marvelous boy as human being and as artist—to correct the chronology of his short life in some places, supplement scanty data in other places, fill out biographical lacunae where possible, and provide appropriate inferences from the documentation available. In places my judgments or interpretations of data differ from those of other critics, editors and interpreters of Beardsley. But I have relied on the documents, while in some cases not accepting the rearranging of hypothetical dates or the "normalizing" of texts of Beardsley's letters, the latter practice flattening out the writer's personality in order to preserve orthographical or grammatical rules he ignored. And I have attempted to refrain from speculations that are novelistic or propagandistic rather than biographical.

What is known about Beardsley—but for trivia and redundancies—is here. Further, the life of an artist, however detailed, is bloodless if not reconstructed in the context of his art. Here that context is many times more full than in the original biography. Yet no biography is as complete as its author would like it to be, and it is likely that this one, too, will need a successor as Beardsley's life and art become meaningful anew to new audiences, and as further material about his life and art inevitably emerges. Until then I leave this book to lady librarians and other readers.

Stanley Weintraub

Preface

When a memorial bust of John Keats was unveiled in Hampstead Church in July 1894, the literary and artistic élite of London gathered there to do homage to the poet. Keats, who had died of tuberculosis in 1821 at the age of twenty-five years and four months, had in his posthumous fame triumphed over the jeers of his detractors so completely that only because of their hostility to him were some of them still remembered by a later generation.

As the congregation streamed out of the church on the hill, a young man broke clear of the throng and cut across the graveyard, awkwardly stumbling over the grassy mounds as he hurried away. Elegantly dressed in a cutaway coat and a tall silk hat that accentuated the leanness of his gaunt frame, he carried lemon-yellow gloves in his long white hands, his slender wrists showing beyond the cuffs. To a lady who greeted him the young dandy lifted his hat, exposing a tortoiseshell-hued crown, the hair curiously combed down onto his narrow, bony brow almost into his eyes. It was Aubrey Beardsley, already a celebrity at the age of twenty-one, artist-in-chief of the newest literary sensation, the "scandalous" *Yellow Book*. Stooping as he went on among the mounds of the dead, he seemed to be catching his breath as if he had already run a long race.[1]

Keats, who had lived his few creative years amid the attacks of critics, once said that he could "die content" if he could "upset the drawling of the blue stocking literary world." At the end, his lungs nearly gone, he had retreated into futile Mediterranean self-exile. "There is no doubt that an

English winter would put an end to me," he wrote Shelley. The lines could have been written by Beardsley, for so would it be with him, too, dying like Keats of tuberculosis in his twenty-sixth year, after outraging the bluestocking prudes with his writing and his art, and withdrawing to perish under a Mediterranean sun.

A fortnight after Beardsley's death in 1898 the *New York Times* had already editorially dismissed him to oblivion:

> . . . Granting that Mr. Beardsley had originality, we can concede to him nothing more. He was at his very best when he produced women of the lowest type and men who were satyrs. Beardsley was incapable of creating anything belonging to a higher and a better art. His influence lowered taste and did not elevate it. His influence was only a passing one. Already his work is well-nigh forgotten. . . . The grotesque and the bizarre, being the unnatural and the abnormal, never can be made to live. . . . A coming age will wonder why there was any brief interest taken in Beardsley's work. It was a passing fad, a little sign of decadence and nothing more. Our pity may come, however, for the long-continued bodily sufferings of the man, and sorrow for one whose work showed that his brain and his hand were affected.

Yet, even in his own lifetime, some of Beardsley's contemporaries were already of a different point of view. John Lane had appended to his Bodley Head edition of *The Works of Max Beerbohm*, a facetiously titled collection brought out in 1895, when Max was a precocious twenty-three, a "Preface to the Bibliography." Mocking pretentious Victorian biographical style Lane recorded the momentous events which occurred at the time of his subject's birth. His choice of events was limited, but significant; in fact there was apparently only one worth recording:

On the day upon which Mr. Beerbohm was born, there appeared, in the first column of *The Times*, this announcement:

> On (Wednesday) the 21st August, at Brighton, the wife of V. P. Beardsley, Esq., of a son.

The mockery emphasized the fame already associated with the name of that son of Vincent Beardsley, a fame noted with as much seriousness as satire in "Diminuendo," the concluding essay of Max's small book, in which the author confessed more prophetically than he knew that he belonged to the "Beardsley period." By the mid-nineties Aubrey Beardsley had been mentioned in the press perhaps as much as any contemporary, but at the time the laconic birth notice appeared it seemed likely that the only other time his name would appear in print would be in the notice of his death.

Vignette in *Bon-Mots of Smith and Sheridan* (1893)

1

Beginnings   *1872-1888*

Aubrey Vincent Beardsley entered life inauspiciously. He was sickly from the start, and his mother's confinement, instead of being concluded by his birth, was extended by puerperal fever. When Mrs. Beardsley was at last able to come downstairs, it was assumed she was well enough to be told that her husband had lost all his money. It was only one more of her marital misfortunes, the earliest of which would seem to have occurred when she first met Vincent Paul Beardsley on the pier in Brighton.

A Brighton beauty, Ellen Pitt—because of her extreme slenderness she was known locally as "the bottomless Pitt"—should have been impervious to the tinsel charms of resort romance among the piers and pavilions; yet she continued to see Beardsley, usually in the Pavilion Gardens. Their meetings often had to be clandestine. Her parents objected to the match, for although Vincent Beardsley—the son of a jeweller—called himself a gentleman, it was not so much because he had some unearned income as because he had no trade. Nevertheless, romance won out over prudence, and the marriage took place in Brighton, in the Church of St. Nicholas, on 12 October 1870. On their honeymoon Beardsley was sued for breach of promise by the widow of a clergyman. To keep the scandal from becoming more public than it already was, the bride's family intervened and forced the bridegroom to sell some houses along the Euston Road which had been left to him. Thus the damages were paid, and an uneasy marriage begun.

Witty, charming and musically gifted, Ellen Pitt Beardsley at first had little chance to use her talents. Ten months after the wedding her daughter Mabel was born, followed almost exactly a year later, on 21 August 1872, by the birth of Aubrey, whose christening was delayed for several months because of the illness of his mother. By that time Vincent Beardsley had managed to complete the squandering of his grandfather's modest fortune. As soon as she was in better health, Ellen had to find employment so that she could help maintain her children. For a while she worked as a governess and music teacher for children of her friends; and her husband, finding no satisfactory alternative to employment, worked first for the West India and Panama Telegraph Company, and then spent nearly ten years in the employ of brewers in the London area—jobs his wife obtained for him through her relatives.

Work made Vincent Beardsley even more difficult. He was jealous of his wife's friendships, brought his salary home irregularly, had a vicious temper and beat his children. When her finances were particularly desperate, Ellen would work all day on a penny bun and a glass of milk, then come home to care for her home and her two frail children. Her earliest memories of Aubrey as a toddler were associated with his fragility. He was "like a delicate piece of Dresden china" to her, and once as a child, she remembered, he used a twig to help himself up a steep flight of stairs.

Ellen Beardsley thought she recognized musical precocity in her son before he was a year old, for he would crawl to the piano when she was playing, and—so she liked to think—"beat perfect time" with a block.[1] When he grew older she gave him piano lessons in the early evening after she returned from work. He was already playing Chopin for her while he was still too young for school.

There was also a sort of home music-appreciation course, probably not nearly so burdensome as it might seem to us today, for it was the pre-electronic age of home entertainment. In the evening, Mrs. Beardsley gave piano concerts for her husband and children from a book of miniature programs she had made up, each six pieces in length. "In this way they did not hear the same thing too often," she remembered. ". . . I would not let them hear rubbish, and it was the same with books. I would not let them read rubbish."[2] Books seemed always to have been part of Aubrey's existence, perhaps because in his loneliness as a child he had such need of them; one of his schoolmasters was later told that "he never in a sense learnt to read, but seemed to be perfectly conversant with the English language from the

Sketch from *Becket* in
the *Pall Mall Budget* (1893)

first moment of handling a book."[3] If the awesome tale meant anything at all, it at least indicated that Aubrey was able to read at an impressively early age.

At four he was taken to a symphony concert at the Crystal Palace, and once accompanied his mother to Westminster Abbey for a service: Mrs. Beardsley was a "sermon-taster" and would visit any church where the preaching was reputed to be good. Aubrey, bored as we may imagine with the homilies, could at least admire the stained-glass windows and the forest of busts. When they left the Abbey, Aubrey tugged his mother's hand and wondered, "Mummy, shall I have a bust or a stained-glass window when I am dead? For I may be a great man someday."

"Which would you like, darling?"

He thought it over. "A bust, I think," he said finally, "because I am rather good-looking."[4]

Ellen Beardsley's working hours began stretching into more and more of the day and evening as she acquired a somewhat fashionable but poorly remunerative circle of pupils. It meant leaving her children alone for greater periods—a situation alleviated only when Aubrey became old enough for school. He was sent to Hamilton Lodge, a boarding school near Brighton, close to his grandfather (who apparently paid the fees) and to Miss Lambe, his great-aunt, who theoretically could look in on the boy to see how he was doing, and corroborate the reports in his letters home. It was the autumn of 1878; he was just past six years old, but could write, in neat, oversized child's script, a letter full of information:

My dear Mother
    I hope you are quite well. I am getting on quite well. . . . The boys do not tease me. . . . I do not do very many lessons. I go lots of times in to the playground. . . . I am very happy. . . .[5]

Soon he was writing his mother and sister that he had pudding every day, that the drilling master's regular Thursday visit to march them on the school lawn was an occasion he looked forward to, and that the school's dog, Fido, came out with them on their walks and drills. Although his family worried about his tubercular tendencies, he was apparently doing as well as he claimed, and thrived through the autumn. At Christmas he sent his uncom-municative father a present he had made—a bookmark decorated with a

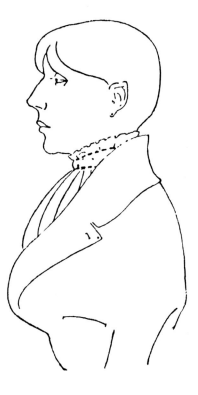

Self-portrait in the form of a bust (1896)

Chapter heading for *Le Morte d'Arthur* (1893-94)

single holly-wreathed word. "It is Affection," he explained, "because I love you."

Life at Hamilton Lodge continued happily. He went—inexplicably—to a local wedding with his schoolmates and, more predictably, to a circus and a bazaar, and a garden fête where the children had tea, cake and eggs, and played all afternoon. The circus and its aftermath were great events. "There were two large elephants who did all kinds of funny things," he wrote his mother. "Last night Miss Wise let us make a bonfire in the playground, and then the boys let off some fireworks. We had great fun and stayed up a little later than usual. I am quite well and happy. Please send me some more money. Mine is nearly gone. . . ."

At Valentine's Day he reported receiving four valentines, which the boys were permitted to open only after dinner; and on Good Friday they had hot cross buns at breakfast. Classes were not onerous, and were interspersed with play, and walks to regional points of interest. One outing was to a "Temperance Fête" at the Chinese Gardens, where Mr. Hannington, a local clergyman, spoke, and then accompanied the boys back to school to play with them in the gymnasium. The class was rehearsing a play it was going to present for the "breaking-up party" to close the school year, and Aubrey and another boy were planning to play a piano duet for the same program. His early reports on his musical progress at school were good-humoredly negative. "At first Miss Barnett was nearly bald with teaching me," he wrote his sister. "I hope I shall begin a tune soon." His mother began sending him music, some of it formidable. "I am learning 'Fading Away,' " he wrote, "and then I shall begin the sonata."

The second year at Hamilton Lodge, when Aubrey was seven, began equally happily, with an unexpected gift of five shillings from his grandfather. Again there was a round of autumnal class jaunts, highlighted by a harvest festival—a traditional "harvest home"—and still no evidence appeared in any of his letters of the illness for which his teachers had been fortified with stocks of appropriate medicines.

Aubrey had begun drawing what he saw and what he imagined—cathedrals, a carnival and a long series of grotesque figures in color. He experimented with Gothic lettering, and wrote pseudo-Chaucerian verses. He had matured in other ways as well; the outward signs of illness his frail body was still suppressing seemed to produce in him a capacity for stoicism.

When for some reason he was beaten by a schoolmistress to force him to cry, he refused, and she gave in.[6] But stoicism could not suppress the symptoms of tuberculosis and, in 1881, when he was nine, Aubrey had to leave school.

For two years he lived at Epsom "to get strong," before returning to his parents in London, where he appeared with his sister at musical entertainments arranged by their mother at the homes of friends. The two children played piano duets, including nocturnes Aubrey had composed; and Mabel initiated her career as an actress by reciting. Rather than mere opportunities for Ellen Beardsley to display the precocious talents of her children, these may have been benefit concerts of a kind, for the family was nearer to destitution than Beardsley's parents pretended.

Before Aubrey was eleven, even his drawing talents had to be called upon. Later his mother was proud of his having earned £30 in six weeks by sketching little Kate Greenaway* figures on menus and guest cards for a fashionable wedding in Scotland; it was a considerable fee for a boy who should have been in grammar school.

Even before his sketches for the wedding in Scotland, Aubrey had done more than a dozen drawings based on illustrations in Kate Greenaway books, which his mother's acquaintance Lady Henrietta Pelham commissioned to help relieve the Beardsleys' financial distresses. "I often do little drawings from my own imagination," he wrote her on forwarding them; "but in doing figures the limbs are apt to be stiff and out of proportion and I can only get them right by copying." Mature beyond his years[7] he added, "I find it very difficult to be persevering but I think I am a little more so than I used to be. I am very fond of drawing and should very much like to make you anything for a Bazaar."[8]

Aubrey also drew dinner place cards, including "Mr. Weller," "Dick

Chapter heading for *Le Morte d'Arthur* (1893-94)

---

*Kate Greenaway designed and illustrated her own books, and her *Under the Window* was a favorite in Aubrey's childhood. (It may have been a subconscious stimulus for the title of a story he was to write, design and illustrate during his few adult years—*Under the Hill*.) Although there were delicacy and a Victorian charm in her flowers, garlands, wreaths, gardens and processions, her children were seldom differentiated by sex, their dancing feet and skipping shoes peering out from under long frocks seldom seen on children the ages of those she drew. This may have been an over-concession to Victorian prudery, but more likely it concealed Kate Greenaway's inability to draw lifelike limbs.

Swiveller," "Mr. Winkle on the ice," "Artful Dodger," "Pecksniff," "Barnaby Rudge" and—misspelled from *Bleak House*—"Little Joe." Each featured, to the left of a rectangular blank for a name, a different humorous miniature of a Dickens character, and each captured the Dickensian flavor as effectively as the original Dickens illustrators had done. Whether Beardsley had read the novels, or only studied the pictures, they were considerable achievements for a boy of ten. But he was isolated in an unnatural life for a child, his only education coming from his own reading and drawing, and his glimpses of the fashionable world. It ended when his mother became too sick herself to make any further pretense of being able to care for her children. Just before his twelfth birthday Aubrey and his sister were sent to Brighton, to stay with Miss Lambe, their mother's strange old aunt, in her house in Lower Rock Gardens.

Life at Miss Lambe's house was hardly more than custodial care, and sometimes resembled something out of the more grotesque pages in Dickens. The children were prodded out of bed at daybreak, and sent to sleep when darkness came. They had no toys, and only one book, Green's *Short History of England*, which set Aubrey off imaginatively to write his own history of the Spanish Armada. Their great-aunt's chief outside interest was going to church, and since she considered High Church people as the only human beings who had leave to enter the gates of heaven, she went regularly and often to Brighton's Church of the Annunciation, in Washington Street. It was the grandest outing Mabel and Aubrey were permitted.

Although Miss Lambe knew that her two lonely and ignored charges were precocious, she pretended that they were backward; it was easier to take care of them that way. Ill in a London nursing home, Mrs. Beardsley could not visit them; but her father lived nearby in Brighton, at 12 Buckingham Road, where Aubrey was born, and sometimes came to see the children. Once Mr. Pitt found them sitting patiently on their little high-backed chairs, with nothing to do. "The children can't be happy like that," he observed. "Oh, no," Miss Lambe assured him confidently: they were "as happy as birds."

"Then all I can say," he retorted, "is that they have damned contented minds."[9]

For Aubrey it was merely another lesson in stoicism, but it was too much for Grandfather Pitt. In the fourth month of Aubrey's stay in Brighton he

Pierrot and cat, from *St. Paul's* (1893, but not used until 1895)

was partially extricated from Miss Lambe's house, becoming a day boy at the Brighton Grammar School in November 1884, with the fees paid by his grandfather. It was cheaper than boarding him, but it brought him back to Lower Rock Gardens each evening. By January he was spared even that; he became a boarding student. He had just about lost touch with any kind of home life, and his unhappiness during his first days at the school, away now even from his sister, was misinterpreted by the other boys as normal homesickness.

C. B. Cochran, later a famous theatre impresario, remembered that at Beardsley's first day at dinner he sat next to him—"a delicate-looking boy, thin, red-haired, and with a slight stoop. He was a particularly quick talker, [who] used his hands to gesticulate, and altogether had an un-English air about him."[10] Another schoolmate recalled him on his first day as a boarder "sitting in a corner of the 'day-room' looking the picture of misery and showing very evident signs of homesickness," and attracting additional attention because of his curious reddish-brown hair, brushed smooth and flat over his forehead, emphasizing his high, narrow brow. He wore knickerbockers, exhibiting a pair of frail, broomstick-like calves, about which he was so chaffed by the other boys, who could not see death in his gaunt frame, that after the term ended and he left on vacation he never wore knickerbockers to school again. When he came back, he was in long trousers and Eton jacket, and his mood had improved.

"I don't know why," a friend of his at school later wrote, "but he always [while at school in Brighton] reminded me of a squirrel—yes—there was a manner about him that certainly gave me that impression. His head was always in a book when he had a moment to spare and I often caught him with his long hands drawn up on one side of his face like the paws of a squirrel." The boys called him "Weasel," perhaps because of his long, bony face and alert, dark eyes—"the oldest eyes I have ever seen," said a classmate, R. Thurston Hopkins, "older than the world . . . once he took up a book you could see the intelligence retreat and retreat from those eyes, until the mind deserted them to adventure in space and eternity. I often noticed him lose his identity in this way in the classroom. It was a disconcerting habit; but the masters understood him after a while and would wait for his return."[11]

Once the masters understood their strange, precocious charge, and he

Vignette from *Bon-Mots of Charles Lamb and Douglas Jerrold* (1893)

became part of the scene to the other boys, Aubrey experienced some of his happiest years. Fortunately, Brighton Grammar School included A. W. King, who doubled as Science Master and Senior House Master. King first discovered Aubrey lecturing the other boys on Shakespeare's plays, an arrogance belying his unease, and quickly dissipated by his classification exams, which proved that, whatever he knew of the tragedies, comedies and histories, he did not know the multiplication tables. Explaining that it was entirely unnecessary, as long as one could count money, and had enough of it to count, he was squelched by an order to stop chattering, and to report for classes in the Lower School.

That evening after tea there was an unnatural silence where sounds of play were usually heard, impelling the House Master to investigate what could only suggest trouble. He found the pale, bony new boy, uncowed by his demotion, entertaining the others with a monologue about the absurdity of a person of his mature years being placed in classes with babies to learn such unimportant skills as spelling and the multiplication tables. Although King enjoyed the performance himself, he thought first of the need to maintain discipline. Aubrey was sent to the Master's sitting-room with orders to tidy up the bookcase and wait there until King arrived. It was the beginning of one of his happiest friendships.

Too frail for games, and without the stamina to be a good swimmer, Aubrey kept his place as a force in school life through King's encouraging him to use his talent as a performer. King had a seemingly incurable addiction to theatricals, in which he quickly enlisted the boy's eager services, and even turned his bent for drawing malicious caricatures of his classmates into approved channels. "Why not give a Shakespearian recital?" he suggested. "And why not try lightning sketches on a blackboard with chalk, or on paper with coloured chalks? And instead of giving annoyance to your victims by these innumerable sketches, use your talents to amuse and instruct without giving offence."[12] Nevertheless, Beardsley continued to caricature the masters as well as the boys, and published some of his sketches in *Past and Present*, the school magazine.

He had a barely satiable appetite for books, and King's personal collection was exactly what he had been seeking, for he preferred drama over everything else. All boys' books except those about pirates he then thought unworthy of his attention, and Dickens, whom he now dismissed as a

"Aeneas on the Links,"
in the *Pall Mall Budget* (1893)

"Cockney Shakespeare," bored him. Congreve and Wycherley were his favorite playwrights — strange reading for so young a boy.* Butler's *Erewhon* was offered to him with reservations that it might be too deep, yet he was at the same time going through Carlyle's *The French Revolution*, Boccaccio's *The Decameron*, the poems of Thomas Chatterton and the tales and poems of Poe. (Later he interpreted several of Poe's stories in striking illustrations—"The Murders in the Rue Morgue," "The Black Cat," "The Masque of the Red Death," "The Fall of the House of Usher.") He showed his feelings about one of his school reading assignments when he got as far as the second book of *The Aeneid*, 1886. Above a caricature of a blasé, pipe-smoking late-Victorian Aeneas, dangling over the roofs and walls of Troy from a small balloon attached to the visor of his helmet, Aubrey added a two-stanza limerick:

> I Aeneas once thought
> He'd have some sport
> So he tied a balloon to his topper
> And he soared up so high
> In the beautifull [sic] sky
> That all thought he'd come down a great flopper.
>
> II If he did, no one knows
> But I really suppose
> That the hero still hangs in the air
> Or has gone for a turn
> To the moon with Jules Verne
> And will write if his time he can spare.[13]

When he visited the home of R. Thurston Hopkins, at Worthing, he borrowed an armful of adult books, but came away most pleased with the juvenile *Lives of All the Notorious Pirates*. It delighted him for weeks, as he read and reread it; while it inspired as well a series of pirate games among the boys. For a week or two afterwards, Hopkins recalled, their speech was larded with pirate jargon. "We addressed other boys as 'ill-looked dogs,' and I remember Beardsley hissing in my ears such imprecations as 'Harkee ye rogue, you will be hang'd because ye have a damn'd hanging look.' "[14]

---

*He would buy the Mermaid volumes of Elizabethan and Restoration dramatists as they were published, and during holidays from school would do dramatic readings from them with his sister.

Grotesque in *Bon-Mots of Lamb and Jerrold* (1893)

Aubrey was inspired to write several pirate tales and poems for school publications, one a ballad called "The Valiant":

> The *Valiant* was a noble bark
>   As ever ploughed the sea,
> A noble crew she also had
>   As ever there might be.
>
> When once at night upon the deep
>   The *Valiant* did sail
> Her captain saw a pirate ship
>   By the moonlight dim and pale. . . .*[15]

There was little sign of the later Beardsley in the verses; but in June 1885, when they were published in the school magazine, he was still only twelve.

He was not much older when he found an admirer in a girl in a nearby boarding school, two letters to whom are among the most recent Beardsley manuscripts to surface.[16] The much-folded sheets to Miss Felton are covered with a crazy-quilt of caricatures, among which are the texts of playful letters from Brighton Grammar School, the second of them addressed to "My own Love." The letters are a travesty of amorous missives. Aubrey asks Miss Felton to hold a handkerchief in her right hand next time they both attend church "as a token that you love me," sends her a doggerel verse in which his heart "is bursting, like fine ginger pop," and signs himself "Your own devoted slave and admirer."

In his own school the letters he exchanged with Miss Felton would have made him a grand figure, but he did not depend upon them, nor upon his star turns in the school magazine, to assure his reputation among his peers, for public practical jokes were even more appealing to his friends, and remembered longer. To make himself the center of attention, he guyed E. J. Marshall, the Headmaster, who had a reputation for firmness in dealing with troublesome boys. Once Aubrey stuffed the corner of Marshall's academic gown into an inkpot while his back was turned. When the elderly schoolmaster strode off, the inkpot went with him, spattering everything in the classroom within range when it finally came loose with a clatter. Not until Marshall saw Beardsley's classmates dissolve in laughter did he realize that something was wrong: he was too deaf to have heard the inkpot crash.[17]

Sketch from *Becket* in the *Pall Mall Budget* (1893)

*The remaining verses of Beardsley's ballad are printed in Note 15 to this chapter.

Beardsley "used to be up to all sorts of mischief," G. F. Scotson-Clark recalled, "and many a clever scheme we concocted together in order to raise a shilling apiece, and then steal off to the theatre."[18] With C. B. Cochran, too, Beardsley would go off to the rococo Brighton Pavilion to see matinées of plays and pantomimes, his angular figure, already in dapper dress and topped with an inverted bowl of red hair, becoming a familiar sight to theatre habitués. The stage was his great love, even more than music or drawing; and when he could not get to the real thing in Brighton he was involved with theatricals in the school. Almost every week there was some kind of performance, usually directed by the stagestruck King, and Aubrey sometimes took his recitation assignment or his script out to the decaying and deserted old Chain Pier, once Brighton's entertainment glory. There, pacing up and down the weatherbeaten planks, he committed his lines to memory. At one school program he recited Thomas Hood's "Mary's Ghost"; at another he gave a reading of the skating scene in *Pickwick Papers*, although it was from the pen of an author he affected to despise. "We played *Ici on Parle Français*," C. B. Cochran noted; "Beardsley was the Frenchman and I took Toole's old part. We also did *The Spitalfields Weaver*, and I remember, too, reciting 'Ostler Joe,' and Beardsley gave a most impressive rendering of 'Eugene Aram.'"[19]

The Christmas performances were the most elaborate. The Annual Entertainment for 20 December 1887 was an original script by Mr. King to celebrate, in appropriate fustian, Queen Victoria's Golden Jubilee on the throne. It starred Beardsley as the Prologue and his friends Clark and Cochran as Henry II and Henry VII. Aubrey was the Spirit of Progress, emoting a lengthy, pseudo-Elizabethan ode to the Queen which reviewed all of English history:

> Until, from age to age, by slow degree
> We reach Victoria's year of Jubilee . . .
> I cannot run through all the thousand years,
> A nation's joyfulness, a nation's tears;
> My duty I must do, and by the power
> Which I possess, will call this very hour
> From regions dark to this mundane stage,
> The ghosts of some, who on past history's page
> Did leave the impress of their vig'rous brains,
> That we might profit by their glorious gains.

Sketch from *Orpheus* at the Lyceum in the *Pall Mall Budget* (1893)

(Spirit of Progress turns to call the Ghosts.)
Arise ye ghosts, come forth that we may see
The sort of folk our rulers used to be!
Come, Conquering William, from thy long repose![20]

Beardsley also designed the programs for some of the school entertainments. His most ambitious achievement was his last, for the Christmas musical *The Pay of the Pied Piper*, performed on 19 December 1888. Not only did he design the program, but the costumes as well. Some idea of them may have been captured in his sketches in the program—the Pied Piper boasting of his rodent-catching prowess to the Beadle, the ladies of the town petitioning the Council, the procession of the Council to an assembly called to consider the crisis, and a procession of children charmed by a turbaned and flowingly garbed Piper. Humorously malicious, with a touch of what Aubrey's master Mr. King called "the cartoon spirit," they reached their climactic point with the "Arrest of the Piper," who was ironically shown making surprise protestations of his good intentions. In the inevitable *Prologue* by King, the program listed Aubrey as Mercury; and in the *Pied Piper* he had the role of Herr Kirschwasser. This virtuoso performance— from program and costume design to parts in the prologue and the play— was by a non-student: he had been withdrawn from Brighton Grammar School by the time the entertainment was held, and had to return to play in it.

Aubrey's final effort for his school was a play for which he not only designed the program, but wrote the lines. It was *A Brown Study*—a one-act "original farce" with five characters, two of whom were "Charles Brown No. 1" and "Charles Brown No. 2," the first played by C. B. Cochran and the second by G. F. Scotson-Clark. Produced at the Royal Pavilion on 7 November 1890 it was part of the entertainment for the Brighton Grammar School's Old Boys' Association. "Beardsly" (his name misspelled on the program) by then had long been an Old Boy himself.

Indifferent to schoolwork, he had achieved most of his education at Brighton Grammar School on his own, doing a little hard study at the last moment to get through his exams, and otherwise reading, writing and drawing as the mood occurred. Without permissive masters who encouraged his theatrical experiments (King) and his art (Payne), he might have gone more submissively from school into the world. But H. A Payne, who taught him classics, had also permitted him to read French novels—in French. And his

Illustration for the comic operetta *The Pay of the Pied Piper*, Brighton Grammar School (1888)

translation of the mandatory Vergil was idiosyncratically done in English heroic couplets, illustrated with a thirteen-year-old's comic perspective. Nineteen sketches giving Beardsley's satiric idea of *The Aeneid* have survived, most of them with a touch of the grotesque and the absurd.[21] There was the same flavor in the *Pied Piper* sketches, done when he was fifteen.*

In July 1888, just before his sixteenth birthday, Aubrey was placed temporarily as a clerk in the office of the surveyor for the Clerkenwell and Islington districts of London. This was to help him survive until a clerkship vacancy occurred in a London insurance office to which he was to be recommended. He was clearly as unfit by temperament and training for one as for the other.

From *The Pay of the Pied Piper*

*Kate Greenaway who, as previously mentioned, was a favorite in Beardsley's childhood, had also made much-praised illustrations for *The Pied Piper of Hamelin*.

2

The High Stool

Before he was seventeen Beardsley had written the first act of a three-act comedy, and a monologue he titled *A Race for Wealth*. But there was no promise of wealth in the surveyor's office, and the thought of a literary occupation was only something to tease himself with as he frequented the Bookseller's Row in shabby, narrow (and soon to be demolished) Holywell Street, near the Strand, and the bookshops in Queen Street, while continuing his education at the British Museum. He sensed that his chief chances would come in art, and he browsed among the treasures of the National Gallery on some of his free afternoons. His artist friend Scotson-Clark had remained in Brighton, and whenever either had a holiday he would take the train to visit the other.

On one London trip Scotson-Clark arrived with an invitation to call on the artist G. F. Watts, and took Beardsley along. Both confided to Watts their ambitions to become artists, and he kindly offered his encouragement. Still, other than what Beardsley required for the amateur theatricals he was beginning to stage at home with his sister, or was inspired to do by his visits to theatres, operas and concerts, he did little drawing. Many evenings in London that first year passed in an ecstasy of music which reverberated later in his art.

Often when Beardsley returned to Brighton to stay with Scotson-Clark the two would sit up all night drawing. One morning—Scotson-Clark recalled that it was about six and the sun was already rising—he gave Beardsley oil paints and brushes, unfamiliar tools to his guest, who worked in pen-and-

Opposite: *Le Dèbris d'un Poète*. In Beardsley's weak French, "the wreck of a poet." Beardsley as an insurance office clerk (1892)

ink. Then he curled up on a sofa and went to sleep. When he awoke he discovered that Beardsley had painted a peculiar woman. Her dress was red, her hair green and her face blue.[1] Few of the women Beardsley would draw, even in pen-and-ink, would be less grotesque.*

At home in Cambridge Street in Pimlico, he continued indulging his passion for amateur theatricals. Together with his sister he was proprietor of "The Cambridge Theatre of Varieties," their name for the performances of skits and charades they not only produced at home for their friends but formalized with programs Aubrey drew in pen-and-ink for each occasion. Each production was a Victorian music-hall performance in miniature, and immense after-working-hours effort was devoted to them as well as to the witty drawings Beardsley provided for each program. He was spilling over with undirected creative energy his clerkship failed to satisfy, a fact he afterwards illustrated in a drawing in the shape of a narrow panel, titled (ungrammatically) *Le dèbris d'un poète*. In it he appeared on a clerk's high stool, bent over a ledger, with files and bundles of papers as a backdrop. In the foreground was a carpet with a design of symbolically beckoning sunflowers.

There were several types of productions staged at the Cambridge Theatre of Varieties. Some were composed of songs—"Quite English," "They Call Me a Poor Little Stowaway," "Eighteenpence," "Far, Far Away," "The Happy Fatherland" and "Two to One." There were original entertainments and charades, and productions of Victorian farces—"The Jolly Mashers" (starring Mabel and Aubrey, each in two roles), "The Man of Honour" (with Mabel as both a widow and a landlady), "Box and Cox" (with Ellen Beardsley "in her first performance"), parodies of Gilbert and Sullivan, and Charles Brookfield's "Nearly Seven" (starring Aubrey). Beardsley not only enjoyed all the details of organizing, writing and acting in his skits but was good at them. King recalled that in Brighton days a Beardsley recitation had "secured . . . the loud applause of three thousand not uncritical people." Mabel Beardsley, a striking and high-spirited redhead, did go on to become a professional actress, but her brother was to observe rather than participate. The closest he would ever get to the footlights would be to draw the performers, both from the audience and backstage.

*See Chapter 6 for a reference to later (and perhaps final) Beardsley attempts at painting in oils.

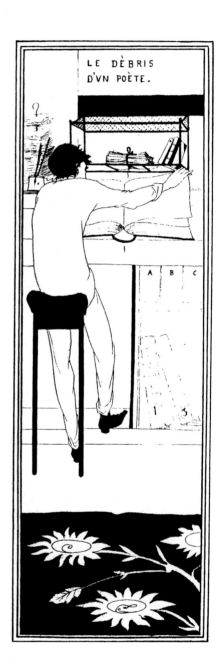

Hand-drawn program for a home entertainment (ca. 1889)

Clerkships seemed destined to be the routine of his life, and he found the work easy and dull. "I don't exactly dislike but am not (as yet) frantically attached to it," he cautiously wrote his former mentor King, in a letter crowded with sketches of things he had seen and done. One was another self-portrait, with Aubrey seated at the traditional Victorian clerk's sloped desk, "looking very wise over an empty ledger." If his letters were any augury, no one could have then predicted any future for him in literature. He was always a poor speller, and had hardly improved his prose style over that of his first year at school. But his sketches already reflected a sardonic wit he may have only half-sensed, and which he never brought completely under control.

In the summer of 1889 Beardsley shifted from a clerk's stool at the district surveyor's office to a clerk's stool in the Guardian Fire and Life Assurance office, in Lombard Street. He might have remained there to work his way up the drab routine of ascending titles and petty responsibilities, acquiring in the process a bowler hat, furled umbrella and commuter ticket to a small red-brick house in the burgeoning suburbs, but by autumn he was immobilized in bed. He had suffered the first severe hemorrhages of the lungs since his childhood.

Dr. Symes Thompson, called in to treat Beardsley, wondered how he had existed so long in such a deplorable condition before the relapse, but offered his patient more platitudes than facts about his case. There was no lung disease involved, Thompson inexplicably told the patient: his heart and lungs were merely weak, and any exertion, the doctor warned, would bring on the bleeding. Instead of a Christmas holiday routine of concerts, visits and entertainments, Beardsley had to live on a diet of soft invalid fare, leaning regularly over basins. In dressing-gown and slippers he sat up over an easel when he felt strong, read hungrily for lack of any more strenuous activity, and even tried writing. He read Daudet's humorous tales in French, and found to his satisfaction that he could still read French almost as easily as English. He wrote and offered a short essay (actually a piece of thin fiction) to *Tit Bits,* and received his first income as a professional writer for it: £ 1.10.0.

"The Story of a Confession Album" earned its author the strange sum because *Tit Bits* offered one guinea per column for "original contributions," and Beardsley's ran to nearly a column and a half of the weekly's tiny type.

Tit Bits was a *Reader's Digest* of its day, serving up snippets "from all the Most Interesting Books, Periodicals and Contributors in the World" to a circulation of almost half a million subscribers; and Beardsley's story shared a page of the 4 January 1890 issue with "How 400 Tons of Fish Comes to London Daily," an essay on the great fish market of Billingsgate. "Confession Album" was a trifle in the form of a first-person lament by a young man whose fiancée jilts him after taking seriously a facetious "confession" in an album on a friend's drawing-room table. He had tried to be funny when answering such traditional questions as "Your beau ideal of happiness?" and made matters worse by flippantly signing his piece as while "sitting beside Emily." Unfortunately, the story went, Emily was not the name of his intended.

As Beardsley's fiction indicated, he was not strong on plot, but he was delighted to have become—at seventeen—a published author. Weak and more frail than ever, he could see no extended future in the insurance office, and daydreamed about a literary or artistic career which would not require a walking invalid to journey daily to a place of business and remain an allotted time for his £70 or £80 a year. But he returned to Lombard Street, "with a vile constitution, a sallow face & sunken eyes, long red hair, a shuffling gait & stoop."[2] Yet at least twenty-two drawings survive from the period, all accomplished during 1889 and the first half of 1890, and nearly all from Beardsley's reading. There were four drawings illustrating *Manon Lescaut,* a "Dame aux Camélias," several scenes from *Madame Bovary,* illustrations for novels by Daudet and Balzac, a depiction of the fifth scene in Act II of *Phèdre.* Inspired by French fiction and theatre, they were otherwise uninspired, for his clerkship and his wheezing lungs left him too tired at night to do more than an occasional pencil or wash drawing. For the rest of the year, and into the next, he even tried unsuccessfully to suppress the urge to draw. It had become too painful to tease himself about a future in art.

By the spring of 1891 Beardsley had decided that the grave would have to wait. The hemorrhages had not returned, and the stronger he felt, the more convinced he was that he had a future he could do something about. On his evenings and Sundays he worked with new enthusiasm on his drawing, assembling a small portfolio of what he thought was his best work. Then, on a Sunday in July 1891, he ventured with his sister Mabel to the house of Sir Edward Burne-Jones, in the North End Road in West Kensington. At one time the renowned artist had permitted visitors at his studio

Chapter heading from *Le Morte d'Arthur* (1893-94)

on Sundays, but Aubrey, not knowing that the practice had been discontinued years before, wrote to Scotson-Clark of his intentions, and went off several days later, Mabel in tow and portfolio under his arm.

At the door he presented his visiting card—the prescribed procedure for admittance, he thought. But one then needed, he discovered, an appointment to see the pictures. Disconsolately, the two teenagers turned away. What happened next was described by Aubrey, in ungrammatical and breathlessly innocent detail, in a letter to King:

I had hardly turned the corner when I heard a quick Step behind me, & a voice which said "Pray come back I couldn't think of letting you go away without seeing the Pictures, after a journey on a hot day like this." The voice was that of Burne Jones; who escorted us back to his house & took us into the Studio, Showing & explaining everything. His kindness was wonderful as We were perfect Strangers he not even knowing our names.

By the merest Chance I happened to have some of my best drawings with me, & I asked him to look at them & give me his opinion.

I can tell you it was an exciting moment when he first opened my portfolio & looked at the first drawing "Saint Veronica on the evening of Good Friday" "Dante at the Court of Con Grande de la Scala."

After he had examined them for a few minutes he exclaimed "There is *no* doubt about your gift, one day you will most assuredly paint very great & beautiful pictures."

Then as he continued looking through the rest of them ("notre dame de la lune," "Dante designing an angel," "Insomnia," "Post Mortem," "Ladye Hero" &c &c) he said "All are *full* of thought poetry & imagination. Nature has given you every gift which is necessary, to become a great artist. I *seldom or never* advise anyone to take up art as a profession, but in *your case I can do nothing else."*

And all this from the greatest living artist in Europe. Afterwards we returned to the lawn & had afternoon tea. Mrs. Burne Jones is very charming. The Oscar Wildes & several others were there. All congratulated me on my success, as "Mr. Burne Jones is a very severe critic."

During tea B. J. spoke to me about art training. "I will" he said "immediately find out the very best school for you, where two hours daily study would be quite sufficient for *you*." "Study hard, you have plenty of time before you, I myself did not begin to study till I was 23."

"You must come and see me often & bring your drawings with you. Design as much as you can [for] your early sketches will be of immense service to you later on. Every one of the drawings you have shown me would make beautiful paintings."

After some more praise & criticism I left feeling, in the words of Rossetti, "A Different crit'ter." We came home with the Oscar Wildes—charming people—.[3]

From *Bon-Mots of Foote and Hook* (1894)

The drawings with which he had armed himself, Beardsley added to King, had been done only "within the last few weeks, as prior to that I don't think I put pencil to paper for a good year. In vain I tried to crush it out of me but that drawing faculty would come uppermost. So I submit to the inevitable."

His reception in every way had made that submission easy. Mabel afterwards thought that it was only after tea, before the Wildes were to drive them home in Oscar's carriage, that Burne-Jones had taken them to see the paintings in the garden studio, and that only then had the artist observed Aubrey's portfolio and asked "if he drew." "I am going to say to you," Mabel remembered Burne-Jones as advising after he looked through Aubrey's drawings, "what I say to very few, and that is—give up whatever you may be doing for Art." Only after Aubrey explained that he was dependent upon the Guardian Fire and Life Assurance Company for a livelihood did Burne-Jones offer the alternative suggestion that the boy try a night class with Frederick Brown at the Westminster School of Art. Beardsley almost immediately took the advice, beginning the only formal art study he ever had.

"I am just now enthused to the highest degree about pictures," Beardsley wrote to Scotson-Clark; and he added that he was busy studying the life and works of Andrea Mantegna, "who . . . has inspired Burne-Jones all along." Off he went to the Royal Collection at Hampton Court, to view the Mantegna works there, drawing a sketch for Scotson-Clark of himself standing astounded before several Mantegna engravings, and praising Mantegna's "Triumph of Caesar"* and accompanying works as "an art training in themselves."[4] What Beardsley's new hero admired was good enough for him.

It was no coincidence that Beardsley's drawing began to take on, too, some evidences of immersion in Burne-Jones; and later, William Rothenstein recalled, when the veteran painter was being attacked by younger artists, Beardsley jumped to his defense. In the realm of design, at least, he

---

*Profuse in its details, Mantegna's engraving provided—in quantity if in no other way—a lot for Beardsley to study. It was a conventional procession, but crowded with heralds, riders, a nude boy, elephants, horses and other animals, all against the backdrop of a walled city seated upon a cliff. On the garlanded and ornately blanketed elephants were platforms bearing tall and elaborate torches, the pedestals and legs of each carved into the figures of women and animals. Later Beardsley would adopt the practice himself.

From *Bon-Mots of Foote and Hook* (1894)

insisted, the master was inimitable. From the sidelines Rothenstein corrected, "Imitable, Aubrey, surely; imitable." Beardsley understood and was delighted.

In the aftermath of his artistic resurrection his routine until 5:30 each day remained the same. At 9:30 Beardsley was due in the City, at the insurance office. At lunch hour he would browse in the second-hand bookshops. But in the evenings he would either go home (now 59 Charlwood Street) to draw, or to Westminster, to work with Frederick Brown, for whom he quickly developed great admiration; and for a while he regularly submitted to his two hours' instruction. Burne-Jones sensed that Beardsley was a boy in a hurry, and cautioned him to bear with formal study. "I should like," he wrote him, "to see your work from time to time, at intervals, say, of three to six months. I know you will not fear work, nor let disheartenment languour you because the necessary discipline of the school seems to lie so far away from your natural interest and sympathy. You must learn the grammar of your art, and its exercises are all the better for being rigidly prosaic."[5]

Meanwhile, King tried to help Beardsley financially by offering to sell some of his work in Brighton, and Aubrey—who needed funds for art supplies—suggested ten shillings each as a fair price for a drawing. Even so, King could find a buyer for only one. The Gurneys—old friends of the family—tried to help too by commissioning Aubrey to design Christmas cards for them. Not unexpectedly, they turned out to echo the style of Burne-Jones.

Another place to which Beardsley paid homage was the famous Peacock Room at the London town house of the late Frederick Leyland, a wealthy Liverpool shipowner. Leyland, a patron of James McNeill Whistler, in 1876 had commissioned Whistler to redecorate the dining-room at 49 Prince's Gate,[6] and Beardsley—who had become attracted to Japanese prints—was as much interested in the Japanese-influenced architecture of the room and furnishings as in what Whistler had done with them. The walls, woodwork, shutters and ceiling, Beardsley found, had been prepared as a setting for two Whistler paintings by being covered with a peacock design in blue paint and gold leaf. Even the priceless Spanish leather wall covering had received Whistler's gratuitous brushwork.

Leyland had been horrified at the desecration of the room, and offered Whistler a thousand *pounds* for his labor rather than the two thousand

Chapter heading from *Le Morte d'Arthur* (1893-94)

guineas the artist felt more appropriate for so distinctive a product. After brooding over the insult, Whistler had pocketed the money, but not before he had retaliated by painting two peacocks—a rich one and a poor one—on the place on one wall reserved for one of his paintings. Under the claws of the rich peacock were silver shillings, each one of which represented the difference between pounds and guineas, Whistler more indignant over that aspect of his remuneration than over the difference between one thousand and two thousand, for tradesmen were traditionally paid in pounds, and gentlemen in guineas. Malicious criticism and gossip had made a notorious joke of the ornate Peacock Room; but Beardsley was impressed by the marriage of wit to art and of English to Japanese style, and awed by the peacock shutters and the "gorgeously painted" central portrait.

His mother and sister were away at Woking for the remainder of the summer, and he had remained in London with "the pater." That their relationship had not improved with the years may be inferred from Aubrey's remarks to Scotson-Clark that he was "not having a particularly lively time of it." But the Peacock Room had brought him alive as nothing since the visit to Burne-Jones in mid-July, and he filled a long letter to his friend with detailed sketches of what he had seen. One depicted him reverently walking through an art-filled room. Another showed a large Whistler portrait, flanked by pairs of peacocks, of a woman in Japanese dress. As added information he included drawings of other things he had done and seen—a Holbein at the National Gallery ("a damned ugly picture I assure you"), and Whistler's portrait of his mother, which he admired without reservation ("the accompanying sketch is a *vile* libel").

At one of the bookshops he had begun visiting regularly in Queen Street Beardsley sometimes bartered his own drawings for books; and somehow he was also acquiring the beginnings of a personal collection of art. Inevitably his newest acquisition had to be—he wrote Scotson-Clark about his trophy—"a gem in the shape of an etching by Whistler." It was an 1859 etching of fishing craft tied up at a wharf at Billingsgate—not in the painter's later Japanese style, but nonetheless a Whistler.[7]

As Beardsley's own style matured, traces of Whistler and of Japan began to show through the Burne-Jones influences. In another way, too, the Whistler influence worked upon Beardsley. The year before, Whistler had published his anthology of wit and personal malice, *The Gentle Art of Mak-*

Chapter heading from *Le Morte d'Arthur* (1893-94)

ing Enemies. His book was signed with the familiar Whistler symbol of a butterfly, which might more appropriately have been a wasp; but Beardsley delighted in the image of the great artist who could also create elegant, and stingingly witty, retorts. It added a new dimension to his ambitions. More importantly, the impact of Whistler—whom he had yet to meet in person—meant that no sooner had he begun to imitate Burne-Jones's style, and to draw Pre-Raphaelite figures in medieval garments, than a counter-stimulus had taken hold. Inspired by the patterns in the Peacock Room, Aubrey began to seek out Japanese art wherever he could find it, and experimented with a personal amalgam of Burne-Jones and Utamaro. Since he had no other way to survive but by retaining his clerkship, he had to do his drawing at night.

Like Des Esseintes, the hero of Huysmans's *A Rebours* (1884), a book he admired, Beardsley cultivated darkness and seclusion when summoning his muse. Before he started drawing he often darkened his workroom, laboring by the light of candles set in two tall ormolu Empire candlesticks. He could not help but see that in some ways Des Esseintes was a remarkable foreshadowing of himself, and where nature did not follow art Beardsley began to imitate. The fictional Des Esseintes was a disillusioned aristocrat of immensely ancient lineage and sickly sensibility, "a young man anaemic and nervous, with hollow cheeks, steel blue eyes, a thin yet aquiline nose, and dry, tapering hands . . . and an ambiguous expression, at once weary and subtle." His house at Fontenay, where he lived in solitude, was designed to exclude the daylight; and was lit by candelabras and decorated in orange (as most in harmony with the "sensual nature of a true artist") and indigo.* His tastes in everything ran to the perverse and the unnatural: in literature to the decadent late Latin writers like Petronius, and to medieval church writings; and in art to such canvases as an ornately decorated Salome in the ecstasy of her "lascivious dance."

As the novel indicated, Huysmans had consulted works on dozens of exotic subjects, to fill it with the "quintessence of everything under the sun: literature, art, floriculture, perfumery, furnishing, jewellery, etc. . . ."[8] Its pose caught on, and for a decade its deliberate unhealthiness and artificiality

Vignette in *Bon-Mots of Lamb and Jerrold* (1893)

*Afterwards, when Beardsley was briefly affluent, he had Aymer Vallance decorate several of the rooms in his house at 114 Cambridge Street, Pimlico, in orange and black (see also Chapter 4).

made it, amid cries of outrage from respectable critics, "the Bible and bedside book" (in Valéry's phrase) of readers for whom the author had given expression to their scorn for accepted aesthetic and moral standards, and who wanted to extend the boundaries of emotional and spiritual experience.

Even had "the breviary of the Decadence"[9] escaped Beardsley before 1891, he could not have been unaware of it that year, for in the scandalously successful *The Picture of Dorian Gray* Oscar Wilde celebrated the allure of *A Rebours*. As Wilde's hero turned its pages, "it seemed to him that in exquisite raiment, and to the delicate sound of flutes, the sins of the world were passing in dumb show before him. Things that he had dimly dreamed of were suddenly made real to him. Things of which he had never dreamed were gradually revealed. . . ." The book which Lord Henry Wotton, the evil genius of Wilde's story, had lent Dorian in order to hasten the process of corruption had been a yellow-backed French novel easily recognizable as *A Rebours*:

It was a novel without plot, and with only one character, being, indeed, simply a psychological study of a certain young Parisian, who spent his life trying to realise in the nineteenth century all the passions and modes of thought that belonged to every century except his own, and to sum up, as it were, in himself the various moods through which the world-spirit had ever passed, loving for their mere artificiality those renunciations that men have unwisely called virtue, as much as those natural rebellions that wise men call sin. The style in which it was written was that curious jewelled style, vivid and obscure at once, full of argot and archaisms, of technical expressions and of elaborate paraphrases, that characterises the work of some of the finest artists of the French school of Symbolistes. There were in it metaphors as monstrous as orchids and as subtle in colour. The life of the senses as described in terms of mystical philosophy. One hardly knew at times whether one was reading the spiritual ecstasies of some medieval saint or the morbid confessions of a modern sinner. It was a poisonous book. The heavy odour of incense seemed to cling about its pages and to trouble the brain.

Working on ledgers by day and drawing at night was hard on Beardsley, who was still recuperating from his lung hemorrhages of the previous winter; and the strain resulted in a new cause of anxiety—weak and inflamed eyes. He was doing well at art lessons, and knew it; he hoped he would get as far as the life class before eyestrain would force him to give it up. It was the wrong time to revisit G. F. Watts, but Beardsley went to the old artist looking for reassurance that he was doing the right thing. Instead, Watts growled that not only was Aubrey in the wrong school but that all schools were

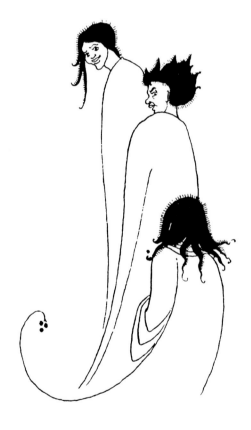

Vignette in *Bon-Mots of Smith and Sheridan* (1893)

worthless—that he was better off teaching himself. Then, with an air of courtesy and hospitality, Watts ushered Beardsley out again into the street, where the young artist, just twenty, could reach for the reassuring bulge of the latest letter of encouragement from Burne-Jones in his pocket. Back at his stool in the insurance office his sketches became more numerous, and (according to King) so did the mistakes in his ledgers.

Beardsley's visits to Burne-Jones and to the Peacock Room had directed his enthusiasms, but beneath them he was troubled. He was still mired in the insurance office, and he was realistic enough about his health to realize that he was not destined for a full endowment of creative years. In verses he had set down just after his nineteenth birthday, the brooding had already taken shape:

> The lights are shining dimly round about,
> The Path is dark, I cannot see ahead;
> And so I go as one perplexed with doubt,
> Nor guessing where my footsteps may be led.
>
> The wind is high, the rain falls heavily,
> The strongest heart may well admit a fear,
> For there are wrecks on land as well as sea
> E'en though the haven may be very near.
>
> The night is dark & strength seems failing fast
> Though on my journey I but late set out.
> And who can tell where the way leads at last?
> Would that the lights shone clearer round about![10]

King was now at the Blackburn Technical School, where he dabbled at arts and letters by issuing *The Bee*, a magazine theoretically under the school's auspices. It became an outlet for Beardsley's drawings, the November 1891 issue reproducing a Burne-Jonesesque drawing of Hamlet following the ghost of his father ("Hamlet patris manem sequitur"). It was, Beardsley had boasted to Scotson-Clark, "a stunning design I can tell you," and he confided further that he hoped to include it in "a grand show of drawings" he was preparing for a return visit to Burne-Jones.[11]

More than Beardsley's artistic instincts were at work, for he was intently studying the best models he could observe, and beginning to develop his own theories about technique, writing to his former headmaster, "I am anxious to say something somewhere, on the subject of *lines* and line drawing.

Vignette in *Bon-Mots of Smith and Sheridan* (1893)

How little the importance of outline is understood even by some of the best *painters*. It is this feeling for harmony in *line* that sets the old masters at such an advantage to the moderns, who seem to think that harmony in *colour* is the only thing worth attaining." But such theorizing would have been lost in *The Bee*.

Like many little magazines, *The Bee* ignored the nominal date of issue fixed in an earlier moment of editorial optimism, the November issue arriving at Beardsley's house on Christmas morning. "On reading your 'notice on the illustration,'" Aubrey wrote King the same day, "I scarcely knew whether I should purchase to myself a laurel wreath & order a statue to be erected immediately in Westminster Abbey; or whether I should bust myself."

The Christmas holidays of 1891 bore additional promise. For more than a year the Rev. C. G. Thornton, a Brighton parson who had known Beardsley in his schooldays, had urged Aymer Vallance to look up the promising boy. Vallance, a fortyish antiquary whose main interest was church decoration and architecture, had attached himself to the William Morris circle, and Thornton saw in him a way for Beardsley to approach one of the great men in the contemporary arts. Finally, in what may have been a burst of Christmas spirit, Vallance journeyed to Pimlico and spent an afternoon examining the drawings Beardsley had arranged for him. It was a considerable portfolio, and Vallance was impressed by its quantity as well as its quality. ("His drawings were nothing less than a revelation.") Beardsley reacted with "childlike delight," and explained that although it was his custom to begin sketching at nine in the evening, after a day in the Guardian office, he made up for the late start by working far into the night.

"You must live by it—you are an artist," Vallance insisted to the insurance office clerk.

Beardsley was sardonic. "What? And give up making out insurance policies in Lombard Street? Impossible."[12]

Vallance remained too enthusiastic to be amused. The boy, he was sure, was a genius, and his work in the pseudo-medieval Burne-Jones manner would impress Morris. He asked Beardsley if he were interested in being introduced to Morris and others whom Vallance knew in the London art world; and the name of William Morris impressed Beardsley. He knew Morris's work in decorative art, and had just read, and been enchanted by, his

Vignette in *Bon-Mots of Foote and Hook* (1894)

The Earthly Paradise. When the antiquary left Charlwood Street, it was with Beardsley's promise that he would reopen his portfolio to Vallance's friends.

At about the same time additional support for Beardsley's hopes arrived from a totally unexpected quarter. He had been left a small legacy by his old great-aunt in Brighton, who once had him sit on a high stool for hours at a time with nothing whatever to do, unaware that he might have been happier any other way. It had turned out to be useful preparation for enduring the monotony of the Guardian clerkship. Although the amount of the bequest was only £500, suddenly the prospect of leaving Lombard Street seemed no longer impossible.

Vignette in *Bon-Mots of Smith and Sheridan* (1893)

3

The Well-Traveled Portfolio   *1892-1893*

Sensing "great power of good or evil" in what he had seen of Beardsley's work, Aymer Vallance was convinced it was his mission to see that the young genius should "fall under good influences." To Vallance, the best possible influence—and the most accessible—was William Morris, the sage of Kelmscott House.

Morris was then searching for a frontispiece for his Kelmscott Press edition of *Sidonia the Sorceress*, and the need provided Vallance with his opportunity. He urged Aubrey to do a specimen frontispiece drawing, then took him to Morris with it. Unimpressed, the bearded old Viking told the pale, gaunt youth that the face of his Sidonia wasn't half pretty or attractive enough, adding, in faint praise, "I see you have a feeling for draperies, and I advise you to cultivate it." Stifling his rage, Beardsley went home to try to improve the design, altering Sidonia's hair in an unsuccessful attempt to better the face. Finally he gave up and destroyed it. After that, Beardsley refused to visit Morris again. Not knowing that, Bernard Shaw later suggested to Morris "that he should take the lad in hand and lead him to nobler levels. But Morris, never jealous on his own account, was blindly and fiercely so on that of Burne-Jones, whom Beardsley had dared to imitate (not without success). . . . He had already spotted the boy's talent and cast him out for ever. He would not listen to my plea; and Aubrey's genius was left to find its own way."[1]

The next important personage on Vallance's list was a much younger man, a twenty-three-year-old art critic named Robert Ross, who knew such

Vignette from *St. Paul's* (1894)

of the famous as Oscar Wilde, and had access to the drawing-rooms of the fashionable. On St. Valentine's Day 1892, Ross awaited Beardsley in Vallance's rooms, prepared for an extraordinary personality. When the youthful apparition arrived, Ross saw only a shy, nervous, self-conscious boy with hair brushed smoothly down over his immensely high and narrow brow, and a face terribly drawn and emaciated. It took Beardsley half an hour to thaw, after which he was talkative and gay as he explained his work.

He was full of Molière and "Manon Lescaut" at the time; he seemed disappointed that none of us was musical; but he astonished by his knowledge of Balzac an authority on the subject who was also present. He spoke much of the National Gallery and the British Museum, both of which he knew with extraordinary thoroughness. He told me that he had only been once to the New Gallery, where he saw some pictures by Burne-Jones, but had never been to the Royal Academy.

Without suggesting that he had ever attended the scholarly exhibitions at Burlington House, Beardsley diplomatically "defended that institution with enthusiasm," saying that he would rather be an Academician than an artist, and quoting the familiar witticism that "it takes only one man to make an artist, but forty to make an Academician."[2]

As soon as Ross withdrew the "Procession of Joan of Arc" from Beardsley's portfolio he decided that he had to buy it. Aubrey quickly objected. It was only a pencil sketch, and besides, he protested, it was the only work of his in the entire group he had brought with him which he personally considered to have any merit. Finally, he agreed to make Ross a pen-and-ink replica of it, which he did not deliver until May. Sick a good deal during the early months of 1892, he had little energy to expend in his art after inscribing insurance policies all day. Still, he managed to assemble more work and paid another call on Burne-Jones, who looked over the collection in Beardsley's well-traveled portfolio and advised sympathetically that it was possible to have assimilated too much from independent study of the Old Masters, and that his eager protégé still needed the discipline of formal art schooling. A few days afterwards Aubrey ruefully produced a caricature of himself being kicked down the stairs of the National Gallery by Raphael, Titian and Mantegna, while Michelangelo dealt him a blow on his head with a hammer.

The chief result of seeing Sir Edward again was an introduction to the Parisian academic painter Puvis de Chavannes, president of the Salon des

Beaux Arts and then as well-known as Degas and Renoir. Through the spring Beardsley prepared for his first voyage across the Channel by experimenting with what he called "an entirely new method of drawing;—Fantastic impressions treated in the finest possible outline with passages of 'black blot.'"[3] (Later he suggested that his technique was to drop an ink blot on the paper and move it around.) His method of composition borrowed still from Burne Jones and the school of Utamaro, but now also from the eighteenth-century French artists who consistently fascinated him by their toying with eroticism. It was, he thought, "something suggestive of Japan, but not really Japonisque," with subjects which were "quite mad & a little indecent. Strange, hermaphrodite creatures wandering about in Pierrot costumes or modern dress; quite a new world of my own creation."[4] Among the less decorous creations of Kitagawa Utamaro was the *Uta-makura* ("Poem of the Pillow"). It, and lesser equivalents in the Japanese art of *Shunga*, or "spring drawing," the generic name given to the erotic art which ranged from orgies to couplings to solitary pleasure, and in mood from lyrical to ugly, had begun appearing in Europe in the mid-nineteenth century, when the home tradition had become regarded as debased and vulgar, and the once-fashionable prints first came to the West—particularly to Paris and Amsterdam—as wrapping paper for imported Japanese pottery. To Beardsley they were a revelation, and his unusual creatures borrowed from several cultures. Sometimes they were flat-chested harpies or bosomy eunuchs, sometimes freakish humans with heads of fetuses he researched in medical textbooks, or with satyr-like legs inspired by the fantastic inhabitants of Mantegna's engravings. Puvis de Chavannes was impressed, introducing Beardsley to another Parisian artist as "un jeune artiste anglais qui fait des choses étonnantes."

After three weeks, Beardsley returned from France convinced of his future in art; still, he had to return to the insurance office, having no other funds he could count upon but what was left (after Paris) of his great-aunt's small inheritance. In London music he found solace and subject matter; after visits to the opera at Covent Garden he produced a Tristan and a Tannhäuser, and then, inspired by the second act of Wagner's music drama, a large imaginative representation of Siegfried. He presented it to Burne-Jones, who hung it in his drawing-room.

Much of Beardsley's routine remained the same. He went irregularly to

Vignette from *Bon-Mots of Smith and Sheridan* (1893)

Title page panel
for *Le Morte d'Arthur* (1893)

Frederick Brown's evening classes, and spent numerous lunch hours at the Jones and Evans bookshop in Queen Street, Cheapside. To Bernard Shaw, Frederick Evans was "an odd little man, a wild enthusiast about music and acting," and "the best amateur photographer in London." Evans's mild, unprepossessing appearance belied his many artistic enthusiasms; he had made the shop a place where booklovers browsed for hours without being pressed to buy, and often came in merely to discuss books and ideas with the proprietor. Long before he and Beardsley became acquainted, Evans had noticed the pale, thin youth regularly dipping into eighteenth-century volumes, and almost always at the same time each day. Almost as regularly, he would leave without buying anything. Eventually, when Beardsley began inquiring about specific books, Evans, intrigued by the boy's appearance and tastes in reading, asked some questions of his own. "I draw a little," Beardsley confessed, and one day came in with some samples. An informal working arrangement resulted—that now and then the boy from the insurance office in Lombard Street could have a book in exchange for a drawing.

Occasionally, the two went to Wagnerian opera, where Aubrey often listened with score in hand, or while drawing a performer; and sometimes Evans would keep a sheaf of Beardsleys overnight to decide whether to buy or barter for any of the lot. While he had one group in the shop he was suddenly tempted to send for his friend J. M. Dent to look at them, recalling

that the publisher, just back from a business trip to America, had been discussing with him the idea of producing a new edition of Malory's *Le Morte
d'Arthur* in a form which would appeal to the general reader, with illustrations in keeping with the medieval spirit of the text. It was proving difficult,
Dent had confided, to find the right artist, for what he wanted, in effect, was
a Burne-Jones without the Burne-Jones fee.

He had some drawings by a young man who might be good enough for
the *Morte* assignment, Evans told Dent, adding the hope that he could come
down to look at them, for they were only in the shop for the day, until the
artist came to retrieve them. The publisher left at once for Queen Street, and
Evans brought out the specimens. Peering through his bifocals, Dent agreed
that he saw force and balance in the young man's work; but he wanted to
know more. As Evans began explaining, while showing Beardsley's drawing
"Hail, Mary," the artist quietly walked in, intent on his daily lunch-hour
browse. Nudging Dent's arm, the bookseller pointed towards the strange-
looking youth, then barely twenty. "There's your man!" said Evans.

At forty-four, Dent looked even older. He walked with a limp, sucked his
teeth, and flourished a large, drooping moustache as well as a venerable
greying beard which reached half-way down a substantial torso. The boy
who had entered was so pale and thin that he looked even younger than he
was, and "it was evident," the publisher thought, "that without great care he

Panel for the preface
to *Le Morte d'Arthur* (1893)

could not be long for this world." Bewildered and unprepared, Beardsley was fulsomely introduced to Dent as the ideal illustrator for his *Morte d'Arthur*. Evans's recommendation was enough, Dent said, while Beardsley was searching for appropriate words; and, if he could be provided with a specimen drawing for the book, a commission could be arranged.

Burne-Jonesesque medievalism was all Beardsley knew: he had never examined closely one of the ornate pseudo-medieval books William Morris had designed for his Kelmscott Press, and Evans had to pull one off his shelves to give Beardsley an idea of what Dent had in mind.

After turning some of the pages, Aubrey agreed to try, and left the shop overwhelmed by the unsought opportunity. At the door he murmured to Evans, "It's too good a chance. I'm sure I shan't be equal to it. I am not worthy of it."[5]

Intently studying the Kelmscott style, with its careful attention to typographical details, about which Beardsley cared nothing, and its period-researched designs for woodcut initials, borders and ornaments, which fascinated him, he grafted elements of it to his method in preparation for the drawing he was to submit to Dent for approval. William Morris, he realized, was an amazing man, among his other enterprises producing such volumes on hand presses. But the proposed *Morte* assignment was for mass production on modern presses, and Beardsley knew he did not have a long lifetime of preparation—in the Morris manner—as literary scholar, poet, painter, embroiderer, weaver, dyer, sculptor, calligrapher, illuminator and wood engraver. In a few weeks he brought to Dent's office his first masterpiece, "The Achieving of the Sangreal." The publisher was awed by the "marvellous design,"* and commissioned Beardsley—at £250 for the job—to design a graphic framework for the text of the legend, with double-page and single-page illustrations, chapter headings and initial letters, ornaments and borders. The first monthly parts were to be published within a year after commencement of the project, and Beardsley estimated that the task would require at least twelve months and four hundred designs. It was an enormous venture for an untried youth, who up to then had published his work in nothing more imposing than a school magazine. Eventually it took twenty full and double pages, and nearly 550 borders, ornaments, chapter head-

Initial letter from
Le Morte d'Arthur (1893-94)

---

*It became the frontispiece for the volume.

Merlin and Nimue,
from Le Morte d'Arthur

How Four Queens found Launcelot
Sleeping, from Le Morte d'Arthur

ings, initials and tail pieces. (And eighteen months, during which the book began appearing monthly in mid-1893 in 2s. 6d. segments.)

With the *Morte* assignment settled, Beardsley had no misgivings about quitting his clerkship at the end of the summer of 1892. Mabel had urged the step and Aubrey quickly gave his notice; but he waited to tell his parents until he had passed his last day in Lombard Street. "I left the fire office," he wrote wryly to King,

to the great satisfaction of said office & myself. If there ever was a case of the □ boy in the ○ hole, it was mine. I left the Office and informed my people of the move afterwards. There was ructions at first but of course now I have achieved something like success and getting talked about they are beginning to hedge and swear they take the greatest interest in my work. This applies however, principally to my revered father.[6]

Another responsibility Beardsley had grown weary of was Frederick Brown's school in Westminster. The early enthusiasm had worn off quickly, especially when winter illness haunted Beardsley with thoughts of mortality and set him back in his lessons, which he had been attending irregularly. With Brown's appointment as professor at the Slade School of Art, Beardsley found an excuse to cut his vague academic tie. After signing with Dent, he gave up formal art study in favor of the shops, galleries and museums; they had always been his real university. The result was that the medievalism which was supposed to pervade his *Morte* project sometimes emerged only by accident, for his imagination was a fever of incongruous and unschooled influences. Some of the illustrations were ripe achievements, although others

were wide of the text. Most of them showed traces of the Burne-Jones style deliberately marred, so to speak, by uncanny thoughts; and since he was learning as he went along with this towering job, his designs often reflected features in the works of other artists he admired at the time. He seems to have adapted figures, forms and compositional ideas from paintings by Botticelli, Crivelli and Pollaiuolo which he saw in the National Gallery, and from prints by Dürer and Mantegna which he saw mainly in reproduction. Moreover, he was deeply attracted by Whistler, as a sort of human wasp, and as an artist. The craft of achieving asymmetrical balance in two dimensions as shown in those Japanese prints and fans so fashionable during the Aesthetic period appealed to him also, and this Japanese note was struck with dissonant effects in some of the *Morte d'Arthur* designs, against a medievalism in the Burne-Jones manner. To chords like these were added further notes, notes of grotesque humour, of an odd vein of fantasy. . . . Two of the full-page illustrations had to be reproduced in photogravure, they were so complicated, and in one of them dated [in the drawing] 8th March 1893, Beardsley introduced hair-line details in nightmare profusion, including his own initials, the treble clef sign, a phallus, a spider's web and various types of calligraphic flourish.[7]

Outwardly unassuming, Beardsley was privately intoxicated with auguries of success. He was about to illustrate "the life of the great wonder worker Merlin," he confided to Scotson-Clark, apparently referring to the first parts of the *Morte*. And his "latest productions," he judged, "show a great improvement [—] 'The flower & the leaf' from Chaucer, & Two pictures from Aeschylus' 'Libation Bearers' . . . , 'Orestes and Electra meeting over the grave of Agamemmon' & 'Orestes driven from city Argus by the 3 Furies.'" On the last page of the letter he drew a large sketch of himself climbing Parnassus, a walking stick clutched in his hand.

Vallance, meanwhile, was still trying to direct the initial enthusiasm he had found for Beardsley's work into meaningful opportunities, and these required good timing and an ear sensitive to new developments in art and publishing. On the fringes of this society, rather than part of it, Vallance found most people he approached lukewarm to the idea of meeting yet another boy who could draw. One of the invitations he did succeed in getting for Beardsley was for a Sunday late in the summer of 1892.[8] C. Lewis Hind, then sub-editor of *Art Journal*, was spending the afternoon with Alice and Wilfrid Meynell* at their home in Palace Court, a rendezvous for artists and writers. It was almost teatime, yet still only a few people were there, including Hind and Vernon Blackburn, who was singing his setting of Mrs. Meynell's "Love of Narcissus." Blackburn stopped when additional visitors arrived. Hind glanced up and saw Aymer Vallance. "Oh, Hind," said Vallance, "I've brought a young artist here, Aubrey Beardsley. I wish you would look at his drawings: they're remarkable."

After introductions, Aubrey proceeded gravely to untie the ribbons of his black portfolio and present it open to Hind, who Vallance had said was seeking support for a new magazine of art he wanted to establish. "I turned over the drawings," Hind recalled, "and then looked up at him—amazed."

---

*Afterwards Alice Meynell had some misgivings about the young artist who found one of his paths to recognition through her front door. As "A.M." in the *Pall Mall Gazette* for 2 November 1904, she wrote that Beardsley "never sets himself to arrange, to balance, to fill his corners, to weigh his blacks, to sweep the fine line, without busying his imagination to express an infernal evil—not, needless to say, passion or any of the ardours, but explicit evil standing alone. . . ."

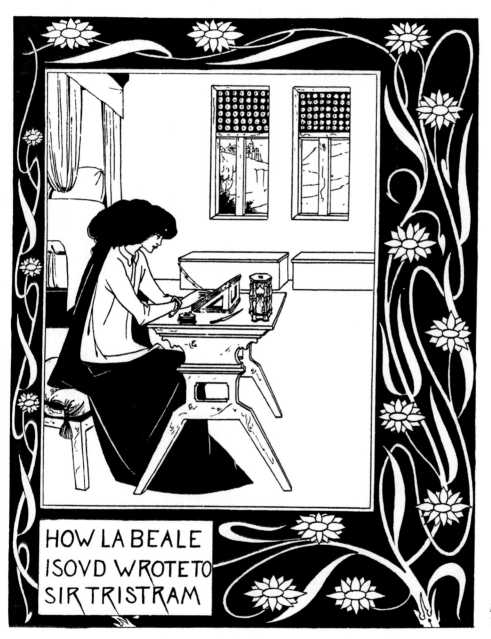

How La Beale Isoud Wrote to Sir Tristram, from Le Morte d'Arthur

Two steps away Beardsley stood quietly, while Vernon Blackburn, uninterested in the fuss, touched the keys of the piano again to play his setting of another Alice Meynell verse:

> No, I shall live a poet waking, sleeping,
> And I shall die a poet unaware. . . .

Beardsley (wrote Hind)

waited for my admiration, but his eyes were watchful. I saw a tall youth of blonde complexion with a prominent nose . . . projecting from his thin, hatchet face; hair lightish cut in a fringe and falling evenly over his forehead. I have never seen such strong capable hands with long fingers full of latent power. . . . In each [drawing] there was mastery. . . . When I tell you that the portfolio he showed me that Sunday afternoon in 1892, his years being 20, contained, among other drawings, "The Birthday of Madame Cigale," "Les Revenants de Musique," and the drawing from Act II of "Siegfried," all of which were reproduced in the first issue of "The Studio," you will realize what an astonishing degree of proficiency his art had reached . . . I carried the drawing away with me, confident we had found the unique thing for the new magazine.[9]

Chapter heading from *Le Morte d'Arthur*

Hind had already had a dummy issue privately printed in order to interest a backer or publisher, and found both before the end of the year—Charles Holme, a businessman and art dilettante, and publisher John Lane. Then came the planning for the first actual issue. "What we want, Hind," Charles Holme told him before they parted for other business, "is a sensational send-off article for the first number." When Hind showed the Beardsley drawings, Holme was more than convinced. "I shall buy some of them," he told Hind. "Will you write the [Beardsley] article?" Hind backed away from the idea, and suggested instead that art critic (and artist) Joseph Pennell do it: "His name carries weight."

Through Vallance, Beardsley had met Ross as well as Hind, and through Robert Ross's intervention the travels of the portfolio continued. Critic D. S. MacColl had been told by Frederick Brown about a student of his, a boy "who drew like Burne-Jones," but it was through Ross that he finally came upon Beardsley, in December 1892. Like others then, MacColl was impressed by "the stamp of the consumptive upon him, the look of eager fire and hurry that often go with the disease." To MacColl Beardsley talked nervously, but without shyness, "in impatient, almost petulant snatches, and with the preoccupation of a young man full of his own ideas, and indifferent to

La Beale Isoud at Joyous Gard, from *Le Morte d'Arthur*

Chapter heading from *Le Morte d'Arthur*

everything outside of them." Beardsley's elders "were frequently disconcerted by the sharp decisions of his admirations and indifferences, the way he pounced on everything that was dainty, naughty, witty, extreme in expression, . . . erratic, confident, flippant. . . ." Still, MacColl found it "astonishing . . . that a boy of his years should be so equipped in knowledge, knowledge of the important things in literature and the arts. There were magnificent gaps, ignorance of whole worlds of mediocre commonplace, but his instinct for what was vivid . . . stood him in stead of painful schooling and acquirement."[10] MacColl may not have considered that Beardsley's "astonishing knowledge" — like his "fire and hurry" — was directly related to his near-invalidism. Often on his back in bed, or restricted to inactivity, Beardsley had more time than most people to indulge a passion for books.

A few days later, MacColl met Beardsley again, at a dinner party Ross gave to introduce the artist to influential people in the London art world. "I have found an artist— at least I think I have," he had told Joseph Pennell modestly. "Would you care to come to a dinner I am going to give in a few days, and meet . . . Beardsley?" George Moore (a painter before he turned writer) was already there when Pennell arrived, as well as Justin McCarthy, Lewis Hind and Gleeson White. Then

there appeared in the room a boy, almost a child, and this boy who came into the room was Beardsley. He was dressed very simply, and didn't at all look like an artist, but very like a swell. He carried a portfolio, not an artist's portfolio, but more like something a young lady would carry, prettily decorated on the sides. In that portfolio, there were a number of drawings which he proceeded to show us. That was what he came for, and we came to see. . . .

To MacColl it was "a whole world of fanciful vision expressed in fine-spun lines and cunningly arranged blots."

Pennell was struck by one drawing which combined "in a remarkable manner the work of the pre-Raphaelites and that of the modern designers, with a medieval feeling running through it." Like the other guests, he praised it, and Beardsley matter-of-factly noted that Sir Edward Burne-Jones had liked it too ("which rather staggered us"). Caught up in the atmosphere of admiration, the boy fibbed that William Morris had also liked it. But, he explained, he was having his drawings reproduced by the line-block process "and not by wood-cutting, as he had no use for Morris's hidebound mannerisms."[11] The revelation that Morris had admired Beardsley's work "waked us up," Pennell remembered. No one contradicted it, and he remained impressed, agreeing to do the introduction to Beardsley's work which Hind and White wanted for the first number of *The Studio*. Before Beardsley left, several guests offered to lighten his portfolio by buying some of his specimens.

Through Elizabeth and Joseph Pennell, and their Thursday nights at their home in Buckingham Street, Beardsley met more of artistic and literary London. Not all the introductions proved happy or rewarding, for burly, bearded W. E. Henley, a poet ("Invictus") and then editor of the *National Observer*, was a habitué of Buckingham Street. A formidable presence, he wore a large-brimmed hat—often indoors—and walked with crutch and cane. In his newspaper he busied himself inveighing against sham, affectation and sentiment, and loved argumentation in any form, stirring up a storm among whatever collection of people he joined at London "at-homes." It was much the same role he played in his *Observer*, where he rewrote all contributions until they resembled his own style, one full of brawling vitality and (sometimes unwitting) brutality.

Ready to show his drawings to anyone in a position to help who wanted to see them, Beardsley arranged an appointment with Henley. As he went up the two steep flights of stairs to Henley's Great College Street rooms, portfolio in hand,

Chapter heading from *Le Morte d'Arthur*

he heard a voice, loud, angry, terrifying; at the top, through an open door, he saw a youth standing in the middle of the room listening in abject terror to a large red [faced] man at a desk whom he knew instinctively to be Henley;—one glance, and he turned and fled, down the stairs, into the street, the little portfolio under his arm, his pace never slackening until he got well beyond the Houses of Parliament, through the Horse Guards into the Park.[12]

The date of the first number of *The Studio* had been optimistically fixed for February; but by February Hind was no longer its editor, and no issue had been published. William Waldorf Astor had bought the *Pall Mall Gazette* as well as the *Pall Mall Budget*, and had offered Hind an attractive salary to edit the *Budget*. As a result Beardsley made his début in that journal instead, on 2 February 1893, while the first issue of *The Studio* was being delayed by the shift until April, under the editorship of Gleeson White. Afterwards Hind realized that he had wasted Beardsley on the slight things the *Budget* could use; but Beardsley found "news" drawing a diversion after the

How a Devil in a Woman's likeness would have tempted Sir Bors, from a double-page panel in *Le Morte d'Arthur*

Chapter heading from *Le Morte d'Arthur*

painstaking work for the far-from-finished *Morte d'Arthur*. He "had little reverence for existing institutions, or for authority," and enjoyed venturing forth from the *Budget's* Northumberland Street offices, in Charing Cross, to sketch a play or a local event. He drew Henry Irving in Tennyson's *Becket*, playwright Henry Arthur Jones, Ellen Terry, Émile Zola, Pope Leo XIII, a caricature of a golfer. He and Hind even went to the Royal Mint to examine the plaster casts in competition for the New Coinage of 1893; and Beardsley made comic versions, some of which Hind suppressed as carrying irreverence too far. Four coin designs "that were not sent in for competition" were published, but one "coin," showing Queen Victoria as a Degas ballet dancer, merely survived the wastebasket. Afterwards, Beardsley's contributions to the *Budget* dwindled, to no one's sorrow.

The *Budget* had been Beardsley's first chance to reach an audience beyond the art coteries, and his head was beginning to dizzy from the sudden eruption of praise and opportunity. He saw, too, Pennell's "A New Illustrator" article before it was published, and had visions of a Beardsley vogue. Still carefully quiet and reserved in professional company, he could contain himself no longer when he began a letter to Scotson-Clark in February 1893. "I should blush to quote the article," he commented about Pennell's forthcoming piece.

My weekly work in the "Pall Mall Budget" has created some astonishment . . . I have . . . already far distanced the old men at that sort of thing . . . My portrait of Irving made the old black-and-white duffers sit up; and my portrait of Verdi, this week, will make them sit up even more . . . Clark my dear boy I have fortune at my foot. Daily I wax greater in facility of execution. I have seven distinct styles and have won success in all of them . . . .

Scotson-Clark was in America at the time, and Beardsley exhorted him not to be "a fixture in the land of the Philistines. Come out from among them if you can manage it. England after all is the place for oof and fame!" And he illustrated his point with a drawing of a rising sun and a sack of money marked £ s. d.[13]

Some of the *Morte d'Arthur* drawings circulated in originals and in proofs before the first number appeared in June 1893; and four designs were published in the April *Studio* — an initial letter, an ornamental border, a frieze of six soldiers, and a full-page plate, "Merlin taketh the child Arthur into his keeping." Dent found it useful publicity, while it also did much to extend Beardsley's reputation and acquire new commissions for him. As early as December 1892, Aymer Vallance had brought some of the first drawings to Kelmscott House, including "The Lady of the Lake telleth Arthur of the sword Excalibur," and Morris looked at several, then pushed them away in anger. It was "an act of usurpation," he raged. "A man ought to do his own work."[14] The news quickly reached Beardsley, who by then was so swamped by offers of commissions, and the praise of critics and publishers eager to climb aboard his bandwagon, that he had little sympathy with Morris's accusation. "William Morris," he wrote Scotson-Clark, "has sworn a terrible oath against me for daring to bring out a book in his manner. The truth is that while *his* work is mere imitation of the old stuff, mine is fresh and original."

Too naïve about business matters—and too eager for the *Morte* assignment—to insist upon a contract, Beardsley delivered his drawings for the first serial issue early in 1893 without the deadline pressure of a formal agreement. But the loose arrangement may have frightened Dent, once printing was actually under way, and he realized on what flimsy basis—Beardsley's former need for funds—such a large undertaking rested. Before the artist delivered the second installment, Dent prepared a contract for signature. It was silent about Part I (since all the drawings for it had been delivered), beginning instead with the stipulation that sufficient matter was to be furnished to illustrate "the opening chapters of the 4th and 5th books" and to complete Part II "of the said work by the 17th day of April 1893." The number of full-page and minor illustrations was spelled out in detail, part by part for each of the eleven installments still to be delivered, with deadlines for each, the last to be supplied by the artist by 12 June 1894.

It was easy to see why smaller-scale undertakings suddenly appeared more alluring to Beardsley than the eleven formidable segments of the Dent project still due. "Better than the *Morte d'Arthur*," he told Scotson-Clark, was a new assignment he had accepted—at £100—from Lawrence and Bullen. He was to do thirty small drawings to illustrate Lucian's *True History*, one of the earliest imaginary voyages. "I am illustrating this entirely in my new manner or rather a development of it. The drawings are certainly the most extraordinary things that have ever appeared in a book, both in respect to technique & conception. They are also the most indecent."[15] The combination of elements was appearing simultaneously in an explosion of new projects Beardsley was somehow managing to juggle. Free of the Guardian office, and spending some of his time

Chapter heading from *Le Morte d'Arthur*

How Sir Tristram Drank of the Love Drink, from Le Morte d'Arthur

in Aldine House, Dent's establishment in Great Eastern Street, Shoreditch, he heard about new publication ventures as they originated, and involved himself in some of them. At least the first of them was Dent's deliberate effort to diversify Beardsley's work, for it quickly became apparent that the *Morte* undertaking was too extensive to be done without a paralyzing monotony setting in. Although Beardsley would sometimes turn up at Evans's bookshop to show him a half-dozen Arthurian drawings he had pushed himself to do the previous night,[16] he was often bored with the problem of finding something new to say for the ornamental letters, chapter headings and other small-scale parts of the assignment. But he was developing artistically through forced growth, and was accruing an income available to few youths of twenty.

Initially, as a diversion from having to flog his invention for the *Morte*, Beardsley was asked by Dent to make some drawings for three small volumes of *Bon Mots* by famous wits, to be published as a trial for a possible series of them. Most of the sketches turned out to be humorous grotesques done in Beardsley's Japanese style — small vignettes which had nothing to do with the texts they accompanied but had a considerable relationship not only to Japanese prints but to seventeenth-century pen-line masters and to antique medical diagrams. Strange as they were as embellishments to *bon mots* by Goldsmith, Sheridan, Sydney Smith, Charles Lamb and others, they nevertheless ran on to more than a hundred drawings as the series expanded.

It was a confident, recognized artist, rather than a diffident boy, who traveled to Paris for the New Salon in May 1893, while Joseph Pennell's article about him was already in circulation, and the first part of the *Morte* about to be released. Elizabeth Pennell was amazed that when Aubrey arrived "he seemed at once to know Paris in the mysterious way he knew everything." Apparently he never told her that he had been there the year before.

A group of visiting artists, including Beardsley and the Pennells, stopped at the curiously named Hôtel de Portugal et del l'Univers, where the *concierge*, who knew many of them from previous visits, greeted them effusively. Beardsley was shocked at having to undergo being ceremonially kissed, but submitted, and then went off with his portfolio to see other painters, many of them Englishmen who had crossed the Channel when he did, all of them for the annual Salon of the Champs de Mars, where each year the same veteran artists, augmented by a flock of fledgling aspirants, hoped it would be the season when the new vogue, whatever it would be, would include them.

Detail from the title page of *A Child of the Age*, by Francis Adams, for John Lane's *Keynotes* series of novels (1894)

Merlin, design for the verso of the contents page
in *Le Morte d'Arthur*

The New Salon drew strikingly attired artists, and also, as Mrs. Pennell noted, "many beautiful women present, many women in beautiful or extraordinary gowns, many unmistakably at a glance the models for portraits and pictures on the walls." But no one of either sex, she thought, was more noticed than Beardsley. Taking advantage of his new affluence, he arrived in costume he thought appropriate for Paris and for Art. In an elegantly carried-out harmony of grey coat, grey waistcoat, grey trousers, grey suède gloves, grey soft felt hat, and grey tie knotted wide and loose in the French style, he achieved a small triumph of underplayed affectation. In that ensemble, among the bohemian-garbed and the formally dressed, a light, gold-headed cane swinging in his hand, Beardsley became the most striking figure at the Salon, upstaging the event's *cher mâitre et président,* the splendidly tailored and barbered Carolus Durand.[17]

Whistler and de Chavannes were there, as well as writer-critics of the Robert Ross and Henry Harland generation; and the crowds climbed on chairs to see such celebrities as Zola and Durand walk by, leaving the artists to peer at each other's pictures. Beardsley left as little as he could to chance. It was premature for him to have had anything on exhibit, but while most of the artists arrived daily in the traditional tail coats and top hats, he turned up on one occasion not only in his grey ensemble but in a very noticeable straw boater. There was something he could display at the Salon after all — himself.

An English professor of architecture was among the visitors that year, and the group of artists in which Beardsley and the Pennells were traveling decided to host the professor at lunch. Infected by the bohemian atmosphere, they airily chose a location outside the Palais Royal, where their guest arrived in top hat and frock coat, matching their own formal dress. Bob Stevenson (Robert Louis's artist cousin) placed himself at the head of the table, which they had carefully set in the gutter in a spot ordinarily used by cabmen. Predictably, the confusion and noise were so great after the luncheon had lasted only about five minutes that the police arrived to move them on and take the table away. The survivors took cabs to a café to finish the lunch.[18] On another day during the Champs de Mars they gaily took the professor on an excursion boat on the Seine to Saint Cloud, their straw hats blowing away into the river and being replaced by large handkerchiefs tied about their heads. Looking disconcertingly like a cluster of mumps victims, they first joined a wedding party, as a lark, and then visited the palace's park to play "living statues," posing as gods and

How Sir Bedivere cast the sword
Excalibur into the water, from Le
Morte d'Arthur

goddesses on the empty pedestals, the professor a self-conscious Apollo. "Meanwhile," Joseph Pennell recalled, "we worked, looking at pictures, writing about them, and talking of them. Some of us even made sketches. . . ."

That spring Pennell clambered about the towers of Notre Dame in preparation for a project of his own, and several times Beardsley went with him, once caricaturing Pennell as a cathedral gargoyle in a parody of Charles Méryon's etching *Le Stryge* (1853). One of the Gothic monster grotesques of the Notre Dame towers, the Stryge had been used by the intermittently mad Méryon as the figure in the foreground of a hallucinatory view of Paris, its elbows propped on the ledge of a balcony, brooding with its head in its hands and its tongue lolling out of its mouth, over the city far below, while jackdaws circled in the air above the towers. Later the caricature became the last Beardsley to appear in the *Pall Mall Budget* (4 January 1894) as "A New Year's Dream, after studying Mr. Pennell's 'Devils of Notre Dame.' " The gardens at Luxembourg and Versailles also absorbed Beardsley, as well as the palaces of Saint Cloud and Saint Germain, details and images from them appearing in such later work as *Under the Hill* and *The Rape of the Lock*. Another experience would also have its repercussions in Beardsley's work, for he could not help but notice a Parisian literary review which celebrated newness and called itself the *Revue Blanche*. Some called it by less flattering names.

In Paris on Saturday night Beardsley and Pennell went to the opera to see *Tristan and Isolde*, sitting on the side of the parquet, on the steps. Afterwards Aubrey produced, from memory, his first sketch of what he later called "The Wagnerites," a great design almost entirely in black, which later helped make his French reputation. But he was running low on ready cash, and sold a sketch of it at the Hôtel Druout for fifty francs. After the opera they went across the street to the Café de la Paix, and noticed Whistler there, who affected a very aloof air as soon as he saw them. After Beardsley went back to the Hôtel de Portugal to bed, Whistler sniffed to Pennell, "What do you make of that young thing? He has hairs on his hands, hairs on his finger ends, hairs in his ears, hairs on his toes, hairs all over him. And what shoes he wears—hairs growing out of them! Why do you take to him?"

"You don't know him," said Pennell. "Do you mind my bringing him to your place this Sunday afternoon?" Whistler was dubious about the idea, although he loved to show off the beautiful garden by his new flat in the rue du Bac. Eventually he murmured something like "Well, you come and bring him too,"

*How Queen Guenever Made Her a
Nun, from* Le Morte d'Arthur

and the next day the two went to the rue du Bac, Beardsley in a little straw hat similar to the one he had seen Whistler wearing. The great man was in the garden with a number of his admirers, including Mallarmé, and, when most had drifted away, a wealthy English dilettante who had lingered asked the Whistlers, Pennell and Beardsley to be his guests at dinner at one of the cafés in the Champs Elysées. As they left the rue du Bac to dress for the occasion, Whistler whispered appealingly to Pennell, "Those hairs—hairs everywhere!"

"But you were very nice," suggested Pennell, "and of course, you'll come to dinner."[19] But Whistler never made an appearance, and Beardsley took it as a personal affront. That Sunday he worked out an acidulous caricature of the artist, and offered it to Pennell; but somehow Walter Sickert acquired it instead, losing it afterwards in a cab, before it could do any immediate damage.* The snub from the man he admired more than any other living artist continued to rankle, and he later tried to even the score by drawing a gratuitously nasty caricature of Whistler's plump and pretty wife. When it was published a year later as "The Fat Woman," Whistler recognized who had inadvertently sat for the portrait. He was offended, and Beardsley was glad.

The memory of the visit to Whistler's garden lingered. Beardsley drew a small ($8'' \times 4\frac{1}{2}''$) sketch of the Master sitting on a frail garden seat, wearing an oversized Wildean carnation in his buttonhole and a straw hat over outrageously bushy hair, while pointing his finger at—and possibly hectoring— a butterfly, the famous Whistler signature. It was, he confided to André Raffalovich, "a very malicious caricature." For a time Beardsley privately savored his joke, but a year later he and Mabel hung it on their Christmas tree. The season of good will toward all men —at least for Beardsley—excluded Jimmy Whistler.

Whatever the rebuffs and frustrations, it had been an idyllic season for Beardsley and his well-traveled portfolio. He was beginning to banquet from life, and in Paris even the *vin ordinaire* was at first something to savor. It was always possible for him in 1893, still short of his twenty-first birthday, to forget how limited his life expectancy was; but if his shallow breathing provided no constant reminder, Bob Stevenson in Paris did. With the aggravating superi-

Vignette intended for the *Bon-Mots* series, the butterfly suggesting that caricature of Whistler may have been intended

*It turned up much later, and was published. Beardsley caricatured Whistler several times, once as a faun on a settee, in a panel for the title page of one of John Lane's *Keynotes Series* novels, *The Dancing Faun*, by actress Florence Farr (1894).

ority of his years he called Beardsley young, and in soothing tones suggested what Aubrey might learn as he aged and matured. It was a cruel irony to Beardsley, who had not quite reached his legal manhood yet understood without being told that the years of his artistic maturity would be few. He would turn on Stevenson fiercely, while the artists and writers within hearing in the café would laugh at the game.

Young and unsophisticated in the ways of the exotic world to which he had attached himself, Beardsley was taking his small Parisian triumphs and tragedies seriously. Yet even then his reputation was not being made there but in London — by publishers unknown to him the year before, and by writers to whom he never anticipated getting closer than reading their books. It was something Beardsley should have recognized, for he had almost taken his trip to Paris that season of the Champs de Mars with Oscar Wilde himself.

Title page panel
from *The Dancing Faun* (1894)

4

1893-1895

Aubrey and Oscar

Talking about Aubrey Beardsley with a friend, Arnold Bennett remarked that there were people who said they had seen him in the flesh after his death. The friend countered with a story about a man who had met Oscar Wilde in the Pyrenees while Oscar was in prison.[1] Even in death (and both were dead by the time of this conversation in 1904) the two men could not escape what in life had been a mutual abomination—being linked to the other. Yet Beardsley had once, on a postcard to Arthur King, crowed, "I'm off to Paris soon with Oscar Wilde."[2]

In mid-April of 1893 almost anything, even that unpredictable excursion, began to seem possible for Beardsley. Wilde had talked of going to Paris for the New Salon, and had even used Paris as his excuse for begging off attendance at a benefit dinner (for which he sent two guineas). Apparently he never was in Paris that May, and Beardsley quietly went alone, rather than in Oscar's formidable shadow. The postcard remained one of the few times Beardsley was recorded as using Wilde's name with a sense of pleasure and delight.

When the French (and original) version of Wilde's *Salome* was published in Paris early in 1893, Beardsley was still far from completing his *Morte d'Arthur* drawings in the pseudo-medieval style he had already outgrown. His "Peacock Room—Japanese" phase was then influencing his work; and when he read Wilde's play he almost immediately put its most powerful image in a drawing, inevitably in his developing Japanesque style. It was "Salome with the head of St John the Baptist"—with the caption appended, "j'ai baisé ta bouche Iokanaan, j'ai baisé ta bouche." With his instinctive sense of theatre, Beardsley had visualized that line from *Salome* which had caused the greatest controversy in the French press.

The *Salome* drawing was intended as one of the illustrations to accompany Joseph Pennell's article "A New Illustrator: Aubrey Beardsley," in the April (and first) issue of *The Studio*, but it obviously had a large pre-publication audience. Possibly what happened is that Wilde's friend Robbie Ross, who had entrée to Beardsley, saw it almost before the ink had dried, and recommended that John Lane, prospective publisher of the yet-to-be-commissioned English translation of *Salome*, see it too. By March, Wilde himself had seen it, either in an advance copy of *The Studio* or an even earlier state, for that month he presented Beardsley with a copy of the Paris edition, inscribed "For Aubrey: for the only artist who, besides myself, knows what the dance of the seven veils is, and can see that invisible dance. Oscar."[3]

Beardsley designed the cover for the first number of *The Studio*, April, 1893. Joseph Pennell's article on Beardsley, accompanied by a selection of the artist's work, helped establish Beardsley's reputation.

Beardsley would have preferred a commission to translate *Salome* rather than to illustrate it, but Lane instead offered the twenty-year-old artist fifty guineas for one of the most desirable artistic opportunities then available. Wilde had either encouraged Beardsley to work out his own translation, or, as Lord Alfred Douglas afterwards said, "yielded to the solicitations of Aubrey Beardsley, who declared that he could do a splendid translation, and that he thoroughly understood the spirit of the play." As far as the publishers were concerned, Beardsley was the *artist* they wanted.

Although he had agreed to illustrate *Salome* before he left for Paris, the contract was not signed until after he returned, on 8 June 1893. It stipulated that Beardsley would provide ten full-page drawings and a cover design for a fee of fifty guineas, the illustrations to be the "exclusive property" of the publishers. The plum he really wanted—although his sole literary achievement had been a less-than-mediocre short story in *Tit Bits*—passed to Wilde's closest crony, Douglas, whose translation Oscar found unsatisfactory and freely altered. He liked Beardsley's pictures even less as, one by one, he saw them delivered to the Sign of the Bodley Head in Vigo Street. Then Wilde brought the drawings to artist and stage designer Charles Ricketts, who would have liked to illustrate the play himself. To Oscar's disappointment, Ricketts was enthusiastic about Beardsley's accomplishment. "They are too Japanese, while my play is Byzantine,"* Oscar insisted, while to another friend he complained, "They are like the naughty scribbles a precocious boy makes on the margins of his copybooks."

One of the naughty scribbles made as an apparent reference to Oscar's scholarship in *Salome* was Beardsley's private commentary upon Oscar's boast—after having written his drama in French—that he never had to look anything up. Titled "Oscar Wilde at Work," it showed the smug playwright in his study, writing at a desk piled high with large volumes which included a Family Bible, *Dorian Gray, Trois Contes*, volumes of Swinburne and

---

*Oscar's play was Byzantine in the Flaubertian manner in the way that Beardsley's drawings were Japanese in the Whistlerian manner. Both, of course, assumed that they had improved upon their masters. According to Will Rothenstein, "Wilde admired though he didn't really like, Beardsley's *Salome* illustrations; he thought them too Japanese, as indeed they were. His play was Byzantine. When he gave me a copy on its first publication in its violet paper cover, he knew at once that it put me in mind of Flaubert. He admitted he had not been able to resist the theft. 'Remember,' he said with amusing unction, 'Dans la littérature il faut toujours tuer son père.' But I didn't think he had killed Flaubert; nor did he, I believe." (*Men and Memories*, p. 184.)

The Woman in the Moon,
frontispiece from *Salome* (1894)

The Stomach Dance, from Salome

Gautier, the histories of Josephus, a French dictionary and a "First Course" in French, as well as "French Verbs at a Glance."

"It would have been difficult to imagine," an art critic wrote a generation later, "a man less competent to create the true atmosphere of the times and Court of King Herod than Oscar Wilde—but he could achieve an Oxford-Athenian fantasy hung on Herodias as a peg." Beardsley was no more qualified, but he made a virtue of the fact by weaving "a series of fantastic decorations about Wilde's play which were as alien to the subject as was the play. Beardsley imagined it as a Japanese fantasy. . . ." Like the *Morte*, *Salome* was a vehicle for his art, the drawings fashioned not so much after the story as after moods and impressions the story communicated.⁴ His second thoughts seemed to dominate his *Salome* drawings, for his original *Studio* drawing, done before the commission, was a serious comment on the grotesque eroticism of the play. Although the later illustrations often retained that mood, they added some sly additional perspectives Oscar quickly understood.

Whether it was at Oscar's urging, or merely the cautiousness of respectable Victorian publishers, Elkin Mathews and John Lane examined with great care each drawing Beardsley supplied, for, although they wanted their edition to gain public attention, their artist was fast developing a reputation for getting impish delight out of concealing improper detail in ornate decoration. Beardsley's art, Wilde quipped, "was cruel and evil, and so like dear Aubrey, who has a face like a silver hatchet, with grass-green hair." What Oscar may have really worried about, and with good cause, was that the completed pictures were reversing the usual relationship of writer and illustrator. They were as serious as they were impudent, and possessed so much power independent of the text—some of them, in fact, had nothing to do with the text—that Oscar's play was in danger of being in the embarrassing position of illustrating Aubrey's illustrations. This nurtured the kind of feeling which is difficult for a young man to conceal, and Beardsley made little effort to do so. Afterwards Max Beerbohm would suggest waggishly to a friend that *Salome* was "the play of which the drawings are illustrative. . . . I have just been reading it again—and like it immensely—there is much, I think in it that is beautiful, much lovely writing—I almost wonder Oscar doesn't dramatise it."⁵

Wilde, whom Holbrook Jackson characterized as being

as amiable as he was vain, did not seem to object, possibly because he was a showman as well as an artist, and recognized the advantage of having his play decorated,

Enter Herodias, from *Salome*. First state of the illustration to which Beardsley's publisher insisted that a fig leaf be added to cover the unexcited genitalia of the male figure. The fig leaf blurred the innuendo of the illustration, for the youth with the mask appears to be homosexual, or at least not excited lustfully by Herodias, while the fetus-headed but sexually normal figure on the left shows his lust in the way his clothing is strained. Clearly, publisher John Lane missed this point.

even a little outrageously, by the most discussed artist of the moment. So Herod, Herodias, and even the Moon, which plays a leading part in the drama, were allowed to appear with some of the author's features. . . ."[6]

Perhaps with the idea that his personal magnetism could help control Beardsley, and perhaps too because he was immensely curious about the marvellous boy, Oscar tried the desperate expedient of securing his friendship. It outlasted their abortive jaunt in tandem to Paris, but few friendships can have been as uneasy.

With Wilde at Kettner's in Soho, at the Café Royal or in Willis's Rooms, Beardsley was discovering a personality for himself. He enjoyed the world of the evening, the life of the dandy, the dinner-table duels of wit. The Café Royal itself might have been a later Beardsley drawing, with its "smoky acres of painted goddesses and cupids and tarnished gilding, its golden caryatids and its filtered, submarine illumination, composed of tobacco smoke, of the flames from chafing dishes and the dim electric light within. . . ."[7] At one dinner party there given by Frank Harris and attended by Max Beerbohm, William Rothenstein, Robert Ross, Beardsley and Wilde, Harris boomingly monopolized the conversation with tales of his social successes among the aristocracy; and, although he may have been the most impervious to insult of any man in England, Wilde silenced him with "Yes, dear Frank . . . you have dined in every house in London—*once*."[8] In a society which included such opposites in the sensual spectrum as Oscar and Frank Harris, Wilde baited Beardsley incessantly, making fun of the frail artist's asexuality. "Don't sit on the same chair as Aubrey," Oscar would warn. "It's not compromising." Still later, Wilde dismissed Beardsley as not flesh-and-blood, but rather "a monstrous orchid."

Immature and largely self-taught, Beardsley found himself at first rationalizing for his inability to cope with the repartee, or with its felicitous letter-writing equivalents, at which Oscar excelled, by pretending that his style of words was fashioned to parallel the "archaic sympathies" of his art. But he had reached a point in precocity where he could telescope the development of his talent into an amazingly brief span. "Shortly afterwards," Frank Harris recalled, "I got a letter from him written with curious felicity of phrase, in modish polite eighteenth-century English. He had reached personal expression in a new medium in a month or so, and apparently without effort."[9]

Beardsley aped Wilde's dandyism as well as Wilde's *bon-mot*-punctuated conversation, on one occasion apologizing for appearing even more wan than usual by explaining that he had caught a cold by inadvertently leaving the tassel off his cane. "Dear Aubrey is always too Parisian," Oscar once observed, using a variation of the remark with which he had demolished Frank Harris; "he cannot forget that he has been to Dieppe—once."[10] Knowing that Beardsley admired Pope above all other English poets, Oscar brought a literary discussion with Douglas and Beardsley to an abrupt end by observing that there were two ways of disliking poetry: one was to dislike it, and the other was to like Pope.[11] Beardsley and Wilde were at lunch one day when, to the others present. Oscar declared with flattering insincerity,

Absinthe is to all other drinks what Aubrey's drawings are to other pictures; it stands alone; it is like nothing else; it shimmers like southern twilight in opalescent colouring; it has about it the seduction of strange sins. It is stronger than any other spirit and brings out the subconscious self in man. It is just like your drawings, Aubrey; it gets on one's nerves and is cruel.

Baudelaire called his poems *Fleurs du Mal*, I shall call your drawings *Fleurs du Peche*—flowers of sin.

When I have before me one of your drawings I want to drink absinthe, which changes colour like jade in sunlight and makes the senses thrall, and then I can live myself back in imperial Rome, in the Rome of the later Caesars.

"Don't forget the *simple* pleasures of that life, Oscar," said Aubrey. "Nero set Christians on fire, like large tallow candles; the only light Christians have ever been known to give," he added languidly.[12]

Beardsley worried that Wilde would somehow bring him bad luck, but he continued with the uneasy friendship, and went on with the *Salome* drawings, diabolically inserting caricatures of Oscar into four of them. The frontispiece, "The Woman in the Moon," showed Oscar, rather than a female face, an implication that should have given the playwright some cause for alarm. In a later illustration, "A Platonic Lament," Oscar again appeared in the moon, this time literally under a cloud. He was also in "The Eyes of Herod" and "Enter Herodias," while a broad-beamed nude figure in one of the *Morte d'Arthur* chapter headings,[13] drawn during the period he knew Oscar, looked like a sybaritic and feminine Wilde.

While working on *Salome*, Beardsley drew a frontispiece for John Davidson's *Plays*, again caricaturing Wilde, and he added a face almost equally recognizable by the public, that of impresario Sir Augustus Harris. The artist was getting even with Harris for having oversold his house, accepting

John and Salome, from *Salome*

The Peacock Skirt, from *Salome*

Beardsley's half-crown at the Covent Garden Opera House without providing him with a seat. When the book was published, the *Daily Chronicle* took Beardsley to task:

An Error of Taste

Mr Beardsley has contributed a frontispiece *à propos* of "Scaramouch in Naxos" in which one or two well-known faces of the day are to be recognized*—an error of taste which is to be regretted.

The next day the *Chronicle* published Beardsley's rebuttal of the criticism:

An Error of Taste

Sir,—In your review of Mr. Davidson's plays, I find myself convicted of an error of taste, for having introduced portraits into my frontispiece to that book. I cannot help feeling that your reviewer is unduly severe. One of the gentlemen who forms part of my decoration is surely beautiful enough to stand the test even of portraiture, the other owes me half a crown.

I am, yours truly,
Aubrey Beardsley

The more Beardsley knew of Wilde, the less he appreciated being patronized by him. Oscar was gross and sybaritic, had strange young fawning friends, and complacently accepted adulation as his due. One of his sallies making the rounds in London was particularly infuriating to the young artist: "I invented Aubrey Beardsley." Countering, Beardsley was contemptuous of Oscar's artistic obtuseness. "At noontide," he told Frank Harris, knowing that it would get back to Wilde that way, "Oscar will know that the sun has risen." Still, Wilde knew most of the literary and artistic establishment worth knowing, and a link to him meant introductions and connections in the right places. Whether to satisfy his ego or to mortify his soul, Beardsley even kept— for a while— an autographed portrait of Oscar (swathed in a fur-collared coat) on his mantel.

Since Beardsley still had the huge *Morte d'Arthur* project on his hands, as well as other commissions, the work on *Salome* progressed slowly, and he

---

*Actually, more than "one or two" faces were recognizable, for (from left to right across the drawing) Beardsley had caricatured Henry Harland (as a satyr), Oscar Wilde, Sir Augustus Harris, and Richard Le Gallienne. The women have been inaccurately identified as Mabel Beardsley and Adeline Genée.

delivered pictures to Elkin Mathews and John Lane one or two at a time. He redrew and simplified his original *Studio* "Salome," adding it to the series, and drew the swirling, Japanesque "The Peacock Skirt." Although influenced by Wilde's play, the drawing showed, too, how much Beardsley was still under the influence of Huysmans's novel. (Wilde's Herod tries to bribe his daughter with peacocks—"my beautiful white peacocks, that walk in the garden between the myrtles and the tall cypress-trees. Their beaks are gilded with gold and the grains that they eat are smeared with gold, and their feet are stained with purple.") There were peacocks, too, in Whistler's Japanesque decorations for Frederick Leyland. But the texture of Beardsley's "Peacock Skirt" seems right out of *A Rebours*, in which one of the paintings in Des Esseintes's gallery had been a Salomé, described in one of Huysmans's most famous purple patches:

With a face withdrawn, solemn, almost august, she began the lascivious dance which was to awaken the exhausted senses of the aged Herod; her breasts quivered and, at the touch of her whirling necklaces of jewels, the nipples rose; diamonds, attached to the dampness of her flesh, scintillated; her bracelets, her girdles, her rings gave out sparks on her triumphal robe sewn with pearls, of which each scale was a stone, seemed to be on fire, little snakes of flame swarming over the pale flesh, over the tea-rose skin, like splendid insects, with dazzling shards, marbled with carmine, shot with pale yellow, diapered with steel-blue, striped with peacock green.*

It was about this time that the Beardsleys moved to a more spacious house in Pimlico, at 114 Cambridge Street, and Aubrey had the rooms he used himself decorated as Des Esseintes had done. Newly prosperous, he had Aymer Vallance design the alterations. "The walls of his rooms," a shocked visitor observed, "were distempered a violent orange, the doors and skirtings were painted black." It was "a strange taste," he thought, but after all, Beardsley's tastes were "all for the bizarre and the exotic."[14] Apparently the visitor had not read *A Rebours*.

Although long afterwards Beardsley's mother, who was preoccupied with being his nurse but had little idea of his professional associations, thought that her son's friendship with Wilde lasted only six weeks, it was still in progress through the summer of 1893, possibly because the most question-

---

*Huysmans was inspired by a "Salomé" of Gustave Moreau, first exhibited in 1876; and Moreau in turn had been influenced by Flaubert's evocations of oriental imagery in his *Tentation de Saint Antoine*.

The Dancer's Reward, from *Salome*

The Climax, from *Salome*

able drawings for *Salome* had yet to be delivered to Lane. While it lasted, Aubrey could be seen with the usual Wildean coterie in all the fashionable restaurants and theatres. Oscar's *A Woman of No Importance* was playing at the Haymarket, and Beardsley was included in the party at its final performance on 16 August. Apparently they had all drunk, if not dined, well before the performance, for Aubrey was the only sober one in the group—his chronic illness restricting his intake. Max Beerbohm saw them there, Oscar with "Bosie and Robbie and Aubrey Beardsley. The last of these," Max noticed, "had forgotten to put vine-leaves in his hair, but the other three wore rich clusters—especially poor Robbie. I have never seen Oscar so fatuous. . . ."[15] Max left no record of how uncomfortable Aubrey may have felt with the tipsy trio.

Towards the end of the summer he had a recurrence of hemorrhaging, and was weak and wan from overwork and illness. His mother packed him off to Haslemere, hoping that the Surrey countryside would do him some good. By early September she had to write to Robert Ross, "Haslemere was a failure, Aubrey took a dislike to the place directly he got there and wanted to rush back to town at once. . . . I persuaded him to stay from day to day, but his depression was so great and the life he led me so dreadful that at the end of a fortnight I gave it up and let him come home."[16] It had been a disastrous way for Aubrey to celebrate his coming-of-age: 21 August 1893 had been his twenty-first birthday.

By the end of September he was hard at work again, although he had had more hemorrhaging earlier in the month. To King he apologized for a "long silence" by admitting that he found letterwriting "a terrible strain on me now, as my health is very feeble and my work very exacting." "Certainly for the moment," he added, "I have fortune at my foot, but I can tell you I have worked & work very hard for it . . . I have had no rest this summer at all & indeed shall get none this side of Xmas. My drawings for Salome have aroused great excitement & plenty of abuse. . . ."[17]

At the beginning the abuse came from the people most concerned with the publication of *Salome*—the publishers. Like Wilde, they were torn between admiration and horror. Wilde, who understood the theatrical, self-advertising personality, very likely would have gone along completely with the drawings; but he was more and more under "Bosie" Douglas's influence, and Douglas and Beardsley had had little time for each other, since their rivalry for the

A Platonic Lament, from *Salome*

translating commission for *Salome*. Undiplomatically, Beardsley even commented once to Robbie Ross, best friend of Oscar and Bosie, "Both of them are really very dreadful people." Late in 1893, Douglas, acting for Wilde, asked John Lane to send the completed set of Beardsley drawings over to the Hotel Albemarle, and the issue was joined.

"I suppose you've heard about the *Salome* row," Beardsley wrote to Ross. "I can tell you I had a warm time of it between Lane and Oscar and Co. For one week the numbers of telegraph and messenger boys who came to the door was simply scandalous. I really don't quite know how the matter really stands now . . . I have withdrawn 3 of the illustrations and supplied their places with 3 new ones (simply beautiful and quite irrelevant). . . ."[18] Writing to another friend, Beardsley inquired whether he was "ready to join the newly-formed anti-Lane society"; and soon afterwards, having become ill while driving himself to complete the sketches, reported on an additional ordeal. "I have been very ill since you left—rather severe attacks of blood-spitting and an abominable bilious attack to finish me off. This is my first day up for some time. The *Salome* drawings have created a veritable *fronde* with George Moore at the head of the *frondeurs*."[19] It would not be the last time George Moore would be scandalized by Beardsley's work, and intrude into attempts to suppress it.

Beardsley admitted that one of the drawings—the original title page—"was impossible." "You see," he later explained to Ross, "booksellers couldn't stick it up in their windows." He did a replacement drawing, with Salome and "a little grotesque Eros . . . a great improvement on the first."[20]

The publishers' sense of scandal and decorum affected Beardsley's drawings with grotesque inconsistency. After passing by the "Woman in the Moon" frontispiece, with its nude male figure in the foreground, they insisted that the artist remove the genitals from two figures on the title page. Another sketch, "Enter Herodias," was canceled in its first state, and Beardsley was asked to make some concessions to good taste by altering a proof copy, from which a new block would be made. Strangely, this preserved the since-reproduced original, while the artist added a large fig leaf to an "indecent" figure in the proof. On one copy of the proof which Beardsley retrieved and gave to Frank Harris, he scrawled a wry quatrain in the upper left corner:

> Because one figure was undressed
> This little drawing was suppressed.
> It was unkind, but never mind,
> Perhaps it all was for the best.[21]

Rather than continue attaching fig leaves or otherwise expurgating drawings with which he was satisfied, Beardsley withdrew several originals and replaced them with—as he had told Ross—"beautiful and quite irrelevant" substitutes. As even a critic not entirely noted for sympathy with Beardsley realized,

whilst his will compelled him to make two new drawings as substitutes in fulfilment of his covenant, and his hand's skill endeavoured to create them in the same convention, he had so markedly advanced to a new creative intention and a new hand's skill that he could not recall the atmosphere of the thing he had wrought so well; he had left it behind him for ever, and by the very fulfilling of his covenant he came near to wreck[ing] the design of *Salome* . . . We could not have a more marked proof that so rapidly was Beardsley advancing from stage to stage of artistic utterance that even when he attempted to go back, and did not refuse to go back he found that with the best will in the world he could not do so.[22]

The relatively innocent "John and Salome"—it endowed Salome with a pronounced navel—was replaced with "The Black Cape," a burlesque on nineties vogues in dress, which showed a fashionable woman in a narrow-waisted, wide-skirted, multiple-caped black coat. It could have offended no one except a reader who expected the illustrations to have some connection to the text. "The Toilet of Salome" also became a nineties scene, with a masked pierrot adjusting the broad-brimmed hat of another fashionably-gowned lady, while the background was a modern Venetian blind and the foreground an Art Nouveau dressing-table. On the bottom shelf, below the paints and powders, was a group of books, ancient and modern, but uniformly scandalous to the philistines: Zola's *Nana, Manon Lescaut*, a volume of de Sade, and *The Golden Ass*. The anachronistic dressing-table, as well as some of the books, had appeared in the original, as well as a pierrot hairdresser, but there had also been several nude figures, including Salome, most of them complete to—by Bodley Head standards—erotic physical details. But Beardsley affected innocence. As Frank Harris put it, "Looking a mere boy, Beardsley would point to this scabrous detail and that: 'I see nothing wrong with the drawing; do you?' as if pudenda were [merely] ears to be studied. . . ."

Some of the most powerful and imaginative drawings, such as the final full-sized one showing Salome clutching Jokanaan's head ("The Climax"), had balance and magnificence; but they were sufficiently sadistic and sanguinary to be repellent as well, had the Victorian mind dwelt on any other offenses to decorum than sexual ones. Fortunately the drawings remained, and the book went to press, both Wilde and Beardsley apparently happy with the final

The Black Cape, from Salome

The Toilet of Salome, from *Salome*

result, as far as each other's parts in the enterprise were concerned.* Possibly the "Pictured by" rather than "Illustrated by" on the title page helped mollify Wilde—and was clearly more accurate. But both Beardsley and Wilde were now unhappy with Lane, who had devised coarse-grained blue canvas boards for a cover. "The cover of *Salome* is quite dreadful," Oscar wrote Lane.

Don't spoil a lovely book . . . The texture of the present cover is coarse and common: it is quite impossible and spoils the real beauty of the interior. Use up this horrid Irish stuff for stories etc: don't inflict it on a work of art like *Salome*. It will really do you a great deal of harm. Everyone will say it is coarse and inappropriate. I loathe it. So does Beardsley.[23]

Here the curious collaborators apparently won out over Lane. The decorative splendor of the green-and-gold peacock-feather binding Beardsley designed had a luxuriance which communicated more of the atmosphere of Wilde's play than most of the pictures inside.

Early in 1894 the Bodley Head *Salome* was released, the notoriety of the event giving Oscar and Aubrey additional reason for mutual, but guarded, admiration. Yet Beardsley should perhaps not have felt so secure in his success with *Salome*. As brilliant as some of the drawings were, he had made publishing history of a sort not always useful to a career: some of the illustrations in the volume finally printed included more "erotic" details than had ever been seen before in a book openly published and distributed in England. And although Beardsley could point to other concealed caricatures he had made, including Whistler as a faun and Max Beerbohm as a fetus, his method of illustrating Oscar's play as well as the fact of its publication inevitably associated him in the public mind with a public figure not only near the pinnacle of his reputation, but also on the edge of ill-fame.

If Wilde had pretended not to notice the obvious caricatures of himself in *Salome* before publication, he could not evade them after the book's release, for critics—generally malicious when it came to Wilde anyway—

---

*"I fancy Beardsley was relieved to get his *Salome* drawings done. The inspiration of Morris and Burne-Jones was waning fast, and the eighteenth-century illustrators were taking the place of the Japanese print. Conder, and also Sickert I think, influenced Beardsley just at this time. I have some hesitation in suggesting that paintings of mine—the *Souvenir of Scarborough*, for instance, and the studies of the girl in an 1830 bonnet exhibited at the New English Art Club, were not without their effect on Beardsley's outlook. . . . This is not for a moment to take away from the originality of Beardsley's conceptions; but this change from the Japanese to the eighteenth century was as marked as that from Morris to the Japanese." (Rothenstein, *Men and Memories*, pp. 184-5.)

The Eyes of Herod, from *Salome*

thought the illustrations either an outrage or a huge joke. To the *Saturday Review* it was a prank:

Mr. Aubrey Beardsley is a very clever young man, but we cannot think his cleverness is quite agreeable to Mr. Wilde. Illustration by means of derisive parody of Félicien Rops, embroidered on to Japanese themes, is a new form of literary torture; and no one can question that the author of *Salome* is on the rack . . . Mr. Beardsley laughs at Mr. Wilde. . . . Let us turn to the "Toilette of Salome" . . . no wonder her conversation had an irreligious effect upon the Tetrarch. But what a fantastic way of illustrating a Biblical tragedy! We should like to test Mr. Aubrey Beardsley's *bona fides* by entrusting the *Athalie* of Racine to his care. Would he play the same pranks with *Samson Agonistes* as with *Salome*?

The Times agreed that Beardsley's pictures were a joke, but found less fun in them, condemning them as

. . . fantastic, grotesque, unintelligible for the most part, and, so far as they are intelligible, repulsive. They would seem to represent the manners of Judaea as conceived by Mr. Oscar Wilde portrayed in the style of the Japanese grotesque as conceived by a French *décadent*. The whole thing must be a joke, and it seems to us a very poor joke!

Loyally—but prudently—*The Studio* supported Beardsley, and (since it had introduced him to the public) by inference, itself:

Audacious and extravagant. . . . Those who dislike Mr. Beardsley's work will be happy in the possession of the documentary evidence to support their opinion, while those who find it the very essence of the decadent *fin de siècle* will rank *Salome* as the typical volume of a period too recent to estimate its actual value, and too near to judge of its ultimate influence on decorative art. All collectors of rare and esoteric literature will rank this book as one of the most remarkable productions of the modern press.

By publication time of *Salome*, Beardsley was doing preliminary work for the first issue of *The Yellow Book*, for which he was to be art editor, and although Wilde had not yet been asked to contribute to the new quarterly (he never would be) he seemed to be on good terms with the young artist. In February he even took Beardsley to the St. James's Theatre to see *The Second Mrs. Tanqueray*, and escorted him backstage afterwards to meet its star, Mrs. Patrick Campbell, whom Beardsley wanted to draw. From a box in the theatre Wilde sent her a note:

Mr. Aubrey Beardsley, a very brilliant and wonderful young artist, and like all artists a great admirer of the wonder and charm of your art, says that he must once have the honour of being presented to you, if you will allow it. So, with your gracious sanction, I will come round after Act III with him, and you would gratify and honour him much if you would let him bow his compliments to you. He has just illustrated my play of *Salome* for me, and has a copy of the *edition de luxe* which he wishes to lay at your feet. His drawings are quite wonderful.[24]

When the first number of *The Yellow Book* appeared, it contained a Beardsley drawing of the actress. Oscar, not being otherwise involved with the venture, naturally found little about it he liked. Max Beerbohm met Wilde one afternoon in the Domino Room of the Café Royal, and was told that Beardsley had just been displaying the drawing for the cover of *The Yellow Book*. "What was it like?" Max asked. "Oh" said Oscar, "you can imagine the sort of thing. A terrible naked harlot smiling through a mask — and with *Elkin Mathews* written on one breast and *John Lane* on the other."[25]

Once *The Yellow Book* was offered for sale, Wilde found the quarterly "horrid," "loathsome," "dull," and — worst of all — "not yellow at all." "*The Yellow Book* has appeared," he wrote to Alfred Douglas. "It is dull and loathsome, a great failure. I am so glad."[26] He confided to Charles Ricketts that he had invested five shillings in the first issue, and when Ricketts praised it Wilde countered sweetly,

> My dear boy, do not say false things about *The Yellow Book*. I bought it at the station, but before I had cut all the pages I threw it out of my carriage window. Suddenly the train stopped and the guard, opening the door, said "Mr. Wilde, you have dropped *The Yellow Book*." What was to be done? In the hansom, with the subtlety of the poet, I cunningly hid it under the cushions, and paid my fare. . . . When came a loud knocking at the door, and the cabby appearing, said "Mr. Wilde, you have forgotten *The Yellow Book*."[27]

During the first year of *The Yellow Book*'s life, Robert Hichens, who, through his friends Reggie Turner and Lord Alfred Douglas, had met Wilde several times, poked fun, in a satirical novel, *The Green Carnation*, at Wilde's hostility to the publication he associated with Beardsley — and Beardsley's love of masked figures and linear economy. Wilde became the aesthete Esmé Amarinth, who, rather than spoil his afternoon by taking a walk, explains,

> "I will stay at home and read the last number of *The Yellow Disaster*. I want to see Mr. Aubrey Beardsley's idea of the Archbishop of Canterbury. He has drawn him sitting in a wheelbarrow in the gardens of Lambeth Palace, with underneath him the motto *J'y*

Salome on Settle, intended as a replacement for one of the more obviously erotic drawings for *Salome* but not used, perhaps because the publisher interpreted the back view of the figure as indicating an open kimono, and the wand or baton, therefore, as dildo. It was first published by Lane as part of a portfolio of *Salome* drawings in 1907.

suis, j'y rests. I believe he has on a black mask. Perhaps that is to conceal the likeness."

"I have seen it," says Mrs. Windsor, "it is very clever. There are only three lines in the whole picture, two for the wheelbarrow and one for the Archbishop."

"What exquisite simplicity!" Lord Reggie exclaims.[28]

Beardsley had learned a lot about affectation from Wilde, and in the early days of his glory often outmaneuvered and surpassed his reluctant teacher. The effort brought him the friendship of caustic-tongued Ada Leverson, whom Oscar called "Sphinx." "Though not affected myself, I like other people to be," she would say; and in one of his few facetious remarks about the disease which would, more and more often, leave him hemorrhaging and gasping, Beardsley observed, to her delight, "Really I believe I'm so affected, even my lungs are affected." One of her favorite memories was of his leaving the Brompton Oratory on a brilliant, sunny morning and startling the departing congregants by exclaiming, as he looked up at the sky. "What a dear day!"[29] Beardsley became a favorite dinner- and theatre-guest of hers, and once he reciprocated, writing to her the day before he was to give a party, "Will you come an hour earlier than the others, and help me to scent the flowers?" When she arrived she discovered that he took his pose seriously: he was spraying bowls of gardenias and tuberoses with opoponax. As Sphinx entered, he handed her a spray of frangipani for the stephanotis.[30]

John Gray was another of Mrs. Leverson's young friends. He had become a fashionable poet, and mingled with Wilde, Pierre Louÿs, Ernest Dowson, and—soon—Beardsley. His first and most curious book had been the narrow, thirty-five-page *Silverpoints* (1893), the costs of publication by the firm of Elkin Mathews and John Lane paid for in part by Wilde, their friendship sufficiently close to give the writer of a gossip column in the London *Star* the idea that Gray was "said to be the original Dorian of the same name" and had "cultivated his manner to the highest pitch of languor yet attained." Gray had sued, and without Wilde's help (and Oscar denied everything) the *Star* could not prove its allegedly libelous allegation in court, and had to publish a meek retraction. (Seventy years later a letter from Gray to Wilde turned up beginning "My dear Oscar" and ending "Yours ever, Dorian.") Gray would become later one of the most influential people in Beardsley's life, but was then still a librarian at the Foreign Office, with a busy after-hours career. A civil servant by day, he frequented at night the Café Royal, the Florence Restaurant, the Crown in Charing Cross Road, the Cheshire Cheese. His slender book of poems, handsomely designed by Charles Ricketts, but printed in nearly unreadable italics, had been intended primarily for distribution to Gray's friends.

Mrs. Leverson was more impressed by the expanse of white on each page than by the letterpress. "There was more margin," she wrote afterwards;

margin in every sense of the word was in demand, and I remember . . . when I saw the tiniest rivulet of text meandering through the very largest meadow of margin, I suggested to Oscar Wilde that he should go a step further than these minor poets; that he should publish a book *all* margin; full of beautiful unwritten thoughts, and have this blank volume bound in some Nile-green skin powdered with gold by Ricketts (if not Shannon) and printed on Japanese paper; each volume must be a collector's piece, a numbered one of a limited "first" (and last) edition: "very rare."

Wilde approved. "It shall be dedicated to you," he told Sphinx, "and the unwritten text illustrated by Aubrey Beardsley. There must be five hundred signed copies for particular friends, six for the general public, and one for America."[31]

Wilde sent Mrs. Leverson a ticket for a box for the opening night of *The Importance of Being Earnest*, on 14 February 1895; and she invited Aubrey and Mabel, and other friends of hers and the author's. It was to be Wilde's greatest—and last—moment of success, and between the acts, beaming and bloated, he joined Ada and Ernest Leverson and their guests in their box, while the opening-night audience gaped. Glancing at the young Beardsleys in their evening dress, he quipped tiresomely to the Leversons, "What a contrast the two are! Mabel a daisy, Aubrey the most monstrous of orchids." The attention from Oscar on the greatest evening of his career must have fed Beardsley's cockiness, yet a curious premonition of the disaster to come had already appeared in his note of acceptance to the Sphinx: "I look forward eagerly to the first act of Oscar's new Tragedy. But surely the title 'Douglas' has been used before."[32] Beardsley knew that Wilde's play was advertised as a comedy, and that Lord Alfred Douglas would be at the opening with Oscar. For the Sphinx the note could have been little more than a private joke, referring to the title of John Home's laborious 1756 Scottish tragedy and to Oscar's closest friendship—which would lead to an arrest, his three trials in April and May, and a conviction which would shatter the career of such an innocent onlooker as Beardsley himself. Aubrey was, Bernard Shaw wrote, "boyish enough to pose as a diabolical reveller in vices of which he was innocent." And when Wilde fell, Beardsley mischievously remarked ("with an air that did not impose on me," G.B.S. added), "I suppose I shall have to leave the country."[33]

The Burial of Salome
(cul-de-lampe), from *Salome*

5

1893-1894

The Beardsley Boom

The month in which *Salome* went to press was the month in which *The Yellow Book* went into proof. Beardsley's burgeoning fame seemed never to wait for the actual appearance of its latest justification. Once he had begun working on the *Morte*, the news of something he was doing, or even beginning, seemed sufficient. In his "A New Illustrator" article for *The Studio* of April 1893, where it had all started less than a year before, Joseph Pennell had been careful not to make flamboyant pronouncements about Beardsley's personal potential. Instead, he had used his "new illustrator" to represent the values of line-block (as opposed to old-fashioned wood-block) reproduction of prints and drawings. "It is most interesting," Pennell had observed, implying several slaps at William Morris,

. . . that though Mr. Beardsley has drawn his motives from every age, and founded his styles—for it is quite impossible to say what his style may be—on all schools, he has not been carried back into the fifteenth century or succumbed to the limits of Japan; he has recognised that he is living in the last decade of the nineteenth century, and he has availed himself of mechanical reproduction for the publication of his drawings, which the Japs and the Germans would have accepted with delight had they but known of it.

Whatever Pennell's prudence, *The Studio's* small initial audience was composed of sophisticated readers in the arts and in publishing, and they were able to assess the new illustrator's abilities for themselves. Curiously, Holme, the owner of *The Studio*, paid his writers but not his artists, who had even less opportunity for earnings from their work; and Beardsley received nothing for the eleven reproductions of his drawings—nothing, that is, but an influential readership.

Some of the eleven drawings were mediocre mimicries of Mantegna and Burne-Jones, but there were also four from the *Morte d'Arthur* (not due to begin serial publication until that June), and Japanesques representing an even later style. More significantly, there was the "Salome with the Head of John the Baptist," the germ of the *Salome* series and perhaps the most striking single drawing knowledgeable professionals in London had come upon in years. Yet it had been an afterthought, produced after Hind and Holme had gone through Beardsley's portfolio, and, in fact, after Hind had left *The Studio*. Pennell's text—which acted as careful confirmation—was hardly needed to announce that, at twenty, Beardsley had arrived.

To the London public in 1893, Beardsley still hardly existed. Almost none of the myriad dailies, weeklies and fortnightlies which appeared in the city took notice of his *Studio* debut, and, for the few which mentioned his name, only the minor *London Figaro* (20 April 1893) seemed interested:

. . . they are the quaintest things I ever saw. His men and things are like nothing (I hope) that is in heaven above, or in the earth beneath, or in the waters under the earth, but we are called upon by Mr. Pennell to bow down and worship them all the same. I refuse. The drawings are flat blasphemies against art. Burne-Jones I admire and the oddities of Japanese draughtsmen I can appreciate, but when a man mixes up impotent imitations of Burne-Jones at his very worst with pseudo-Japanese effects, and serves up the whole with a sauce of lilies and peacock feathers I think it is only charitable to think that the author of all this rococo business has a twist in his intellect. His decorative borders, however, show that if his gifts were directed into the right channel. . . .

Although the popular press largely ignored him, the silence was of little professional consequence. After his grand reception in Paris that spring, his dogged work on the *Morte* installments, and new commissions like *Salome* undertaken, Beardsley had more to do than time to do it, a problem quickly aggravated by renewed lung hemorrhages. Despondently, he talked of giving up the elaborate and time-consuming *Morte* drawings, although serial parts were already on sale. He was pushing himself physically, and running low on invention for the dozens of chapters still remaining. Exhausted, he complained that Malory's book was "very long-winded," and Mrs. Beardsley took him seriously enough to intervene with his friends, pressing Vallance and Ross to persuade Aubrey to persevere with the work. "To me," she wrote Ross without her son's knowledge,

it seems monstrous that he should even contemplate behaving in such an unprincipled

Silhouette, a self-portrait

Design for chapter heading for *Le Morte d'Arthur*

manner. His "Morte" work may be a little unequal—that is his own fault and because he is wilful enough not to exert himself over what he pretends he doesn't like—but take it on the whole it is beautiful work and does him credit. But that isn't the point, he undertook to do it, and Mr. Dent has spent money over it and subscribers too, and if Aubrey gives it up it will be disgraceful.[1]

"He was disappointed," Vallance thought,

. . .with the printing, and finding how much the beauty of drawings on which he had bestowed infinite pains was lost in excessive reduction. . . . Whether it was these causes or because he had taken upon himself a burden beyond his strength . . . Beardsley declared he would not go on with it: every subsequent drawing was wrung from him by threats and promises and entreaties. The publisher was in despair. . . . Not one of the outside public knew . . . [Beardsley would] put off the irksome duty as long as he could, and then, as the day approached when the month's work was due . . . he had to strain every nerve, working early and late, to get it done.

As a result, Vallance concluded, the *Morte* contained "some of the artist's very best, together with some of his most indifferent and slovenly, work."[2] But the work continued.

The ebbing of enthusiasm in the *Morte* was not obvious to any but the few possessing inside information, for some of the most inspired drawings appeared in the closing sections of the work. They had been done earlier, and laid aside for their appropriate places in the sequence. Yet even the uninformed reader could see some small designs repeated, and some printed in unfinished states only superficially disguised. A horseman appeared, with only the hindquarters of his mount shown, the unfilled space covered with a wash of black. A double-page drawing of "La Beale Isoud at Joyous Gard" was printed with a figure strangely alone at the right. In the original draft Beardsley had penciled in a group of figures, but to spare himself work on their details he rubbed out all but one, extending Isoud's wide, sweeping train to fill in most of the foreground and blacking in the background with "grass."* One of the chapter headings had a fountain in the background and a peacock (one of some two dozen peacocks among the drawings) in front. As lacking in detail as the fountain was, it had more precision than the peacock, which lacked legs, and had only a patch of white for a tail. What had begun in enthusiasm and

*Yet there was a Picassoesque (although pre-Picasso) border of suggestively detailed pears, each shaped like a female torso, and complete in most cases to lopsided breasts and a pubic area. One wonders whether Beardsley was relieved or disappointed that his inspiration went unnoticed.

vigor was ending in indifference and relief. As with the *Salome*, which encompassed a much briefer creative period, by the time Beardsley completed the project he had so outdistanced the phase of his development in which he had begun it that he had to create forgeries of his earlier style in order to complete the work.

Looking in on the *Morte* project towards the end of 1893 was a bespectacled young painter with whom Beardsley had become friendly in Paris, Will Rothenstein. The curious orange-and-black color scheme of the Cambridge Street rooms took him by surprise, and he wondered whether to accept an offer to share temporarily a drawing table enclosed by such "distempered" walls. None of Rothenstein's misgivings were intimated to Beardsley, who would not have understood. He was too busy creating a persona for himself, much of it acquired at second-hand from Whistler, Wilde, Huysmans and others, yet like his art developing characteristics which were becoming uniquely his own. He wanted to be known for his tastes for the bizarre and the exotic, tastes which began at the extremes and eventually moderated with success, and Will Rothenstein provided him with an early opportunity.

Rothenstein had picked up a Japanese book in Paris, realizing afterwards that its explicit pictures were "so outrageous that its possession was an embarassment." When Beardsley seemed pleased with *The Book of Love*, he gave it to him; and the next time Rothenstein visited in Cambridge Street he found that Beardsley had removed the most indecent prints from the book and put them on display in his bedroom. "Seeing he lived with his mother and sister," Rothenstein wrote later, "I was rather taken aback. He affected an extreme cynicism, however, which was startling at times; he spoke enormities. . . ." The gift prints may have been the beginnings of a larger collection, for a later visitor claimed that "Beardsley owned the most beautiful Japanese woodcuts one could see in London, all of them of the most detailed eroticism. They were hanging in simple frames on delicately shaded wallpaper—all of them indecent, the wildest visions of Utamaro. Seen from a distance, however, they appeared very dainty, clear and harmless."[3]

Before going on to Oxford to paint portraits of university personalities, Rothenstein took up Beardsley's offer to make use of the Cambridge Street workroom while in London. They would sit at opposite sides of a large table, Beardsley keeping up a constant flow of talk while he concentrated on his drawing. He would do a preparatory design in pencil, only suggesting the

Design for chapter heading for *Le Morte d'Arthur* very closely resembling Beardsley's title page for *Salome*

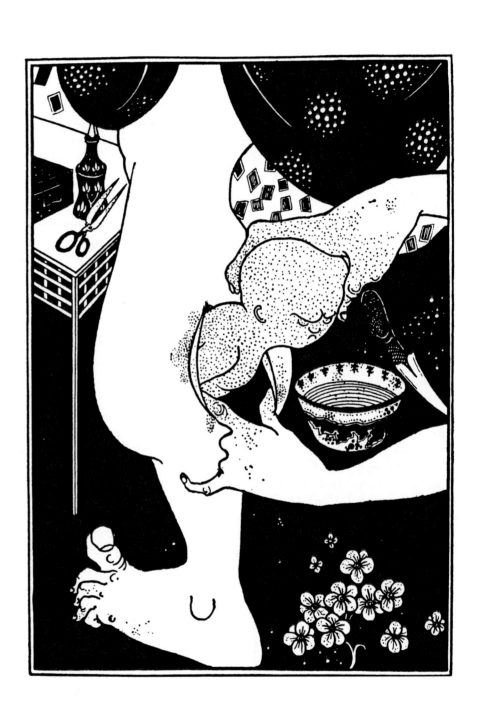

complicated patterns he had in mind; afterwards, while Rothenstein pretended not to watch, Beardsley would draw over them, sometimes performing complicated traceries with his pen.[4]

In London and in Paris, by the end of 1893, he was being talked about more and more, and in both cities was becoming the subject of articles in the press. In mock complaint he wrote to Robbie Ross, "Did you see the 'life' and *atrocious portrait* of myself that came out in the *Morning Leader* last week [?] The Brutes gave my real age too!"[5] Art critic Royal Cortissoz first heard of him from Gleeson White, and found that Beardsley's name now cropped up whenever there was discussion of modern art and artists. One day in Paris Cortissoz asked Whistler's opinion of Beardsley. "He seems to me," said the Master, "like one of those men who stand idle in the market place because no man hired them." With that utterly uninformed dictum, Whistler dismissed further thoughts of the upstart artist with a wave of his hand.[6]

In Cambridge Street, Beardsley was beginning to establish himself in London social life. It was obvious from a self-caricature of the period, which reflected his habit of walking into publishers' offices in morning coat and patent-leather pumps, "doubtless causing a slight uncertainty as to whether the latter were a remnant of the night before or an early anticipation of the night to be."[7] A famous public figure when *Salome* was released at the beginning of 1894, he drew curious stares wherever he went, and had well-attended at-homes, presided over by his sister and his mother. For his Thursday afternoons he prepared the house to reflect meticulously his persona. Haldane MacFall, who attended some of the later Thursdays, recalled that Beardsley

dressed with scrupulous care to be in the severest good taste and fashion, delighted to play the host—and an excellent host he was. All his charming qualities were seen at their best. The lanky, rather awkward, angular Aubrey, pallid of countenance, stooped and meagre of body, with his "tortoiseshell-coloured hair" worn in a smooth fringe over his white forehead, was the life and soul of his little gatherings. But he paid for it with a "bad night" always when the guests departed.

The little theatricals he and Mabel had given when they were innocent teenagers had given way to the more formal give-and-take of conversation, but the new Cambridge Street house had something of the theatrical about it too, in the orange-and-black décor of Beardsley's studio, and other walls in

Birth from the Calf of the Leg (left) and *Lucian's Strange Creatures* (above), both intended as illustrations for *Lucian's True History* (1894), but published finally by Leonard Smithers in 1906. Note that the horned figure with the grape-like hair is one of Beardsley's many sly caricatures of Oscar Wilde.

the house decorated with stripes running from ceiling to floor. "The couch in his studio," MacFall observed, "bore sad evidence to the fact that he had to spend all too much of his all too short life lying upon it."[8]

While working on *Salome* and the *Morte,* Beardsley had begun the art work for what became a series of books which made him better known than the limited-audience publications on which he had been spending so much time. He did a title-page design and cover for "George Egerton's" novel *Keynotes* (1893), and for the back of the book devised an ornamental "key" combining the initials of the author. Actually the author was Mary Chavelita Dunne, who wrote feminist novels under a masculine pseudonym. By nineties' standards *Keynotes* was "sexy" enough to be a notorious success for Elkin Mathews and John Lane, giving them the idea of publishing a series of novels under the *Keynotes* colophon. For them Beardsley designed title pages, covers, and monogram "keys," but, although the series ran to thirty-four volumes, his own part in the ingenious promotion ran only to twenty-two covers and fifteen "keys"; the remainder were designed in his style by successor artists. Among the ones he did himself were such then-notorious novels as Grant Allen's *The Woman Who Did,* and fiction by Arthur Machen, Kenneth Grahame, Florence Farr (whose book bore a Whistler caricature) and a clutch of younger-generation writers who were to appear with Beardsley again in *The Yellow Book. The Keynote Series* were among the most popular books of the decade, and for years afterwards Beardsley's work circulated through them when it was otherwise unavailable.

John Lane knew a good investment when he saw it, and Beardsley was soon taken in hand by the publisher in a way that let the young man know his value. For example, Lane took him to the writers' haunts which he assumed that Beardsley, in the diffidence of youth and near-invalidism, would not have frequented, among them the Crown, a public house in the music hall district where, according to Arthur Symons—one of whose passions was the music hall and another of which was a music hall dancer—, "Young England—poets, painters and others—had the friendly habit of meeting, most nights in the week, and where aesthetics and metaphysics were discussed (after Alhambra hours) to the accompaniment of the cheerful chatter of Alhambra ladies."

Symons's first impressions were negative ones, but he had no idea of

Design for *St. Paul's* (1894). See page 88.

THE WOMAN WHO DID
BY GRANT ALLEN

BOSTON: ROBERTS BROS, 1895

LONDON: JOHN LANE, VIGO ST

Title page for the most famous of the *Keynotes* series
of novels, with its "key"

Beardsley's innocence in bohemian society, for the artist had only weeks before signed the *Salomé* contract, and was still relatively unknown. He was also, to Symons, "the thinnest young man I ever saw, rather unpleasant and affected," as he wrote to Herbert Horne on 23 August 1893, on returning from an evening at the Crown; "Give my love," he concluded, "to La Mumu (to whom I am going to write a charming letter about all your imaginary iniquities)." "Mumu" was Horne's exotic mistress, Muriel Broadbent, whom Symons had first met on the promenade of the Empire Theatre, where she was then plying her trade as a prostitute. Horne had since given her full-time employment.

What neither Horne nor Symons could have predicted then was that "Mumu" would, under curious circumstances, also meet Beardsley, or that Symons would become—if only for a hectic year—Beardsley's publishing partner.*

The urge to do everything he was asked to do, however much it seemed hack work, was irresistible to Beardsley. He wanted to earn what he could while he could, and to draw as much as he could while he could, even when a hack assignment was a substitute for inspiration. As a result, early in 1894, he took on still another commission, to do illustrations for *St. Paul's*, a new paper directed to the market then captured by the *Graphic* and the *Illustrated London News*. Initially, there were some conventional things to do, such as devising illustrations to be headings for each of the magazine's departments—Music, Art, Books, Fashions, Drama. None of the headings excited the proprietor, until he looked more carefully at one. In order to exasperate or titillate the readers of *St. Paul's*, Beardsley had done a drawing of a woman seated at a table, upon which was a glass dome then in fashion to house flowers or a curio. Under the dome, grotesquely, was a fetus. When the headpiece was published, it was without the macabre fillip.

Feverishly trying to accomplish everything, Beardsley reacted to the Toulouse-Lautrec posters he had seen in Paris by experimenting in poster art. Suddenly the poster had become an art form, in London through the work of the "Beggarstaff Brothers" and in Paris through the designs of a

---

*Symons later did not recall this first encounter with Beardsley. See Ian Fletcher, "Symons and Beardsley," *Times Literary Supplement*, 18 August 1966, for the full text of the letter to Horne.

Frontispiece ("The Landslide") to Bjørnstierne
Bjørnson's novel *Pastor Sang* (1893)

dozen artists besides the notorious dwarf. Without being overly concerned whether his drawings fitted the textual matter, Beardsley produced striking posters for children's books and adult books, and hopefully foresaw a day when advertising would brighten the walls of modern cities, rather than blight them. He published his observations in the *New Review*:

Advertisement is an absolute necessity of modern life, and if it can be made beautiful as well as obvious, so much the better for the makers of soap and the public who are likely to wash.

The popular idea of a picture is something told in oil or writ in water to be hung on a room's wall or in a picture gallery to perplex an artless public. No one expects it to serve a useful purpose or take a part in everyday existence. Our modern painter has merely to give a picture a good name and hang it.

Now the poster first of all justifies its existence on the grounds of utility, and should it further aspire to beauty of line and colour, may not our hoardings claim kinship with the galleries, and the designers of *affiches* pose as proudly in the public eye as the masters of Holland Road or Bond Street Barbizon (and, recollect, no gate money, no catalogue)?

Still, there is a general feeling that the artist who puts his art into the poster is *déclassé*—on the streets—and consequently of light character. The critics can discover no brush work to prate of, the painter looks askance upon a thing that achieves publicity without a frame, and beauty without modelling, and the public find it hard to take seriously a poor printed thing left to the mercy of sunshine, soot, and shower, like any old fresco over an Italian church door.

What view the bill-sticker and sandwich man may take of the subject I have yet to learn. The first is, at least, no bad substitute for a hanging committee, and the clothes of the second are better company than somebody else's picture, and less obtrusive than a background of stamped magenta paper.

Happy, then, those artists who thus escape the injustice of juries and the shuffling of dealers, and choose to keep that distance that lends enchantment to the private view, and avoid the world of worries that attends on those who elect to make an exhibition of themselves.

London will soon be resplendent with advertisements, and against a leaden sky skysigns will trace their formal arabesque. Beauty has laid siege to the city, and the telegraph wires shall no longer be the sole joy of our aesthetic perceptions.

Now, as to the technicalities of the art, I have nothing to say. To generalize upon any subject is to fall foul of the particular, and 'twere futile to lay down any rules for the making of posters. One's ears are weary of the voice of the art teacher who sits like the parrot on his perch learning the jargon of the studios, making but poor copy and calling it criticism. We have had enough of their ominiscience, their parade of technical knowledge, and their predilection for the wrong end of the stick. But if there be any who desire to know—not how posters are made—but how they

Vignette of a lady of fashion,
from *Bon-Mots of Foote and Hook*

should be, I doubt not that I could give them the addresses of one or two gentlemen who, having taken art under their wing, would give all necessary information.[9]

Beardsley made his most conspicuous contribution to the poster movement by what was then considered a daring design for the Avenue Theatre, for a short season of plays produced by Florence Farr early in 1894. It showed a broad-shouldered woman, standing behind a polka-dotted transparent curtain, and was intended by Beardsley for a variety of uses, including reduction for printing on programs sold in the theatre. "Of course," Beardsley explained to Miss Farr, "I should make my design in black & white so that a zinc block can be made, & from that you can print in any colour you like."[10] At the time he wrote, Miss Farr and her anonymous financial backer, Miss Annie Horniman (who later built the Abbey Theatre in Dublin), had not yet found a theatre, which held up final lettering on the poster. Eventually they leased the Avenue for an opening late in March. Not known for successful productions or prominent location (the two may have been related), the Avenue, located by the Thames Embankment under Charing Cross Bridge, was sometimes referred to disparagingly as the "home for lost seagulls." Because the expected Bernard Shaw play was not ready in time, the season opened with a twin bill of W.B. Yeats's *The Land of Heart's Desire* and John Todhunter's *A Comedy of Sighs*. Almost immediately afterwards Shaw wrote Alma Murray, the actress scheduled for his comedy, "The fiasco last night at the Avenue has made it necessary to produce a play of mine with all possible speed, as the only way of rescuing the enterprise." That evening he had received a telegram urging him to come to the theatre immediately. He found Miss Horniman and the theatre manager in despair, with a copy of Shaw's first play, *Widowers' Houses*, in front of them. Clearly they were planning to resort to the expedient of producing it, but Shaw dissuaded them, promising them the new play, which he had brought with him in manuscript. Whereupon he took it "out on to the Embankment Gardens and there and then put the last touches to it before leaving it to be typewritten."[11]

Beardsley's poster for *Arms and the Man* went up, and by 22 April the play, advertised by a wag in *Punch*—after Aubrey's drawing—as "Shoulders and the Woman," was in production. The poster seemed a bit of Paris set down in London, and may have been the first theatrical poster to acquire its own reviews, for journalists seemed obsessed by the need to comment on

Grotesque from *Bon-Mots of Lamb and Jerrold*

the blue-and-green woman behind the transparent curtain. It was, *The Globe* thought, "an ingenious piece of arrangement, attractive by its novelty and clevely imagined. The mysterious female who looms vaguely through the transparent curtain is, however, unnecessarily repulsive in facial type. . . ."

Traffic increased in the vicinity of the Avenue Theatre after the announcement of the new Shaw opening, and Miss Horniman noted that "even the cab horses shied" when the sensational Beardsley female on the poster outside came into view. Inside, on opening night, part of the audience cheered and laughed, and part, considering Shaw's satire as reflecting upon the glory of Her Majesty's Army, sat in silence. The Prince of Wales (afterwards Edward VII) was grim-faced, once bursting into the corridor behind his box to mutter that Shaw "must be mad." Beardsley and Will Rothenstein, already "ardent admirers of Bernard Shaw . . . followed the play intently. We laughed so frequently and heartily that we attracted the notice of an elderly lady who was sitting near." During the intermission, Rothenstein wrote afterwards, the lady "came up to us, saying that our enthusiasm had given her so much pleasure, that she would like to make our acquaintance; she introduced herself as Mrs. Bontine—'Robert Cunninghame Graham's mother,' she added, and 'my son is a great friend of Mr. Shaw.'* She hoped we would come to see her, and at her house in Chester Square, I met Robert. . . ."

Rothenstein, a portraitist, offered to paint the picturesque, swashbuckling, red-bearded Cunninghame Graham, and Graham reciprocated by offering to teach the mild Rothenstein how to fence. In fact, he insisted, and they went to Angelo's, in St. James's Street, for lessons amid the Regency atmosphere, while Beardsley and Max Beerbohm looked on with curious fascination.[12] It was a rare glimpse into the strenuous life for the bespectacled Rothenstein, the gentle Beerbohm and the pale, frail Beardsley.

Max had first met Beardsley when Rothenstein took him to the Cambridge Street house with the curious décor. He was impressed. A Cambridge undergraduate with a precocious talent already on view in print, and with

---

*Shaw based the title role and some of the incidents in his *Captain Brassbound's Conversion* (1899) on Cunninghame Graham's adventures in Morocco; and the pompous Sergius in *Arms and the Man* as well as Hector Hushabye in *Heartbreak House* (1920) owe something to him as well.

AVBREY BEAR DSLEY

Caricature of Max Beerbohm (opposite), emphasizing
his youth, from *Bon-Mots of Foote and Hook*, and
the apparently deliberately similar caricature of
Beardsley by Beerbohm in *The Yellow Book* (1894)

entrée to the theatrical and literary worlds through his half-brother, actor-manager Herbert Beerbohm-Tree, he was only three days younger than Beardsley—who was already famous or, at least, infamous. Beardsley talked with a strained, febrile vitality, and seemed to Max to have read and seen everything in current literature and art worth discussing. Although he used the extravagant clichés of the aesthete ("Really, how perfectly entrancing . . . how perfectly sweet!"), his judgments, Max realized, reflected a "stony common sense." He could see why some thought Beardsley's art corrupt or morbid, but it was also obvious to him that this doomed young man had much about which to be morbid.

They admired each other's work (Beardsley knew Max's caricatures), and took a liking to each other at once; and during Beardsley's few remaining years in London they were close friends.

The records of this period of Max's history [Lord David Cecil writes] are full of glimpses of Beardsley; neatly dressed with a butterfly tie, handing round the cakes at . . . Thursday-afternoon "at-homes": or whiling away the afternoon with Max watching the fencing at Angelo's. . . : or, again, with Max driving off for an evening's pleasure in a hansom, each of them in the full dandy's uniform of top-hat, white tie and tail-coat: or—a more distressing memory—Beardsley in his own house at a party, of which he had been the life and soul, suddenly falling asleep at the dinner table from sheer exhaustion, "with his head sunk on his breast, and his thin face white as the gardenia in his coat." They often went to the theatre together, too, to patronize the new serious drama.[13]

One of the first evenings at the theatre in which Max had joined Aubrey was the opening of *A Comedy of Sighs* and its "curtain-raiser" preliminary, *The Land of Heart's Desire*. (Beardsley, having done the poster for the Avenue production, received passes.) "Yeats was not more than a name to us then," Max remembered; "nor were we sure that it beseemed us, as men of the world, to hurry over our dinner. We did so, however, and arrived in good time. The beautiful little play was acted in nerveless and inaudible manner, casting rather a gloom over the house." Only faint applause broke the silence at the curtain, along with a few faint cries of "Author!" There was

a slight convulsion of the curtains where they joined each other, and then I saw a long fissure, revealing (as I for a moment supposed) unlit blackness behind the curtains. But lo! there were two streaks of white in the upper portion of this blackness—a white streak of shirt-front, and above that a white streak of face; and I was aware that what I had thought to be insubstantial murk was a dress-suit, with the

Caricature of Max Beerbohm with fetus-head and evening clothes, in *Bon-Mots of Lamb and Jerrold*

Author in it. And the streak of Author's face was partly bisected by a lesser black streak, which was a lock of Author's raven hair. . . . It was all very eerie and memorable.[14]

When Rothenstein helped Beardsley use his complimentary tickets for the second Avenue production, *Arms and the Man*, there was an even more memorable curtain. Bernard Gould, who played Sergius (and was a caricaturist himself later for *Punch*, as "Bernard Partridge"), through a slip of the tongue substituted "British" for "Bulgarian" in an uncomplimentary Shavian line, and a youth in the gallery hissed. When Shaw appeared for his call as author at the final curtain, the applause was tremendous. But when it faded, to permit the playwright to speak, there was a loud, solitary "Boo!" from the unknown young man in the gallery. Shaw had too much experience on the platform to be disturbed by heckling, and opened his curtain speech with "My dear fellow, I quite agree with you; but what are we two against so many?"* Still, neither posters nor curtain ripostes saved the play. It died at the box office, running at a loss for eleven weeks.

Later Shaw used his memories of Beardsley in creating the artist side of his rogue-hero, Louis Dubedat, in *The Doctor's Dilemma* (1906); and St. John Ervine, in his *Bernard Shaw*, commented, "There is a little of Aubrey Beardsley, an artist with a delicate sense of line and morbid, almost macabre imagination, in Dubedat. It was Beardsley, no doubt, who gave Dubedat his profession." It was Beardsley, too, who shared with Dubedat his mortal illness, for both young artists were to die of tuberculosis.

Shortly after cab horses began shying at Beardsley's *Arms and the Man* poster, critics were performing similar gestures of horror at the first number of *The Yellow Book*. It was Beardsley, together with an American expatriate writer, Henry Harland, who had conceived the project. The two had met in the offices of Beardsley's physician, Dr. Symes Thompson (Harland was also tubercular, but the disease was not yet so far advanced in him). At the time, although Beardsley was having no trouble finding conventional opportunities, he was searching for some unique medium for his work; and he thought of a *Comedy of Masques* which would tell its story through his art,

Decoration for the spine of the "Pierrot's Library" series of volumes published by John Lane (1894-96)

*The young man was R. Golding Bright, who, when he became a play agent, numbered Shaw among his clients. He later married "George Egerton" (Mary Chavelita Dunne), whose *Keynote* novel Beardsley had designed several months before.

Title page design for *The Yellow Book*,
Vol. I (April, 1894)

and "without any letter press." John Lane had encouraged the project, suggesting that Max Beerbohm might write something in prose or verse which would complement, but not necessarily relate, to it. Max then told Reggie Turner about the proposed "letterpress of a fantastic book of which Aubrey Beardsley is doing the illustrations," but added that "the whole thing so far is rather complicated and vague."[15] Nothing happened, and the idea apparently blended into the conglomeration of proposals which became *The Yellow Book* soon afterwards.

After the meeting in Thompson's office, Harland and Beardsley discovered that they had much more in common than their bacilli. The tubercular, dandified young Beardsley was already as mannered as his art. Harland was a *poseur* of another variety, pretending at first to exotic European ancestry and upbringing, probably because he felt that his American background—even in a country which hailed and harbored James, Whistler, Sargent and Harte—weakened his competitive position in literary London.

On New Year's Day 1894, according to Henry Harland, Beardsley—following up their encounter in the doctor's office—came to lunch at his home in Cromwell Road. It was a bleak afternoon,

... one of the densest and soupiest and yellowest of all London's infernalest yellow fogs. Aubrey Beardsley and I sat together the whole afternoon before a beautiful glowing open coal fire and I assure you we could scarcely see our hands before our faces with all the candles lighted, for the fog, you know. ... We declared to each other that we thought it quite a pity and a shame that London publishers should feel themselves longer under obligation to refuse any of our good manuscripts. ...

"Tis monstrous, Aubrey," I said.

"Tis a public scandal," said he. And then and there we decided to have a magazine of our own. As the sole editorial staff we would feel free and welcome to publish any and all of ourselves that nobody else could be hired to print.

That was the first day of January ... and the next day we had an appointment with Mr. John Lane.

The magazine represented the "new movement," Harland first thought, and Beardsley suggested that their new quarterly's literature and art would require housing in a piece of bookmaking commensurate with its quality—in fact, in book format. "*The Yellow Book*," Beardsley proposed, and the working title stuck.

If Harland dated the event correctly, Beardsley must have spread the news as soon as he returned home, for Max Beerbohm afterwards described in the form of a little dramatic sketch how he was introduced to *The Yellow Book* on a visit to his friend, a visit which could not have occurred much later than that same New Year's Day the editors-to-be lunched together:

Scene: Cambridge Street, Pimlico.
Persons: Aubrey Beardsley and Myself.
A.B. "How are you? Sit down! Most exciting. John Lane wants to bring out a Quarterly—Writings and Drawings—Henry Harland to be Literary Editor—Me to be Art Editor. Great fun. . . ."[16]

As soon as Max returned home from Cambridge Street, he added a postscript to a letter—already dated 1 January 1894—he had been writing to Reggie Turner: "John Lane is just going to start a quarterly magazine called *The Yellow Book* with Harland as Editor and Aubrey as Art Editor. It is to make all our fortunes. . . ."[17]

On a morning a few days later Lane came into his office at the Bodley Head to gather together specimens of type, paper and cloth to take to the leisurely setting of the Hogarth Club, where with Beardsley and Harland he discussed format and a provisional list of contributors to be approached. By that time *The Yellow Book* had become the most poorly kept secret in London, and claimants to have been among the first to know were numerous for two generations. One was Arthur Waugh, then a young sub-editor for the *New Review*, who listened in as Lane and Harland took the news from one club to another. "It happened," he wrote,

that I was lunching at the National Club in Whitehall Gardens in the first week in *January* 1894, when Henry Harland and John Lane had come to tell Gosse all about their new project; and as I made it the theme of my London letter to *The Critic* next day, and that letter still survives in print, I have at hand the earliest documentary evidence of what *The Yellow Book* was intended to be—a very different affair indeed from what it is commonly reported to have been among those who were born after it was dead and have not perhaps taken the trouble to look into the features of its death mask. For the popular report of *The Yellow Book* represents it as the organ of a sere and sallow decadence; while that afternoon Harland and Lane, so far at least as Lane could get in a word edgeways, were acclaiming the advent of a magazine which, in their own words, was to be "representative of the most cultural work which was then being done in England, prose and poetry, criticism, fiction and art, the oldest school and the newest side by side, with no hall-mark except that of excellence and no prejudice against anything but dullness and incapacity". . . There was no sort of hint that *The Yellow Book* was to be the oriflamme of decadence; indeed, if any such suggestion had been made to its publisher, he would have become inarticulate on the spot.[18]

Title page design for *The Yellow Book*, Vol. III (October, 1894)

Design for the cover of the prospectus of *The Yellow Book* (1894), apparently a sketch of the Bodley Head bookshop, caricaturing co-proprietor Elkin Matthews as an elderly pierrot

Beardsley clearly had other ideas. "I am sure you will be vastly interested," he wrote Robbie Ross, "that Harland and myself are about to start a new literary and artistic Quarterly. The title has already been registered at Stationers Hall and on the scroll of fame. It is *THE YELLOW BOOK*. In general get up it will look like the ordinary French Novel. . . ." The title and format Beardsley had in mind could not have connoted "culture" and bland respectability to the English public, whatever the table of contents inside would evidence, and it is easy to believe that the periodical's jaundiced reception derived in no small part from its outward appearance. The color of *The Yellow Book* was an appropriate reflection of the "Yellow Nineties," a decade in which Victorianism was giving way among the fashionable to Regency attitudes and French influences; for yellow was not only the décor of the notorious and dandified pre-Victorian Regency, but also of the allegedly wicked and decadent French novel. It suggested, in fact, exactly what Beardsley had in mind. Inviting Ross to contribute to the first number "in your most brilliant style," Beardsley explained, "our idea is that many brilliant story painters and picture writers cannot get their best stuff accepted in the conventional magazine, either because they are not topical or perhaps a little risque."[19]

Word of the new magazine spread as the editors solicited material and prepared a prospectus. It was important, they felt, to advertise a dramatic roll call of expected contributors, and the proposed list represented a compromise between the tone Harland wanted and the tone Beardsley hoped to achieve. Actually, Harland himself personified much of that compromise, for his outward appearance of unconventionality—the goatee, the unkempt hair, the dressing-gown, the spurious stories of an exotic past and the studied cultivation of "decadence"—masked a conventional bourgeois outlook. He felt the first number needed a balance to whatever shocking design his art editor might create for the cover, and that meant a visit to his literary idol, Henry James, who epitomized to him the art of modern fiction yet was as respectable as the Queen.

On a Sunday afternoon early in the year, James recalled, his Kensington neighbor Harland came to call with a young friend,

and bespeak my interest in a periodical about to take birth, in his hands, on the most original "lines" and with the happiest omens . . . to sound the note of bright young defiance. . . . The project, modestly and a little vaguely but all communicatively set forth, amused me, charmed me, on the spot. . . .

The bravest of the portents that Sunday afternoon . . . I have yet to mention; for I recall my embarrassed inability to measure as yet the contributory value of Mr. Aubrey Beardsley, by whom my friend was accompanied and who, as his prime illustrator, his perhaps even quite independent picture-maker, was to be in charge of the "art department." This young man, slender, pale, delicate, unmistakeably intelligent, somehow invested the whole proposition with a detached, a slightly ironic and melancholy grace. I had met him before, on a single occasion, and had seen an example of his so curious and so disconcerting talent—my appreciation of which seems to me, however, as I look back, to have stopped quite short.[20]

Hardly a part of any "new movement," James represented the search by editor and publisher for a tone of prudence and decorum, something they sought further by barring Oscar Wilde from their pages, although Lane himself was Wilde's publisher. Beardsley was delighted, happily forgoing whatever shock value a contribution from Wilde would have had in order to snub the man who patronized him. The art as well as the literary matter were to be balanced between the traditional and the avant-garde, but Beardsley proposed that the art work should stand on its own, and not be mere illustrations for the text—a philosophy meant to attract the best artists of the time. The "letterpress" would come at first from a select group of invited writers, who, it turned out, also represented from the beginning no "school" or "movement."

By March a publisher's announcement was ready, appropriately, on bright yellow paper, and decorated with a typically elongated Beardsley female:

The aim . . . of The Yellow Book is to depart as far as may be from the bad old tradition of periodical literature, and to provide an Illustrated Magazine which shall be beautiful as a piece of bookmaking, modern and distinguished in its letter-press and its pictures, and withal popular in the better sense of the word. It is felt that such a Magazine, at present, is conspicuous by its absence. . . .

A list of expected contributors of art and literature followed, including some writers—the unlikely triumvirate of Frank Harris, Walter Pater and Israel Zangwill, for example—whose work never did appear. Then the announcement spelled out the advantages of the new magazine for both writers and readers:

In many ways its contributors will employ a freer hand than the limitations of the old-fashioned periodical can permit. It will publish no serials; but its complete stories will sometimes run to a considerable length in themselves. . . . And while The Yellow

Vignette in *Bon-Mots of Foote and Hook*

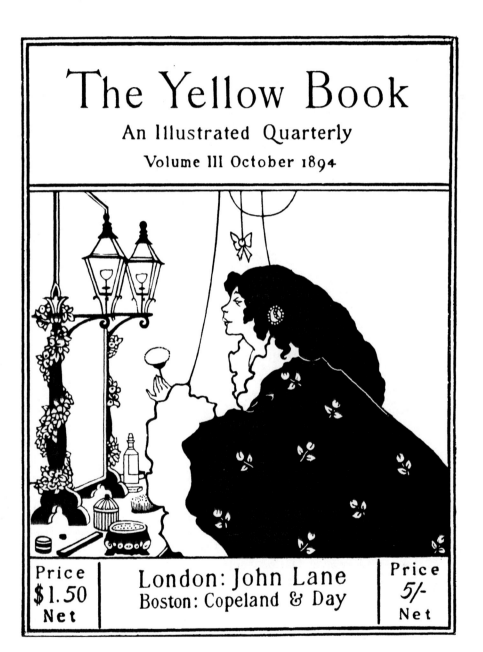

The Yellow Book

An Illustrated Quarterly

Volume III October 1894

Price
$1.50
Net

London: John Lane
Boston: Copeland & Day

Price
5/-
Net

Design for front cover of *The Yellow Book*,
Vol. III (October, 1894)

Design for the title page of *The Yellow Book*,
Vol. II (July, 1894)

Book will seek always to preserve a delicate, decorous and reticent mien and conduct, it will at the same time have the courage of its modernness, and not tremble at the frown of Mrs. Grundy.

Altogether, it is expected that *The Yellow Book* will prove the most interesting, unusual, and important publication of its kind that has ever been undertaken. It will be charming, it will be daring, it will be distinguished. It will be a book—a book to be read, and placed upon one's shelves, and read again; a book in form, a book in substance; a book beautiful to see and convenient to handle; a book with style, a book with finish; a book that every book-lover will love at first sight; a book that will make book-lovers of many who are now indifferent to books.

Indifference to books was exactly what Lane and his then-partner Elkin Mathews wanted most to overcome, hoping that *The Yellow Book* would promote their other books, especially those by contributor-authors, as well as books in general sold from their shop at the sign of the Bodley Head in Vigo Street. It was an ambitious but unprepossessing enterprise, described by J. Lewis May (who began there as a stockboy) as "a little bookshop with a brave array of rare editions cunningly displayed to catch the eye of the passing bibliophile . . . a little box of a place" with books lined "from floor to ceiling."[21] Very likely Beardsley's cover design for the prospectus of the first *Yellow Book* is a fanciful variation upon the Bodley Head shop window, with Mathews as a pierrot.[22]

Beardsley worked furiously to produce drawings of his own for the first number, and to secure art from Charles Conder, Joseph Pennell, Walter Crane and others, some commissions repaying debts of friendship but all up to a high standard he had set. The only art work Lane—as publisher—worried about was Beardsley's own, having learned from *Salome* to scrutinize each contribution carefully. The diligence proved worthwhile, for a disarmingly captioned drawing of a fat woman proved on examination to resemble Mrs. Whistler. Lane had no use for the vain Whistler, yet he had no desire to provoke the artist's explosive hostility. When he refused to permit the drawing for the inaugural issue, Beardsley sent him an appeal illustrated by a self-portrait of the tearful artist contemplating a noose suspended from a gallows. "Yes, my dear Lane," he wrote,

I shall most assuredly commit suicide if the fat woman does not appear in No. 1 of the *Yellow Book*. I have shown it to all sorts and conditions of men—and women. All agree that it is one of my best efforts & extremely witty. Really I am sure you have nothing to fear. I should not press the matter a second if I thought it would give offence. The block is such a capital one too, and looks so distinguished. The picture shall be called, "A Study in Major Lines."

Far from being innocuous, the title called attention to Whistler's method of titling his pictures; yet Beardsley added, innocently, "It cannot possibly hurt anyone's sensibilities. Do say 'yes'. I shall hold demonstrations in Trafalgar Square if you don't, and brandish a banner bearing the device, 'England expects every publisher to do his duty.' "[23] The letter contained as much of the adolescent prankster as had the drawing, and Lane remained unmoved. He wanted a maximum of decorum to counterbalance the self-advertising features of *The Yellow Book*, and took Beardsley's threatened demonstration for what he knew it was worth. Rather than press the issue further, Beardsley prudently offered "The Fat Woman"—he abandoned the overly clever original title—to another magazine, where it was printed within weeks after the first *Yellow Book* appeared.

The editors, meanwhile, were being liberally discussed in the press, partly because of the recent sensation of *Salome*, and more because Lane had set in motion a publicity campaign far in advance of his time in promotional techniques. Henley's *National Observer* even complained about the "judicious advertisements planted and injudicious interviews watered." Obviously inspired by Lane was the *Westminister Gazette*'s paragraph on 31 March beginning, "We understand that orders have already been received for over 5,000 copies, but it is expected that at least 10,000 will be sold. . . ." "What *The Yellow Book* Is to Be" was the title of an interview with the editors in the *Sketch* of 11 April. The new journal, they emphasized, was for the bookshelf, not the wastebasket; for it would contain art and literature of permanent value in a permanent binding, ushering in "an absolutely new era in the way of magazine literature." And illustrating the piece was a reproduction of Beardsley's cover for the inaugural issue. Even before publication, *The Yellow Book* was the talk of the town, and it was inevitable that, whatever reaction the publication would have from critics and the public, any reaction at all would make the already notorious Beardsley—at twenty-one—one of the best-known names of his time.

The Slippers of Cinderella,
from *The Yellow Book,* Vol. II

6

1894-1895

The Prevalence of Yellow

On the evening of 15 April, in a private dining-room of the Hotel d'Italia on Old Compton Street in Soho, contributors and potential contributors toasted, at an inaugural dinner, the success of *The Yellow Book*. It had gone on sale that morning at five shillings—a book price, rather than a magazine price. Still, it had sold well as Lane predicted, and was the leading subject of London literary gossip. The result was that the dinner was a celebration rather than a wake, and more people came than expected. Beardsley and Harland sat at the high table at one end of the room, and Elizabeth Pennell—her husband was away—had the place of honor between them. George Moore, Richard Garnett, John Davidson, Kenneth Grahame, W.B. Yeats, Lionel Johnson, Ernest Dowson and other contributors-to-be and well-wishers were there, and most made speeches or toasts, Walter Sickert suggesting tongue-in-cheek that the time would come when "authors would be put in their proper places by being compelled to write stories and poems round pictures which should be supplied to them. . . ." Beardsley's own oration began modestly with "I am going to talk about a most interesting subject—myself." When the party was over, John Lane took some of the group, including the Harlands, Mrs. Pennell, Max Beerbohm and Beardsley to the Vigo Street headquarters of *The Yellow Book*. Afterwards they repaired to the Monico, where again they drank to the new magazine.[1] Elkin Mathews never found out about either part of the celebration until someone told him afterwards. *The Yellow Book* was the result of Lane's efforts alone, and he was not about to share the glory, lying to the guests with "boldest effrontery" (in Mathews's words) "that he deeply regretted the unavoidable absence of his partner—and that he was not present to join in the general enthusiasm and so on." It was the first public evidence of the breach which would split the firm later in the year, Lane keeping the Bodley Head sign and *The Yellow Book*, but not the premises.*

Some of the literary figures connected with the first *Yellow Book* were also missing at the dinner, but only one of them, Henry James, was so distinguished that his absence was noticed. Settling the estate of a deceased friend, he was prudently abroad in Venice, although it was his long tale, "The Death of the Lion"—a typically ironic Jamesian perspective upon literary life—which had the leading place in the opening number. Nothing succeeds for writers, James well knew, like success, and nothing shattered the personal privacy in which the writer wrote more effectively than that very success. James's hero is lionized to death.

The Master contributed to several later numbers as well, although he confessed uneasiness about some of his bedfellows in "the small square lemon-coloured quarterly," and unnecessary relief (since James should have known the *Yellow Book* policy was that its pictures were to be independent of its prose) that Beardsley hadn't been stimulated to a perverse illustration of "my comparatively so incurious text." Grateful to Harland for allowing him so much space, he felt that such freedom for the writer was "the millennium" for the short story and indicated, on the part of the editor, "the finest artistic intelligence." He and Harland shared, James later wrote, the French ideal of "the beautiful and blest *nouvelle*," and his three long stories for *The Yellow Book*, ranging from fourteen to twenty thousand words, were among his finest in that genre. All had in common, he observed, their concern with the literary life, "gathering their motive, in each case, from some noted adventure, some felt embarrassment, some extreme predicament, of the artist enamoured of perception, ridden by his idea or paying for his sincerity."

It was inevitable that there would be a self-conscious preoccupation with art and artists on the part of *The Yellow Book*'s contributors. Many of them felt a sense of mission in the launching of the venture, and were influenced as well by the aesthetic doctrine—imported from France—that art should serve no master but itself; nor should the artist serve any public, but devote

Design for an invitation card (1894), with *The Yellow Book* prominently displayed

*He cannily moved across the street, retaining a Vigo Street address.

Design for a book plate (1894)

himself uncompromisingly to his craft. (In the same issue with the James tale was "George Egerton's" shorter fiction about art and artists, "The Lost Masterpiece.") The preoccupation renewed itself each quarter, and manifested itself further in such critical essays as Arthur Waugh's "Reticence in Literature," which appeared in the first issue, and was rebutted in the second by Hubert Crackanthorpe. (Together, the two essays provided a *Yellow Book* self-introduction to the literary climate in which its contributors wrote.)

Waugh—Evelyn's father—elucidated the moral perspective of the literary philistine in the nineties, and prepared his position by shewdly tracing both the beginnings and the directions of modern realism. Two distinct directions were clear to him, one towards excess stimulated by effeminacy, "by the want of restraint which starts from enervated sensations," the other towards "the excess which results from a certain brutal virility, which proceeds from coarse familiarity with indulgence." What he missed was "that true frankness which springs from the artistic and moral temperament" where the episodes were "part of a whole in unity with itself." Crackanthorpe upheld frankness in literature by first disposing of Waugh's morality. The modern writer, he declared, could not permit himself to be shackled by an inherited morality in his attempt to get reality and truth—life itself—into his work. Modern realism, he thought, might often be cheerless in its struggle to reach expression, and might not subscribe to the philistine bookselling tastes of Mudie and Smith, but it was not a "gospel of ugliness." All he wanted was the opportunity for the artist "to give untrammelled expression to his own soul." What was sincere, truthful and realistic would ultimately be beautiful as well. That it was not yet beautiful was illustrated by some of the fiction in the first volume, moody stories of dreary realism by Ella D'Arcy ("Irremediable") and Hubert Crackanthorpe ("Modern Melodrama").

From the start Harland courted respectability in a way which went considerably further than the employment of Henry James as *The Yellow Book*'s symbol of prudence. The first volume included poems by Edmund Gosse and Dr. Richard Garnett, and an essay on wine-tasting by Professor George Saintsbury, "A Sentimental Cellar." Possibly all three were needed to balance an essay by Max Beerbohm, "A Defence of Cosmetics." A companion piece to his "The Incomparable Beauty of Modern Dress," which he wrote for Lord Alfred Douglas's *The Spirit Lamp*, it whimsically held artifice above nature. When taken seriously, it was a crucial idea of French aestheticism—

the deliberate rejection of ordinary imitation, and thus of nature as an ideal of beauty. Art—and therefore artifice—was to be the artist's protest against nature.

As art editor, Beardsley, too, bowed in the direction of respectability, including two studies by Sir Frederick Leighton, of the Royal Academy. The gesture failed to convince the staid *Times*, which thundered that the artistic note of the first number appeared to be "a combination of English rowdyism with French lubricity. . . . Sir Frederick Leighton . . . finds himself cheek by jowl with such advanced and riotous representatives of the new art as Mr. Aubrey Beardsley and Mr. Walter Sickert." Quickly, the unhappy Sir Frederick visited the Bodley Head and told Lane that he had been reprimanded by his friends for embarrassing serious art, and that he had promised never to appear in such company again. The *Westminster Gazette* was even more outraged. Like other reviewing media, it thought Max's essay "pernicious nonsense," but not nearly so dangerous as Beardsley's art. "His offence," it said of Beardsley,

is the less to be condoned because he has undoubted skill as a line draftsman and has shown himself capable of refined and delicate work. But as regards certain of his inventions in this number, especially the thing called "The Sentimental Education," and that other thing to which the name of Mrs. Patrick Campbell has somehow become attached, we do not know that anything would meet the case except a short Act of Parliament to make this kind of thing illegal. . . .

Nothing in the first number raised more hackles than the drawing the *Westminster* had condemned. Before it went to press, Aubrey had shown it to Max, who then wrote delightedly to Reggie Turner,

Aubrey has done a marvellous picture for the *Yellow B*: "*l'Education sentimentale*" he calls it. A fat elderly whore in a dressing-gown and huge hat of many feathers is reading from a book to the sweetest imaginable little young girl, who looks before her, with hands clasped behind her back, roguishly winking. Such a strange curved attitude, and she wears a long pinafore of black silk, quite tight, with the frills of a petticoat showing at ankles and shoulders: awfully like Ada Reeve, that clever malapert, is her face—you must see it. It haunts me.[2]

The press thought considerably less of Beardsley's wit. "Who wants these fantastic pictures," the *World* complained,

like Japanese sketches gone mad, of a woman with a black tuft for a head, and snake-like fingers starting off the keyboard of a piano; of Mrs. Patrick Campbell with a black sticking-plaister hat, hunchy shoulders, a happily impossible waist, and a yard

L'Education Sentimentale, from Vol. I of *The Yellow Book* (April, 1894)

and a half of indefinite skirt. . . . Then for the letterpress how little there is to be said. Mr. Henry James in his most mincing mood; a Mr. Beerbohm, whose "Defence of Cosmetics" contains . . . pure nonsense.

Frederick Wedmore, in the *Academy*, after describing Beardsley as "a gentleman of some parts, though not much known to fame," was content to call his drawings "meaningless and unhealthy"; but W.E. Henley, who had inadvertently frightened a more naïve Beardsley from the *National Observer* office two years before, gave the young artist no cause for regretting his flight. Henley's reviewer could only express his "humble, uninstructed amazement at the audacious vulgarity and the laborious inelegance" of *The Yellow Book*'s cover; Beardsley's women, he wrote, "resemble nothing on the earth, nor in the firmament that is above the earth, nor in the water under the earth;* with their lips of a more than Hottentot thickness, their bodies of a lath-like flatness, their impossibly pointed toes and fingers, and their small eyes which have the form and comeliness of an unshelled snail."

The drawing of Mrs. Campbell was missing from his copy, another reviewer complained in his notice, and Beardsley hastened to write a letter of apology, which the *Chronicle* then published. Following the letter was an explanatory editorial note which must have caused Beardsley to regret his haste: "Our own copy, it is true, contained a female figure in the space thus described, but we rated Mrs. Patrick Campbell's appearance and Mr. Beardsley's talent far too high to suppose they were united on this occasion." *Punch* made fun of the exaggerated slimness of the figure under the title of "Played Out; or, The 252nd Mrs. Tanqueray—trained down very fine after a long run"; and a Cambridge satirist inquired,

> Pray, Mr. Beardsley, tell us why
>   Your elongated fancy made you
> Depict this lady nine feet high?
>   What influence conspired to aid you?[3]

Beardsley defended his portrait ("It's just like her . . .") but had much else to defend as well, beginning with his title page, which the *Pall Mall Budget* called "unpardonable affectation." Again he wrote to the editor:

---

*Perhaps the reviewer was the same one who had complained about *The Studio* drawings in the *Figaro* the year before (see Chapter 5).

The Mysterious Rose Garden, from *The Yellow Book*,
Vol. IV (January, 1895), irreverently conceived as an
Annunciation scene and at first titled "The
Annunciation" (see p. 230)

The Wagnerites, from *The Yellow Book*, Vol. III (October, 1894)

Sir,—So much exception has been taken, both by the Press, and by private persons, to my title-page of "The Yellow Book", that I must plead for space in your valuable paper to enlighten those who profess to find my picture unintelligible. It represents a lady playing a piano in the middle of a field. "Unpardonable affectation" cry the critics. But let us listen to Bomvet. "Christopher Willibald Ritter von Glück, in order to warm his imagination and to transport himself to Aulis or Sparta, was accustomed to place himself in the middle of a field. In this situation, with his piano before him, and a bottle of champagne on each side, he wrote in the open air his two 'Iphigenias', his 'Orpheus', and some other works." I tremble to think what critics would say had I introduced those bottles of champagne. And yet we do not call Glück a decadent.[4]

What emerged from his responses—from the drawings themselves—was the literary origin of so much of Beardsley's work. Although his observation was acute, and his imagination prolific, he had an insatiable passion for books, and read (in English and French) specialist publications, exotic and rare books, classical, medieval and renaissance works ranging from poetry and drama to history and philosophy. His inspiration was so often literary that his friends instinctively examined his art to see what Beardsley had been reading. Once, when Beardsley brought some drawings for the *Morte d'Arthur* to Evans's bookshop, Frederick Evans picked one up and instantly recognized that it had been suggested by Blake's "Piping down the valleys wild."[5] Beardsley was delighted. Another illustration—for an initial letter—included a partly visible book, on which he placed the first half of the name of an author he had probably been reading at the time—Boccaccio.[6] Anachronisms never disturbed Beardsley.

He was the artist as intellectual, Holbrook Jackson suggested, "drawing the thing as he *thought* it." His art, according to Jackson, was rarely the outcome of observation, unless it was observation of musical or theatrical performances. His drawings were

thoughts become pictures. And even then they are rarely if ever the blossoming of thought derived from experience; they are the hot-house growths of thought derived from books, pictures and music. Beardsley always worked indoors, without models and by artificial, generally candle, light. On those rare occasions when he did go to life for inspiration he went to life in its more artificial form—to theatres and *salons*, to the Domino Room at the Café Royal, to the Pavilion at Brighton and the Casino at Dieppe.[7]

The same week *The Yellow Book* appeared, the Bodley Head ran off a second printing. Still, the demand could not be met, and over the weekend

A chapter heading from *Le Morte d'Arthur*

The Cambridge A.B.C.

No. 1.   June 8, 1894.

Cambridge : Elijah Johnson

Lane rushed off a third printing, advertising that fresh copies would be "ready on Monday, at all Booksellers, Libraries and Railway Bookstalls." Adverse criticism continued, *Punch* printing an epigram, "Uncleanliness is next to Bodliness." John Lane treated the matter as a profitable joke, ignoring the chance of instituting a libel action, although Kenneth Grahame urged him to take *Punch* to court. There is not, Grahame insisted, "enough impropriety to cover a sixpence" in *The Yellow Book*, "and there is no indecency at all." But the furor embarrassed several of the more staid contributors, including the lion of the first number, Henry James, who confided in a letter to his brother William,

I haven't sent you "The Yellow Book" on purpose; and indeed I have been weeks and weeks in receiving a copy of it myself. I say on purpose because although my little tale . . . appears to have had, for a thing of mine, an unusual success, I hate too much the horrid aspect and company of the whole publication. And yet I am again to be intimately, conspicuously associated with the 2nd number. It is for gold and to oblige the worshipful Harland.[8]

The most "horrid" aspect of the otherwise quite respectable *Yellow Book* remained the cover hue celebrated in the title—a color *Punch* described in a variety of terms:

> LEAVES—like Autumn leaves—the tint of custard,
> Cover like a poultice made of mustard,
> General aspect bilious.
> But, ye gods, the things called "illustrations"!
> Ill-drawn, objectless abominations!
> Supernatural silliness.

Notoriety attracted undergraduate interest too. A group of Cambridge students, among them Maurice Baring, had founded a newspaper, and in search of a daring inaugural issue persuaded Beardsley to design the cover. For a fee of ten guineas the artist, in age hardly more than an undergraduate himself, agreed to do the front wrapper design with which the first number of the *Cambridge ABC* appeared on 8 June 1894. But the ten guineas proved a questionable investment: Cambridge undergraduates persisted in doubting the cover's identification as an authentic Aubrey Beardsley.

A rich crop of press notices of the first *Yellow Book* was being harvested at the Bodley Head, and Beardsley reveled in reading them, especially the most extreme ones. The prospectus prepared to advertise the second issue included a collection of press opinions on Volume I which balanced the favorable with the unfavorable. When the second quarterly volume appeared in July, there was a change intended to prevent at least one variety of gibe, but which instead inspired another. The "Letterpress" and "Pictures" of the table of contents were reduced, in the interest of unpretentiousness, to "Literature" and "Art." All the changes did was provide *Punch* with a new opportunity:

> No possibility of doubt
> Can stop us now in finding out
>   What "literature" should be;
> No longer dazed by rival claims,
> We read a row of deathless names,
> Not yet renowned, but would-be. . . .
>
> And Beardsley shows us now the nude;
> It would not shock the primmest prude,
>   Or rouse the legislature,
> An unclothed woman ten feet high
> Could not make anyone feel shy,
> She's "Art," she is not nature.[9]

La Dame aux Camélias,
from *The Yellow Book*, Vol. III

Poetess and writer of juvenile fiction E. Nesbit (Mrs. Hubert Bland) knew many of the writers and artists in the *Yellow Book* group, contributed to it herself and was deeply under the spell of *fin de siècle* writing. But as a woman, particularly one who advocated freedom in dress, she was more amused than influenced by the fads in fashions Beardsleyesque art was creating. In *A Pomander of Verse* (published in 1895) she wrote a satirical skit about the problem, pointing to the lady whose lover has a passion for the new art, and who, to please him, has changed her dress styles again and again in order to keep up with his endlessly advancing tastes. "The formless form and toneless tones" of Ford Madox Brown and William Morris, the soft frills of Marcus Stone, the shining silks of John Sargent—all these she has, in turn, adopted to gratify his whim; she has even, with misgivings, agreed to appear "as vague as Mr. Whistler's ladies are." But there comes a time when even she must draw the line:

> . . . Now at last you sue in vain.
>   For here a life's submission ends:
> Not even for you will I grow plain
>   As Aubrey Beardsley's "lady friends."[10]

The second *Yellow Book* contained another long story by Henry James, safely unillustrated by Beardsley, "The Coxon Fund," as well as contributions from such writers as Davidson, D'Arcy and Beerbohm, who were to appear in many of the baker's dozen of *Yellow Books*. There was a sensitive story of childhood, "The Roman Road," by Kenneth Grahame, one of the pieces he wrote in seeming preparation for his classic of childhood imagination, *The Wind in the Willows* (1908). Another writer made her appearance at the beginning of her career, Charlotte Mew, then in her mid-twenties, with a haunting (but overwritten) Poe-like tale, "Passed." But compared to the first volume the second was dull, although critics inevitably found cause for complaint in Beardsley's offerings. Yet he had tried to be circumspect. Again he had sought a Royal Academician to replace the retreating Sir Frederick Leighton, and had come up with John Sargent, and his "Portrait of Henry James." It required going to James's rooms to borrow it, and Beardsley wrote for permission after the "worshipful Harland" had made the initial overtures. James was still in Venice, prompting Beardsley to ask James also to look around the local bookstalls for an old copy of Goldoni's plays for him. "Have you heard of the storm that raged around No. 1[?]" Beardsley asked. "Most of the thunderbolts fell on my head. However I enjoyed the excitement immensely."[11]

Eager to retain artists with the Academy cachet, Beardsley tried to commit Sargent to a second contribution, a portrait of Edmund Gosse. The stratagem failed. "From an artistic point of view," Sargent wrote to Gosse, "I dislike that book too much to be willing to seem a habitual contributor." Gosse, given the chance to give his approval, might have been more cooperative, for he liked Beardsley, and was urging him to spend less time on what he considered "work of a trivial kind." Illustrate "acknowledged masterpieces of old[er] English literature" which are in your own spirit, he had suggested. "Set me a task," Beardsley offered; "tell me what to do and I will obey."

"Very well," said Gosse, who enjoyed being pontifical, "I *will* set you a task. You shall illustrate Pope's *Rape of the Lock*, Ben Jonson's *Volpone* and Congreve's *Way of the World*."

He would certainly do *The Way of the World*, Beardsley said, but he didn't "see" the other two. Yet he later did magnificent drawings for *The Rape of the Lock*, and dedicated the volume to Gosse.[12]

"The Comedy Ballet of Marionettes," No. II, from *The Yellow Book*, Vol. II

"The Comedy Ballet of Marionettes," No. I

The "Portrait of Madame Réjane" was Beardsley's equivalent in the second volume to the likeness of Mrs. Campbell in the first, yet it caused fewer protests, the worst of them, legend has it, from Madame Réjane herself, who wept and screamed when she saw the "Cytherean grin" Beardsley had drawn across her face.[13] But William Archer explained, with faint praise, "Mme Réjane happens to be the one woman in the world with a Beardsley mouth."[14] Strangely, one who liked the portrait was the timid Henry James, to whom Beardsley had written before the second *Yellow Book* appeared, "The portrait of Réjane has at last been returned [to] me from exhibition. I am afraid you must have thought me very forgetful—or worse—but now she shall be duly installed at De Vere Gardens if you still find it a pretty picture."[15] Despite both public and private misgivings about Beardsley's art, Henry James apparently wanted a Beardsley decorating his walls, if not decorating his work.

Although his drawings had rapidly become desirable commodities, Beardsley was briefly nagged by the thought that the only truly distinguished art was done in oils on canvas, and early in his *Yellow Book* work (Aymer Vallance mistakenly remembered it as even earlier) he decided to do something about it. He had already drawn three designs for the July 1894 *Yellow Book* he called "The Comedy Ballet of Marionettes." The first design, he thought, might work out well in a variation for oils; and he bought canvas and paints and produced a woman clothed in black with green trimmings, turning towards a beckoning Negro dwarf clothed in red. In the background the outline of a town was visible through an archway. It was for Beardsley a literally large accomplishment, produced on a 30" × 25" expanse, but he was not satisfied with it. "I have no great care for colour," Haldane MacFall quoted him as saying. "I only use flat tints, and work as if I were colouring a map, the effect aimed at being that produced on a Japanese print. I prefer to draw everything in little."[16]

Turning the abandoned canvas over some time afterwards, Beardsley tried working in oils once more, painting what Aymer Vallance called "a grey and leaden representation of a woman (half-length) contemplating a dead mouse" on the unprimed back between the stretchers. After keeping at it long enough to mask the woman's face, he put it aside; and later, when he moved out of the Cambridge Street house, he thought so little of his prowess in oils that he left his Siamese twins of a painting behind.*

By the summer of 1894 Beardsley had definitely achieved celebrity status, and hobnobbed with Henry James at such brilliant affairs as the garden parties of Mrs. T. P. O'Connor, wife of the London editor. One recorded by American novelist Gertrude Atherton, held on a warm summer afternoon in the large garden behind the O'Connor house, was a register of literary figures. There was leonine novelist Richard Whiteing, actor-manager John Hare, Henry James, Sir Walter Besant and Bernard Shaw, American actress Genevieve Ward, Richard Le Gallienne, and Beatrice Harraden, "whose *Ships That Pass in the Night* was still being quoted." Mrs. Craigie ("John Oliver Hobbes") was there—"a short, dark woman who would have been plain but for a pair of remarkably fine eyes"—and "Marie Corelli, with much-befrizzed mouse-coloured hair, wearing pale blue silk, and carrying a lap dog under her arm; Arthur Conan Doyle, dignified and dull; Aubrey Beardsley, who looked as if he might die at any moment. . . ."[17]

Beardsley would often collapse, exhausted, when he reached home; still, for a time he kept up a social pace which might have debilitated a professional music- or drama-critic. Afternoons and evenings were crowded with plays, concerts and operas, sometimes chosen over social engagements, for Beardsley was not only much sought after as a significant name to grace a place card, but was known as a brilliant talker in an age when repartee was prized. At the opera Aubrey and Mabel would sometimes sit, as they used to do, surrounded by other enthusiasts, on the Gallery stairs. Once afterwards, on a cold night, a shivering friend, bundled in furs, met the intense, brooding Beardsley—who was wearing no overcoat—on the steps outside the opera house, and exclaimed, "Aubrey, you will kill yourself!"

"Oh, no," said Beardsley. "I never wear an overcoat. I am always burning."

For the feverish Beardsley, success had not come too fast, nor too soon, for he knew he was dying and that each new morning was a temporary reprieve. Struggling to remain among the walking wounded, he reacted to

"The Comedy Ballet of Marionettes," No. III

---

*The canvas, the only known oils by Beardsley, now hangs in the Tate Gallery as *A Caprice* and *A Lady with a Mouse*. It was discovered by Mrs. Pugh, who took over the lease of the Cambridge Street house, and found its way to the Tate by 1923, sold by Beardsley scholar R.A. Walker, who earlier had purchased it from Mrs. Pugh.

the numbering of his days with an intensity of creative purpose which excluded almost everything else. Even at the opera house and the concert hall he sat in the half-darkness and fashioned drawings in his head, afterwards setting down his memories of actors, singers and musicians, some of them from scrawled hints on his programs. An illustrated survey of London music and drama in the mid-nineties could be made from Beardsley's sketches alone — Madame Réjane and Mrs. Campbell, Max Alvary as Tristan and Frau Klavsky as Isolde, pianist Sophie Menter, scenes from plays, and a corps of dancers, conductors and violinists, some of them disguised in pictures with unrelated captions.

Among his acquaintances was the death-obsessed (and manic-depressive) young writer Count Eric Stenbock, whom Beardsley visited, and through whom critic Ernest Rhys met Beardsley at a Kardomah café, where they disputed for hours on the relative merits of Balzac and Shakespeare. Beardsley even drew a series of four drawings for Stenbock, "The English Flower in the German Conservatory," for which Stenbock provided appropriate captions, as the group was intended for a young friend of his then studying music in Frankfurt, Norman O'Neill, who would later be well known in England as a composer. But Stenbock's commission availed him nothing when he sent a grim story of his, "La Mazurka des Revenants," to *The Yellow Book*. In September 1894 it was rejected. It was his only submission. A few months later he was dead.

When the third *Yellow Book* went on sale in October 1894, only John Lane's name was on the spine, Elkin Mathews having separated from the firm. Mathews kept the premises, and Lane the Bodley Head sign, which he took across Vigo Street to No. 8. Until it reached the end of its run *The Yellow Book* remained at the Bodley Head. Volume III may have assured Mathews that he had departed just in time, for it included Davidson's notorious narrative poem, "The Ballad of a Nun," about a nun who leaves the convent to worship "sinful man" rather than a "righteous God." The issue was more what the non-reading public thought *The Yellow Book* was like than any before or after, for it also published a poem by Arthur Symons about "the joy of sin"; an impressionist essay by Lionel Johnson, "Tobacco Clouds"; and a scandal-courting piece of malice by Max Beerbohm, "A Note on George the Fourth," with a sketch of the pleasure-loving

Portrait of actress Winifred Emery, from *The Yellow Book*, Vol. IV

monarch by Max which as much resembled Oscar Wilde as the dandified George—a trick Max had picked up from Beardsley.

One of its longest pieces was a piece of autobiography by Ernest Dowson, thinly disguised as fiction. "Apple Blossom in Brittany" was about an English writer, who, in love with his French ward, has a rival, a convent in Brittany. Like Dowson, the hero relinquishes the girl and cultivates as a kind of high pleasure the sadness of his loss. Slightly idealizing reality, Dowson made his fictional successful rival something more artistically satisfying—and less personally embarrassing—than another man, and a waiter at that. The idealization of reality was what often kept Dowson going, and it was inevitable that what was part of his life would become part of his artistic method. One of his friends from the Rhymers' Club had seen him in a French café with one who was obviously—so Yeats tells the tale—"a particularly common harlot." The half-drunk Dowson tugged at his friend's sleeve and whispered to him that it was all better than it seemed: "She writes poetry—it is like Browning and Mrs. Browning."

To Volume III Beardsley contributed a "Portrait of Himself" in bed, "The Wagnerites" and several others. Two pictures by hitherto unknown artists appeared, a head of Mantegna by Philip Broughton, and a pastel study of a Frenchwoman in a white cap, by Albert Foschter. Reaction was typified by the *Saturday Review*, which found Beardsley's work "as freakish as ever," while commending Broughton's "Mantegna" as a "drawing of merit," and Foschter's "Pastel" as a "clever study." Both drawings, as Max Beerbohm later put it, "had rather a success with the reviewers, one of whom advised Beardsley 'to study and profit by the sound and scholarly draughtsmanship of which Mr. Philip Broughton furnishes another example of his familiar manner.' Beardsley, who had made both the drawings and invented both signatures, was greatly amused and delighted."[18] When enough critics had been taken in by his hoax, Beardsley admitted it. "I never, before or after, saw him in such a happy frame of mind," one of his friends recalled. "His boyish ruse had been successful, and a thorn had been removed."[19] Whether it was because he enjoyed the practical joke or appreciated the drawing's artistic merits, Bernard Shaw purchased "Philip Broughton's" lone masterpiece.

Beardsley's working methods continued to fascinate the public, as well as

Mantegna, by "Philip Broughton," from *The Yellow Book*, Vol. III

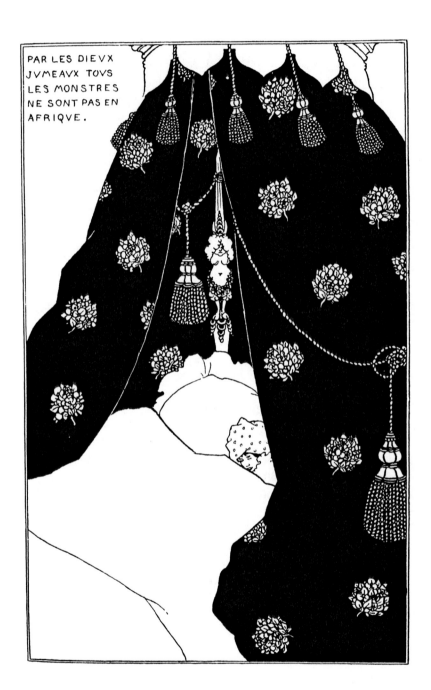

Portrait of Himself,
from *The Yellow Book*, Vol. III

his fellow artists. One chilly afternoon that autumn a young artist looking for *Yellow Book* work called at 114 Cambridge Street and was offered a rare glimpse into the Beardsley sanctum. Taking him by the hand, Beardsley led him into his studio. "Had he not done so," Penrhyn Stanlaws afterwards wrote,

I doubt if I could have entered so easily, as it was very dark. Heavy tapestry curtains were drawn across the windows; the walls were dark; the floor, rugs and furniture were black, or nearly so; the only light came from two altar candles that burned in Empire ormolu candlesticks placed upon his desk. His desk, too, was black, and of the pattern used by priests. Lying on the desk were pens, ink, brushes, an open razor and a half-finished drawing.

While they talked, Beardsley lay back on a lounge placed by one of the draped windows, his long white fingers playing nervously with the curtains. His aching lungs had been troubling him again, he confided, the shadow of a smile crossing his face. "I shall not live longer than did Keats. The doctors give me five years. . . ."[20]

It was not much time, and Beardsley saw his ambitions trapped in the coffin of his worn-out young body. He sought quacks and cures when legitimate medicine gave him little cause for optimism. What kind of relief the therapy of baths might provide for his disintegrating lungs was problematical, but off he went to a hydropathic establishment in Malvern in November, Mrs. Beardsley writing Ross of her son's depression—"at parting with me," she thought—and describing—in her naïveté, perhaps better than she knew—her last view of him in his third-class seat as the train pulled out: "like a little white mouse caught in a trap." (Curiously and even more naïvely she added her thanks to Ross for speaking to Wilde about her daughter's stage ambitions, for her approaching Wilde even indirectly would have infuriated her "white mouse.")[21] At Malvern, Aubrey was miserable, "all day moping and worrying" about his "beloved Venusberg." He was working on what he hoped would be his *magnum opus*, in pictures and text, and had faint expectation that he would finish it.

During the late autumn of 1894 Beardsley worked hard at preparing what he did not know would be the last number of *The Yellow Book* to appear under his signature. He was high in John Lane's esteem, and one story has it that when some friends of Lane's invited him to spend Christmas at St. Mary's Abbey, Windermere, and to bring several friends with him, Lane invited the unlikely group of Beardsley, Beerbohm and the very minor poet William Watson. "After myself," Lane used to say afterwards, "Aubrey was the best behaved of the party. He attended church services regularly and devoutly, and as long as he lived the rector never failed to make inquiries after that 'devout youth.'"[22] The rector could not have known that his "devout youth" was the same "Wierdsley Daubery" and "Awfully Weirdly" people were talking about. "I suffer my critics gladly," Beardsley told an interviewer. And he clearly enjoyed the witty, often inverted, tributes fame provoked. One of the best was Mostyn Piggott's Lewis Carroll-like burlesque:

> 'Twas rollog; and the minim potes
> Did mime and mimble in the cafe;
> All footly were the Philerotes
> And Daycadongs outstrafe . . .
>
> Beware the Yallerbock, my son!
> The aims that rile, the art that racks,
> Beware the Aub-Aub Bird, and shun
> The stumious Beerbomax!
>
> . . . .
>
> Then, as veep Virgo's marge he trod,
> The Yallerbock, with tongue of blue,
> Came piffling through the Headley Bod,
> And flippered as it flew. . . .[23]

The fourth *Yellow Book* appeared on the bookstalls in January 1895—a mediocre issue which forced critics into searching examinations of pictures and text to find cause for sensation. Earlier, Beardsley had shown his cover drawing to a reporter. It featured a small child, drawn simply and without any touch of the grotesque. "I think it is the best of the four [covers]," he said, "and my friends think so too." Unexpectedly he added, "A lot of people will fall in love with that baby." Looking for something to say, the surprised newspaperman asked Beardsley how long it had taken him to do it. "About an evening," he said. "As I told you, drawing is easy, because it's my life."[24] He cultivated the pose of effortlessness, appearing in pubs and cafés frequented by artists and writers, and at concerts, operas and plays, and seemingly never worked. Then he would quietly go home to Cambridge Street and work by candlelight into the morning. In his curtained studio, time had no existence.

Cover design for *The Yellow Book*, Vol. IV

In spite of its unsensational contents, *The Yellow Book*—or, more accurately, Beardsley as a personality—continued to inspire spoofs and satires, some of them paying the compliment of imitation to such an extent that the reproofs intended somehow vanished. *Punch* in February 1895 published a satirical article by a "Max Mereboom" describing a curious sect of decadents which flourished in England in the distant past of 1894. Accompanying it was a drawing "by our own Yellow Book Daubaway Weirdsley . . ." (actually Linley Sanbourne). It was a brilliant caricature of Beardsley's "Frontispiece for *Juvenal*," which had just appeared in the fourth volume. Its central feature was a Roman cart (in a London street) in the shape of a *Yellow Book*, issued—according to a label on it—from "The Bogey Head" in Vigo Street. Pulling the cart (a monkey did it in the original) was a very obvious—and transvestite—Beardsley.

Frontispiece for *Juvenal*,
from *The Yellow Book*, Vol. IV

Cover design for *The Yellow Book*, Vol. I

As the fame of the artist of *Salome*, the *Morte*, and *The Yellow Book* grew beyond professional circles, there were increased demands on Beardsley for interviews and personal data. When, early in the year, a request for biographical details came from his old Brighton friend Palmer, he enclosed a brief account, asked Lane to send a *Yellow Book*, and added to Palmer, "Next year you will I am sure be able to announce my death in addition to other events in my life." He was suffering, he said, from acute hemorrhage of the lungs, yet his work would not permit his going to a warmer climate. He could not even go as far as the forthcoming Old Boys' Dinner in Brighton. It was "out of the question," he finally admitted, not because of the pressure of work but the frailty of his health.[25]

Yet once the fourth *Yellow Book* was released, Beardsley began making plans for a trip to America. Max Beerbohm was going, to tag along with his half-brother's stage company and perhaps find material in Chicago or New York for a *Yellow Book* piece. And John Lane, with Richard Le Gallienne as traveling companion, was going to New York and Boston to look into the possibilities of setting up an American branch of the Bodley Head.

Beardsley wanted to go with Lane, even writing Scotson-Clark as if the journey were assured; and Scotson-Clark published a piece in the April (1895) New York *Bookman* announcing Beardsley's imminent arrival for a lecture tour. Equally certain, Joseph Pennell wrote his young sister-in-law, Helen Robins, in Philadelphia, "Aubrey Beardsley is coming over I believe with John Lane and if you promise to lose your heart to him I'll give him a letter to you."[26] Beardsley may have had in mind the example of Oscar Wilde's American lecturing successes, but seemed to hope, too, that the sea air might mend his chronically failing lungs. "Yes," he told an interviewer, "I am going to Boston and New York, probably in early April. I think the sea will do me good. I'm a poor sailor but I can stand it. My object is partly business and partly health. Perhaps I may lecture if anybody cares to hear me."[27]

Lane sailed, but Beardsley was not with him. Had he gone with Lane, his career might not have taken the catastrophic turn it did. With its publication routine well established, the fifth *Yellow Book* was due for release in mid-April, and featured what was by then a conventional Beardsley cover showing a faun reading to a girl beside a lake. He was busy with new projects, especially his series of illustrations for a rococo version of the story of Venus and Tannhäuser he was then writing, and which Lane was already—prematurely—advertising. Why Beardsley failed to make the sailing with Lane apparently had nothing to do with his various writing and drawing projects: he was too chronically ill to chance the long voyage in the rough North Atlantic. In effect, he remained to mind the shop, for Harland, having put the April issue to bed, had left with his wife to vacation in Paris.

Lane had suspected that eventually he would lose his leading author to the Law, and should have anticipated the disaster's occurring while he was away overseas. Oscar Wilde—as *The Green Carnation* and less public rumor and scandal suggested—had been toying with what he and his young friends facetiously labeled "the love that dares not speak its name." One of the youngest of the friends had for a brief time been Edward Shelley, a young clerk Lane and Mathews had employed at the Bodley Head. Wilde had flattered the boy and, for clearly non-literary reasons, carelessly encouraged his literary aspirations. When he dropped Shelley for another youth, the boy realized that he had degraded himself for nothing and lapsed into self-pitying melancholy. Useless at Vigo Street, he was fired by Lane, who understood the situation yet continued to publish his best-known client. Carefully, however, Lane began to isolate Wilde from the rest of his publishing projects, keeping him out of collaborative ventures—and particularly out of the profitable *Yellow Book*.

Wilde's legal troubles—and the first of the three notorious trials—had begun just before his publisher sailed. Lane had already been frightened, D.S. MacColl recalled, "when Beardsley was mentioned at the Wilde trial as a friend of Wilde's.* He . . . asked me to save the situation by taking on *The Yellow Book* . . . I of course told him that, apart from other reasons, it was impossible for a friend of Beardsley to supplant him, and sent him away with a flea in his ear for running away at a threat of trouble."[28] Worried, but having taken no further action, Lane sailed.

Accused by the half-mad Marquess of Queensberry of "posing as a somdomite" (Queensberry was also a bad speller), Wilde had unwisely sued for

Cover design for *The Yellow Book*, Vol. II

*Beardsley may have been mentioned in gossip. Neither he nor the book he produced with Wilde was ever mentioned in any of the three Wilde trials. That *Salome* was not put into evidence to "establish" Wilde's depravity seems surprising, but the prosecution apparently felt that it had enough "literary" material in *Dorian Gray* and the author's personal correspondence.

libel, whereupon the Marquess's solicitors had hired private detectives and offered rewards to informers. When Lane landed in New York, he was handed a newspaper which headlined, "Arrest of Oscar Wilde, *Yellow Book* under his arm." It was worse than Lane could have imagined. While the April *Yellow Book* was in preparation, Queensberry had been acquitted of the charge of criminal libel. Oscar was arrested on morals charges the same day, and removed in a four-wheeler to the Bow Street police station. Under his arm, the angry, self-righteous mob which had gathered at the Cadogan Hotel noticed, was a volume bound in yellow, and London newspapers predictably reported it to be a *Yellow Book*. Wilde, the press observed, "grasped his suède gloves in one hand and seized his stick with the other. Then he picked up from the table a copy of 'The Yellow Book,' which he placed in security under his left arm." Ironically—the mistaken identification proved accurate the connotation which had inspired Beardsley's choice of color and title—it was only a French novel; Wilde would not have wanted deliberately to give Beardsley's periodical the approbation of being seen in public with him; yet even in the United States his name—although excluded from *The Yellow Book*—had been associated with it. Reviewing the first issue, the American literary journal *The Critic* had headed its notice "A Yellow Impertinence," and identified *The Yellow Book* as "the Oscar Wilde of periodicals." And it was as "the Oscar Wilde of periodicals" that the public reacted to it after the Wilde débâcle. "It killed *The Yellow Book*," Lane later mourned, "and it nearly killed me." Crowds filled Vigo Street and hurled stones through the bow window under the sign of the Bodley Head—a piece of news Lane had not yet heard when he went to the telegraph office to cable Frederic Chapman, his assistant in charge, to withdraw all of Wilde's books from sale. On 18 April there were cables to him from London. Several of his more respectable—and mediocre—authors (goaded by novelist Mrs. Humphry Ward) had declared their outrage and urged that Lane clean house by sacking Beardsley. Otherwise, they felt, *The Yellow Book* was dead or, at the very least, too offensive to contain their work.

Mrs. Ward, W.B. Yeats recorded in the memoirs he did not publish in his lifetime, showed Edmund Gosse the letter she was about to post to Lane, demanding the dismissal of his art editor. "Gosse pointed out that because the British public considered Beardsley's art immoral was not sufficient reason for an act that would connect him in the public mind with a form of vice

Design for the front cover of *The Yellow Book*,
Vol. V (see p. 129)

Design for a *Yellow Book* poster (1894)

with which he had no connection whatever. She said that William Watson, the poet—whose periodical fits of insanity are his sufficient excuse—had asked her to write, and she added, 'My position before the British public makes it necessary for me to write.'"[29] Still, Gosse thought he had dissuaded her, but he had not. She posted her letter, while William Watson pompously cabled Lane, "WITHDRAW ALL BEARDSLEY'S DESIGNS OR I WITHDRAW MY BOOKS."

Within a generation this was the only line of Watson's which had remained memorable, but it struck the panicky Lane as the beginning of the end for his career as a publisher. He had expected some moral posturing, but the vehemence took him by surprise. Cabling Chapman for more information than he could glean from the New York newspapers, he received at first only another piece of Pecksniffery in the form of a warning from the ultra-respectable Wilfrid Meynell, at whose home Beardsley had had one of his earliest triumphs. It was obvious to Lane that Chapman was being pressured to recognize Beardsley's connection in the public mind with Wilde (a connection Lane had apprehensively made earlier himself), and Beardsley's reputation for dandyism and for illustrations which teetered on the brink of indecency. Helplessly, although perhaps relieved that he did not have to do it himself, Lane cabled to Chapman to do whatever had to be done to save the business.

Chapman submitted. He knew of no reason to connect Beardsley's work with debauchery of the Wildean order, but London saw one. To the public as well as to many of Lane's writers, Beardsley was the soul of *The Yellow Book* as well as the young man who illustrated Oscar's *Salome*, a work that evidenced a moral corruption which Beardsley's drawings only reemphasized. Lane privately continued to make that Wildean connection himself, writing weakly to "George Egerton" from Boston after the sacking had taken place, "I have been terribly worried re Oscar-Beardsley-Yellow Book. I have had no peace since my arrival, nothing but cables (Oh! the expense of them!). . . ."[30] He had no idea how expensive other aspects of Beardsley's dismissal would be for him, for *The Yellow Book* had to be quickly retooled to reflect its new purity.

*Patten Wilson, once the dust settled, replaced Beardsley but without the titular authority of the art editorship. He took over instead as cover designer and solicitor of art for the magazine.

With Harland out of touch in France, and Lane only half-aware in America, Chapman had ordered Volume V withdrawn until all traces of Beardsley were expunged. Five plates based upon his designs were removed, and a cover by Patten Wilson* replaced Beardsley's faun and girl. Back went the issue to the printer, Chapman forgetting that the undisturbed spine and back cover were also Beardsley designs. Two weeks later, on 30 April 1895, the purged number appeared.

Beardsley, a contemporary (E.F. Benson) later wrote, "had been the clou* of *The Yellow Book*, for after he ceased to draw for it, it turned grey, as was remarked at the time, in a single night, though it lingered on, feeble and quite respectable, for nine issues more. . . ."

If the hints of scandal had hung about him because of the questionable nature of his art, they now appeared confirmed by his dismissal from *The Yellow Book*. *The Times* even saw "a general tone of striving towards healthiness not hitherto noticeable" in the Beardsley-less April issue. But *The Yellow Book* without Beardsley was *Hamlet* without the Prince of Denmark, although this was small comfort for him. Dismissed from the only salaried position he had occupied since his clerkship days, and cut off from illustrating assignments from "respectable" publishers, Beardsley, not quite twenty-three, was embittered and miserable, and sought the ineffective solace of alcohol. He had first greeted Wilde's arrest with the jest that he would have to go into exile. Now he was not only unemployed, but unemployable.

Back cover design for *Yellow Book*, Vols. I-V

*Star-turn, or staple.

7

1895

Beardsley in Limbo

Just after breakfast one morning in the spring of 1895 unexpected visitors turned up at a hitherto quiet flat in Fountain Court, London. One was Beardsley and the other, Yeats recalled, "a young woman who belongs to our publisher's circle and certainly not ours, and is called 'twopence coloured,' or 'penny plain.'" Yeats—a young Irish poet—shared the flat with Arthur Symons, an equally young* literary jack-of-all-genres. Neither knew Beardsley well; nor had they ever seen him with so wild a look. Still obsessed by his dismissal from *The Yellow Book*, he was a little drunk, and had to steady himself by propping one hand against the nearest wall. A mirror was there, and he stared into it, muttering, "Yes, yes. I look like a Sodomite. But no, I am not that." And he began ruing his birth, and railing against his innocent ancestors, back to and including the great Pitt, from whom—on his mother's side—he claimed to be descended.[1] He might better have railed against Oscar Wilde, then on trial at the Old Bailey.

The verdict at the third Wilde trial had left Beardsley only slightly moved. "I suppose," he wrote a friend, "the result . . . is in the German papers—two years hard. I imagine it will kill him." Like Oscar's harsh sentence—the maximum the law permitted—the jettisoning of Beardsley had been a gesture to the mob, and no more improved the morals of the age than it altered the moral tone of *The Yellow Book*. Instead of saving the quarterly, sacking

*They were both thirty in 1895.

the flamboyant Beardsley insured its demise, for *The Yellow Book* had compromised itself into inevitable dullness, the mortal illness of magazines.

As a result of Oscar's headlines (although Beardsley never figured in the trials), the illustrator of *Salome* unhappily remained lumped together with Wilde and his circle by critics of what was considered "decadence" in art and literature. Wilde's conviction and Beardsley's sacking, they found, were convenient grounds upon which to attack tendencies they did not like. Deserted by fair-weather friends and intermittently ill again, Beardsley alternated between self-pitying moods of black despair and urges to strike back. For one thing, more than his earning capacity had been affected, for he thrived upon public approbation, and had few years left to enjoy it, as well as its artistic stimulus. "When I was a child," he confided to Yeats, "I was a musical genius, and when I came [in]to a room people stared at me. I still wish to be stared at."

The theatre and the opera (to which Mabel often accompanied him) remained his chief consolation during the long weeks in April and May when Oscar was being tried and re-tried; and Beardsley also continued intermittently on those projects which had not yet suffered cancellation, among them a frontispiece for the publisher David Nutt, which out of an excess of caution that spring was rejected because it included a nude female. Beardsley was ripe for a public outburst, which finally occurred when Haldane MacFall, who wrote on art in *St. Paul's* under the name of Hal Dane, declared patriotically that Wilde and Beardsley were really unrepresentative of modern tendencies in English art, for their work, "having no manhood," was "effeminate, sexless and unclean." Wilde—languishing by then in Pentonville prison—may never have heard of the accusation; severe letter-writing restrictions placed on convicts would in any case have prevented him from answering MacFall, but Beardsley was furious. Forgetting his dejection, he dashed off a letter to the magazine's editor:

114 Cambridge Street, S.W.
June 28th

Sir,

No one more than myself welcomes frank, nay, hostile criticism, or enjoys more thoroughly a personal remark. But your art critic surely goes a little too far in last week's issue of *St. Paul's*, & I may be forgiven if I take up the pen of resentment. He says that I am "sexless and unclean."

Vignette of a satyr,
from *Bon-Mots of Lamb and Jerrold*

As to my uncleanliness I do the best for it in my morning bath, & if he has really any doubts as to my sex, he may come and see me take it.

Yours &c.
Aubrey Beardsley

St. Paul's never published the letter, but Beardsley was satisfied when he was shown MacFall's answer to it—that the morning bath about which the irate young artist boasted was "a pretty habit that will soon lose its startling thrill of novelty if he persists in it."[2] Eventually, MacFall and Beardsley became friends, and the critic from *St. Paul's* was later Beardsley's biographer.

For a time Beardsley was obsessed with the desire to prove that his sexual interests were remote from those of Wilde. Both Yeats and Shaw were sure that he had no overt sexual abnormality, and publisher Grant Richards insisted, "I knew Beardsley well, and assuredly there were sides of the Oscar Wilde gospel with which he had no sympathy," but the public saw depravity in his work, not a new Juvenal. If anything, Beardsley had opted for an image as imp of the perverse. Once, for example, he had written to Lane, then in Paris, "I hope that William Rothenstein has done no more than take you to the *Chat Noir* in the daytime, and shown you the outside of the *Moulin Rouge*." Jokingly, he then added, "I am going to 'Jimmie's' [the St. James's Restaurant] on Thursday night, dressed up like a tart and mean to have a regular spree." And he enclosed a drawing of himself in female attire.[3] The letter very likely implied more than it really meant, for although Beardsley's dandyism clearly had traces of effeminacy about it, as did his vocabulary, some of it was as affected as were his sudden evidences of heterosexuality. A letter he wrote to a new and clearly homosexual acquaintance that May even put quotation marks around the word *adorable* once he had been accused of affectation in adopting such well-understood terms.[4]

Beardsley had no close friendships, male or female, except—until she went off to act with touring companies—his sister; yet his professional acquaintances were numerous, and with them he enjoyed visiting clubs frequented by the odd and the unusual, but only to observe, and draw as much from imagination as from life. Once, with friends, he visited a drab drinking establishment called, aptly, "The Failure." More often he appeared at The Thalia, a place haunted "by sodden young Army officers and the ladies they kept." The food was poor, and the liquor was bad, Edgar Jepson

Grotesque from *Bon-Mots of Smith and Sheridan*

Lysistrata shielding her Coynte,
from *The Lysistrata of Aristophanes* (1896)

The Toilet of Lampito,
from *The Lysistrata of Aristophanes*

recalled; but he remembered also one time when art critic Herbert Horne brought Muriel Broadbent, his vivid and pretty mistress, there, and Beardsley "tried to ravish her in the supper-room."[5] It must have been purely a theatrical gesture, for Beardsley was probably as unable to complete the performance as he was unable to be the Sodomite he had thought he looked like in Symons's mirror.* "Once a eunuch always a eunuch," he wrote his publisher, in commenting on a story about a mutual acquaintance. "Perhaps the story might be transferred to me, with equal truth."[6]

The admission was medically inaccurate, but Beardsley seemed to have been implying illness-related or psychosexually-caused impotence. Yeats confided to pages of the memoirs he did not see fit to print the tale that for Beardsley "sexual desire under the pressure of disease had become insatiable," and that he had been told at the time of Beardsley's death "that he had hastened it by masturbation." The concept was a quack-medical Victorian fiction, but it is easy to see in Beardsley's later drawings how the rumor could have gained currency. An isolated personality who lived so much of his life vicariously, he seemed, in the masturbatory daydreams he penned, to reflect his sexually arrested state. His letters to his last publisher (a part-time pornographer to whom Beardsley may have deliberately played up) even state as much. In them his virginity is "broken" only by "reves mouillés," and although a "eunuch" the description of "the lace of her pantalons" in a picture he has drawn is allegedly sufficient to raise an erection † in the writer.

Chronically tubercular since his boyhood, he lived in feverish fantasies arising from illness and from deprivation, and had, he realized, an obsessive intellectual interest in sexual matters. Writing once about a painful extraction

* Among other stories of Beardsley's supposed heterosexual involvements was the inevitable one that suggested an illegitimate child; and the Victoria and Albert Museum's 1966 Beardsley Exhibition displayed a portrait of a young man sitting at a table with a cigarette in one slender hand and a glass of wine in the other, labeling it "Mr. Watkins," and in the catalogue described the figure as "reputed to be a natural son of Aubrey Beardsley." By August 1966, it was proved to be a portrait of Alan Odle (1888-1948), husband of novelist Dorothy Richardson, and son of a bank manager in the service of the Westminster Bank. (*Times Literary Supplement*, 25 August 1966, p. 770.)

† "There. I've given myself a cockstand!" (Beardsley to Leonard Smithers, postmarked 23 December 1896. Huntington Library.)

Grotesque from *Bon-Mots of Smith and Sheridan*

he had submitted to, he drew the tooth, with three long roots, and added, "You see even my teeth are a little phallic." Making wry fun of his inadequacies, he noted a newspaper reference to "*The Rape of the Lock* by Mrs. Beardsley, Illustrated by herself." "You see," he quipped, "how widely spread is the doubt as to my sex." It was a doubt reinforced by the evidence as to who were his friends. He had little choice but to accept and cultivate the approbation of the coterie of aggressively homosexual men in the literary and artistic circles of the nineties who influenced contemporary taste. He could be revolted by the corrupt vulgarity of a Wilde, but he could not reject them all without jeopardizing his livelihood. If anything, his sense of entrapment reinforced the sexual ironies in his work.

Beardsley's thwarted instincts found both expression and release in exotic literature and art, often in its most sardonic and perverse extremes. Similarly, in his own work there was no beauty in the erotic impulse, and he was impelled to the illustration of works like *Lysistrata*, where the mood was morbid, animalistic or otherwise corrupt. He not only would draw people who were emotionally abnormal but would portray mental states physically by portraying people as anatomically grotesque. A human being did not have to wait for birth to become Beardsley's victim. "The little creature handing hats," he once wrote his publisher about a drawing, "is *not* an infant but an unstrangled abortion."[7] Yet he had another side, and could also write, "I read in the papers here that [W. T.] Stead has established an agency for the adoption of children.*[3] Is it true? If so I certainly mean to adopt some nice little girl who would at once satisfy my maternal amatory & educational instincts. This quite seriously."[8]

When Yeats later defended the morbid sexual element in Beardsley's art and writing—"lascivious monstrous imagery," he called it—he told the artist about it, adding, half seriously, "I was defending you last night in the only way in which it is possible to defend you, by saying that all you draw is inspired by rage against iniquity."

"If it were so inspired," Beardsley answered honestly, "the work would be in no way different."

Grotesque from *Bon-Mots of Lamb and Jerrold*

*[3]Stead had been campaigning since 1885 to keep parentless girls in London from being sold into prostitution.

The profusion of grotesque fetuses and embryos in Beardsley's work has suggested to several imaginative critics that he learned about them from life rather than (in his usual manner) from the library. In particular, it has been alleged more than once that he had something to do with an hypothesized miscarriage or abortion of Mabel's, perhaps even providing the seed or presiding at the curtailment of the supposed pregnancy (perhaps the "unstrangled abortion"). A fetid domestic atmosphere, with an oedipal Aubrey unnaturally close to his mother, and/or an incestuous Beardsley in unnatural embrace with his sister, has emerged in several books. Since rumor feeds on curiosity more than on facts, long-posthumous and internally contradictory rumors about the Beardsley ménage have fed upon its undeniable closeness, which for Aubrey, from childhood, was based upon his invalid necessities. That he loved his mother and sister in the open and unaffected manner of close-knit Victorian families is unquestionable. That there was an overt sexual element in Aubrey's affection for his sister is likely to continue to be speculated about because such speculations have been afforded the dubious permanency of print.

The most absurd of the allegations appeared in Frank Harris's *My Life and Loves*:

One afternoon, about 1890, Aubrey Beardsley and his sister Mabel, a very pretty girl, had been lunching with me in Park Lane. Afterwards we went into the Park, and I accompanied them as far as Hyde Park Corner. For some reason or other I elaborated the theme that men of thirty or forty usually corrupted young girls, and women of thirty or forty corrupted youths.

"I don't agree with you," Aubrey remarked. "It's usually a fellow's sister who gives him his first lessons in sex. I know it was Mabel here who first taught me."

I was amazed at his outspokenness. Mabel flushed crimson and I hastened to add, "In childhood girls are far more precocious. But these little lessons are usually too early to matter." He wouldn't have it, but I changed the subject resolutely and Mabel told me some time afterwards that she was very grateful to me for cutting short the discussion. "Aubrey," she said, "loves all sex things and doesn't care what he says or does."

I had seen before that Mabel was pretty. . . . Aubrey caught my eye at the moment and remarked maliciously, "Mabel was my first model, weren't you, Mabs? I was in love with her figure," he went on judicially. "Her breasts were so high and firm and round that I took her as my ideal." She laughed, blushing a little, and rejoined, "Your figures, Aubrey, are not exactly ideal."

Nothing in the purported encounter sounds genuine, least of all the lan-

Grotesque from *Bon-Mots of Smith and Sheridan*

guage. The people in Frank Harris's invented conversations all seem to sound like Frank Harris. Yet Harris may have been elaborating upon a rumor he had once heard. What *is* known about Mabel Beardsley is that she was at home in literary and theatrical circles, liked mannish clothes, had a brief and unsuccessful marriage, was alleged to be a lesbian, and was an ardent exponent of what was then called Free Love. What is even suggested about Aubrey Beardsley in addition to (and even simultaneously with) the incest hypothesis is that he was both a transvestite and suffered from transsexual delusions.[9] The letter to John Lane can be cited as "evidence." And in 1972 an octogenarian Dutch Catholic divine—and medium (who professed also to be in touch with Rembrandt)—"reported," almost as if in corroboration, that in the spirit world Beardsley (who communicated sadomasochistic "emendations" to his drawings to Brother Johannes) is a woman.[10]

It was, Yeats thought, "some turn of disease" in Beardsley which "had begun to parade erotic images before his eyes, and I do not doubt that he drew these images." When Yeats asked what inspired them, Beardsley joked, "I make a blot upon the paper and begin to shove the ink about and something comes." There was almost never in Beardsley, Yeats thought,

any representation of desire. Even the beautiful women are exaggerated into doll-like prettiness by a spirit of irony, or are poignant with a thwarted or corrupted innocence. I see his art with more understanding now, than when he lived, for in 1895 or 1896, I was in despair at the new breath of comedy that had begun to wither the beauty [in his work] that I loved, just when that beauty seemed to have united itself to mystery. I said to him once, "You have never done anything to equal your Salome with the head of John the Baptist." I think, that for the moment he was sincere when he replied, "Yes, yes; but beauty is so difficult." It was for the moment only, for as the popular rage increased, he became more and more violent in his satire, or created out of a spirit of mockery a form of beauty where his powerful logical intellect eliminated every outline that suggested meditation or even satisfied passion.[11]

Paralleling Yeats's diagnosis, another critic wrote that

Beardsley had one great talent apart from the mere mastery of line. Over-civilised himself, he was unequalled in suggesting the tragedy of over-civilisation. . . . He could portray with remorseless truth, though in a convention as strict as that of an old Chinese artist, certain types of modern men and women. He is the limner of the pinched soul, the pampered body, the craving without appetite, the animalism without animal health. . . . There is a sense of joyless depravity about his men and women, as if vice were a . . . solemn social ritual. . . .[12]

The Examination of the Herald,
from *The Lysistrata of Aristophanes*

BATHYLLVS

It may have been that whatever there was of the joyous in Beardsley's work, a mood most visible during the *Yellow Book* period, was extinguished by his dismissal. Afterwards, the public (for the most part) received the perversely sardonic art it expected from him, even when the unnatural did not come naturally to him. He would fulfill his persona: he had painstakingly created much of it on his own, and could not let go of it, nor would it go away.

When Yeats's Fountain Court companion, Arthur Symons, was asked by a minor London publisher to develop and edit a new quarterly to pick up the discarded banners left by the retreat of *The Yellow Book* into respectability, Symons recalled the strange morning visit of Beardsley.* Beardsley would have to be the art editor, Symons thought aloud, and Smithers, the publisher, agreed. The pairing was peculiarly attractive to Smithers, for he had very likely sought Symons out on the strength of such of his writings as "Stella Maris," a poem about a London streetwalker which did as much as any literary contribution to make the early numbers of *The Yellow Book* notorious. Beardsley, if he were available, would confirm the tone of the new venture.

Leonard Smithers in 1895 was thirty-four, and had been in publishing for less than five years. He had practiced—with little success——as a solicitor until 1892, when he went into business, dealing in rare and second-hand books and publishing books as a sideline. His best trade was done in under-the-counter volumes—pornography and other exotica. One of his catalogues offered such rarities as two books bound in human skin, with a comment stressing their scarcity: ". . . owing to the severe restrictions and prejudices of medical men, it is extremely difficult to obtain portions of dead humanity. . . ." His bookselling and publishing interests reflected his personal interests, which, if anything, were unhealthier than his book inventory and grew more so as long as his finances permitted. Oscar Wilde's description of him from memory—he wrote from prison—is unforgettable. "I do not know if you know Smithers," he wrote Reggie Turner;

he is usually in a large straw hat, has a blue tie delicately fastened with a diamond brooch of the impurest water—or perhaps wine, as he never touches water: it goes

*Described by Yeats in *The Trembling of the Veil*. Symons makes no mention of this visit, but cited his later appearance at Beardsley's home—which he recalled as being on 30 July 1895, at 7:30 p.m.—as their first meeting. Yet he had met Beardsley as early as August 1893, and very likely met him repeatedly in *Yellow Book* days.

to his head at once. His face, clean shaven as befits a priest who serves at the altar whose God is Literature, is wasted and pale—not with poetry, but with poets, who, he says, have wrecked his life by insisting on publishing with him. He loves first editions, especially of women: little girls are his passion. He is the most learned erotomaniac in Europe. He is also a delightful companion, and a dear fellow. . . .[13]

Smithers was renowned not only for his unconventional tastes in literature and in women, both of which he probably acquired from Sir Richard Burton, whom he had known and whose works he afterwards published, but for his pasty white face, which someone described as "like the death mask of Nero." The unhealthy aspect was accentuated by eyes sunk deeply into shadowed sockets and long, twitching hands sometimes calmed by drugs or alcohol. Even most of the writers and artists whom he encouraged and published were put off by him and only Wilde, Robert Ross and Ernest Dowson ever thought of him as a person one might want to know. "Smithers," Dowson broad-mindedly wrote a friend, "is, all round, the best fellow I know, and it is astonishing how many people fail to see this, or seeing it temporarily succeed in quarrelling with him." Dowson's relationship with Smithers was sufficiently close that he could utter the truth about the publisher in a jest; planning to meet Smithers in Paris, he wrote, "I want to see your classically sin-stained countenance. . . ." To Ross, who shared other Wildean tastes, "Mr. Smithers was the most delightful and irresponsible publisher I ever knew. Who remembers without a kindly feeling the little shop . . . with its tempting shelves; its limited editions of 5,000 copies; the shy, infrequent purchaser; the upstairs room; the genial proprietor?"

Smithers had first met Beardsley in the early days of his shop in Arundel Street, Aldwych, just off the Strand, when *The Yellow Book* was providing the young artist with a regular income. To the knowledgeable, it was "a perfect little museum of erotica belonging to all times and countries." One evening Beardsley walked in, and Smithers recognized the stooping gait and the emaciated, bony face. Several century-old Fragonards—Smithers displayed paintings and prints as well as books—caught Beardsley's eye, and he expressed his delight with them; yet he left instead with a small volume of eighteenth-century fables at the large price of £6. But Smithers bought as well as sold, and when Beardsley returned it was to sell several books, offering the proprietor the surprising excuse that he wanted to take a pretty girl out to dinner and was short in funds.[14] He left with some of Smithers's money, and, for the first of what were to be many occasions, made

Bathyllus in the Swan Dance (opposite) and *Bathyllus Posturing* (1896), illustrations to the *Sixth Satire of Juvenal*, in *An Issue of Five Drawings Illustrative of Juvenal and Lucian*, published by Leonard Smithers in 1906.

Smithers—through Beardsley's device of buying, then selling back his books—his personal lending library. No other rental library could have boasted such an exotic stock of volumes, nor could any have publicly offered some of them.

Oscar Wilde later called Smithers the "owner of Beardsley," and it became largely true. Smithers, delighted at the prospect of putting an impecunious genius on his payroll, suggested that the artist be offered £25 a week* for his exclusive services, and sent Symons out to find Beardsley and woo him to the magazine venture. Beardsley needed little wooing. He was without any regular source of income, and was finding it difficult to market any of his work. He managed to sell one of his suppressed *Yellow Book* drawings to his old publisher Elkin Mathews, to be used as frontispiece to a book, but after six copies were run off Mathews insisted on an entirely new drawing, having discovered that the original, "Black Coffee," was tainted with yellow. A few drawings were accepted by *The Studio*, which remained loyal. But Beardsley had increasing debts, and practically no funds, and was forced, while fighting renewed hemorrhages, to give up the house in Cambridge Street which had been the symbol of his worldly success.

Towards the end of June 1895, he took a three-year lease on a house in Chester Terrace. † Despite the upheavals in his life he had not lost his sense of humor completely, for he was offered some muslin by Mrs. Savile Clarke, wife of the playwright, apparently for curtains in the house, and answered that he was delighted to have it. "It suits me so well & will be so nice & cool in the hot weather," he added. "If my tailor finds that there is any over I shall get some curtains made."[15] Whether this was the house in which Symons located him is unknown, but finding the artist was an easy assignment. Beardsley's gaunt frame, decorated in dandified clothes, was not easily hidden in artistic London; still, the talk of the town was that he was dying.

---

* In practice, this turned out to be only £12 a week, in the end reduced to £5 a week, irregularly paid, and sometimes with checks drawn on insufficient funds.

† His lease of 57 Chester Terrace was for three years from 24 June 1895, but he lived there only for a few months; it was surrendered on 25 December 1895, with furniture and fixtures, on a valuation, to Sir William Hollingworth Quayle Jones. After Beardsley vacated the house in Chester Terrace he lived briefly during 1895-6 at 10 & 11 St. James Place, S.W.

Symons, entering Beardsley's room, saw him "lying out on a couch, horribly white," and wondered if he had come too late.[16] But the prospect of an income, and—even more—of arming a rival to set against the *Yellow Book* enemy, had a tonic effect on Beardsley. He was suddenly full of ideas for contributors and for drawings and writings of his own; and he even proposed a title for the new magazine—*The Savoy*, suggesting (after the great new London hotel) modernity, opulence and magnificence. Symons and Smithers were first hesitant about the title, but they rejoiced at their acquisition of Beardsley and began the search for contributors to the initial issues.

Symons's connections in London literary circles were wide, and he hoped, besides, that writers and artists who had contributed to *The Yellow Book* but who were disenchanted after the expulsion of Beardsley would find common cause with him. Many did: fourteen of the thirty-five writers who eventually contributed to *The Savoy* had written earlier for *The Yellow Book*. Symons had been earning his living as a critic of music and art, and as a sometime essayist and poet. His closest literary friends were members of the Rhymers' Club, such disciples of Walter Pater and Rossetti as Lionel Johnson, Ernest Rhys, John Davidson, Ernest Dowson, W. B. Yeats and Richard Le Gallienne. Yet his own work was more influenced by Verlaine, Baudelaire and Villon. For Symons *fin de siècle* decadence was intellectual, rather than emotional, something his career as a critic would continue to demonstrate; for after his tenure as literary editor of *The Savoy*, he laid secure claim to a literary reputation with his book *The Symbolist Movement in Literature* (1899), which made the term "symbolist"—transplanted from France—fashionable as well in England.

Some of the Rhymers had created a reputation for their circle by their excesses, but it seemed to Yeats that he, and even more so, Symons, lived the temperate life recommended by Pater. One evening at Fountain Court, comparing their habits with those of the dissipated Dowson, they wondered whether there was some serious lack in themselves. To experiment, they decided to have two whiskies every night at twelve to see if they could do without a third. When at the end of a fortnight they gratefully returned to their glasses of hot water, Yeats said, half seriously, "Symons, if we had a tendency to excess we would be better poets."[17]

It was at that haunt of the Rhymers' Club poets, the Crown, a pub seated between the stage doors of the Alhambra and the Empire, in the Leicester

Juvenal Scourging Woman, illustration to the *Sixth Satire of Juvenal* (1896), published by Smithers in 1906

No. 6   1896

CATALOGUE OF RARE BOOKS

OFFERED FOR SALE BY

LEONARD SMITHERS

EFFINGHAM HOUSE ARUNDEL STREET STRAND

LONDON W.C.

PRICE ONE SHILLING

Square theatrical region, that Symons had first seen Beardsley, who would become a rather difficult collaborator as he would not confine his interests to the artistic side of the journal, fancying himself an unofficial Rhymer. But during the early summer he was too ill to begin playing an active role, even as art editor. When he could, he drew. Joseph Pennell—whose work he solicited for the first number—recalled visiting him at the time in the darkened drawing-room of his house, where, as before, he worked during the day by candlelight, beginning his drawing "by making the pen lines which bound it—two or three of them, sometimes he made a pencil sketch in the space within—sometimes [he] went straight at the subject in ink." Will Rothenstein—whose art was also solicited for the first issue—began collaborating that summer on a "dialogue" with Beardsley—"to no end," he thought, "but our own amusement." Beardsley may have had more serious plans for it, but it was eventually abandoned and forgotten, until years later when Rothenstein "came upon a page or two" and gave them to Robert Ross. In prose as well as in line, the dialogue proved Beardsley was still bent on satirizing Whistler—a one-way vendetta, since the Master never stooped to reply in kind. Discussing him, *R* in the dialogue asks, "What [?] Don't you admire Jimmy[?] Entre nous he has influenced me considerably." "Ah, you suffer, I know," replies *M*, "from severe attacks of Whistlerian tremens."[18]

As he renewed his activity, Beardsley dabbled in prose and poetry on his own, and would read from his efforts to the appreciative Rothenstein, who thought—at least half mistakenly—that his friend wrote "with astonishing ease and command of language." When Beardsley moved to Chester Terrace, Rothenstein recalled, "he would often come round in the morning to my studio, hastily dressed and without a collar. One day he began scribbling some verses about three musicians; afterwards he sent me the whole poem."[19] But even those verses, as easily as they were begun, took Beardsley weeks to hone into a shape which satisfied him.

Once Beardsley set to work, Smithers's weekly checks began arriving. Frugally, Beardsley offered his publisher a variant of his suppressed April *Yellow Book* cover, and the discarded drawing turned up as cover design for Smithers's September catalogue of rare books. By August the hemorrhages had temporarily ceased, and Beardsley was involved with Smithers not only in planning *The Savoy*'s art but in a mild conspiracy to rescue a Beardsley prose work begun and interrupted months before. His version of the Venus and Tannhäuser story, more then a promise than a fulfillment, had been advertised by John Lane in the October 1894 *Yellow Book*, but—whatever its stage of development—the author had no intention of ever delivering it to the traitorous Lane. Perhaps, he suggested to Smithers, the book might be advertised as forthcoming under the innocuous title *The Queen in Exile*: "You see if we gave it that name Lane would not suspect it was his book when your prospectus or announcement appears."

In mid-August, Beardsley took his manuscript, barely begun, to France, and met Symons in Dieppe to plan the magazine. He had hoped to work in London, but Symons had crossed the Channel for a weekend, and ended by staying for two months, which meant that Beardsley had to go to meet his co-editor if *The Savoy* was to get off the ground by December.

The seaside atmosphere and the excitement of the venture resulted in what appeared to be improvement in Beardsley's health (nevertheless his mother generally hovered in the background or remained available nearby). The editors met mainly in a café, and there Symons wrote what he later called his "slightly pettish and defiant" editorial note which prefaced the first number. Dieppe was the meeting place for the younger generation of English writers and artists, and Symons affectionately described the Channel resort setting in an essay written mostly on the scene and also included in *The Savoy*'s first number. Most of the natural glories of the area were lost on Beardsley. He considered himself a city dweller, and felt unable to draw or write out of London. Yet some of his finest work resulted from his stay at Dieppe, when he was restless for London.

"He never walked," Symons exaggerated;

I never saw him look at the sea; but at night he was almost always to be seen watching the gamblers at *petits chevaux*, studying them with a sort of hypnotised attention. . . . He liked the large, deserted rooms [of the Casino], at hours when no one was there; the sense of frivolous things caught at a moment of suspended life, *en déshabillé*. He would glance occasionally, but with more impatience, at the dances, especially the children's dances, in the concert room; but he rarely missed a concert, and would glide in every afternoon and sit on the high benches at the side, always carrying his large, gilt-leather portfolio with the magnificent old, red-lined folio paper, which he would often open, to write some lines in pencil.

Jacques-Émile Blanche, the French portraitist, painted Beardsley at Dieppe, and remembered his arriving late for a Casino concert one afternoon at the "bathing hour." The orchestra was already playing a waltz by Abran,

Design for the proposed title page for *Venus and Tannhäuser*, but first published in *The Studio* in 1898

and Beardsley had just "escaped from the Hôtel des Étrangers without the permission of his mother, who was also his nurse. He was coughing and muffled up, drinking a glass of milk and soda under a coloured umbrella on the terrace." Noticing Blanche, Beardsley showed him a "find" he had made when reconnoitering the local bookshops, a copy of the *Mémoires pour servir à l'histoire de la ville de Dieppe*, by Denis Guibert. With him at the table was a tall, muscular companion with fair, limp hair and a drooping moustache—Charles Conder. Over Beardsley's milk-and-soda and Conder's brandy-and-soda the two were laughing at passages from the book about the role in the area of "English warriors during the Wars of Religion." While the English army was encamped on the plains of Caux, nearby, the *histoire* reported, soldiers enticed into camp the lousy urchins of Pollet in order to teach them the use of the bathtub and to convert them to the "Reformed Protestant Religion."

Beardsley, Blanche remembered,

knew certain of the pages of the learned abbot Denis Guibert by heart, descriptions of processions, of festivals, of Mysteries performed at the Church of St. Jaques, which all delighted him. Conder listened all the more attentively, as he was staying opposite that magnificent church in a room that he had specially rented and from which he was making sketches of the booths, merry-go-round, the theatres at the fair, amidst the turmoil of steam-organs, trombones and cymbals.

Beardsley was carried away by his book. "An amazing town!" he cried. "What a history from Brennus to Oscar Wilde. I can see medieval Dieppe, and the Dieppe of the Renaissance and the town of the powdered wigs and sedan chairs. I see it as clearly as the Rue Aguado at the period of the *Dame aux Camelias* and the Empress Eugenie. We ought to organize pageants, without reviving Charlemagne and his mother Queen Blanche, and, still less, Brennus. I should undertake the staging—and you, Conder? Let us not lose ourselves in legend."

"The French," said Conder, "have no imagination—that's proved by the plays they produce at the Casino. We have plenty to choose from."

When Blanche objected that the revival of local pageants was rather the job of the natives of Dieppe, Beardsley countered, "For centuries the English have here been on conquered soil. We shall re-animate the people's ancestral taste for religious processions, for military and naval parades, for firework displays on board a ship out of commission."[20]

The Bathers (1895), illustration to Arthur Symons's article "Dieppe," in *The Savoy*, No. 1 (January, 1896)

Beardsley was full of plans and ideas, and over drinks with his cronies improvised stories he might write down for *The Savoy*—"so daring," according to Blanche, who was no prude, "that it would have been better had he told them in Greek." But he drew and wrote less than he had planned. He worked best alone, yet feared to be left alone in his hotel room, for no one would then know—until it was too late—if he were to bleed or to collapse.* Beneath his surface gaiety there was a desperate urgency in his search for companionship in Dieppe, and in a crowd he forced enthusiasm and confidence across his tightly drawn, emaciated face, while he spent money more freely than he could afford, losing regularly at the "little horses" in the Casino. And he stayed longer than he should have, explaining to Will Rothenstein—on stationery decorated with an engraving of the ornately domed and beflagged Casino—that he had meant to get back to London sooner, but missed the boat one day "& so stopped on here indefinitely."

Symons's "I never saw him look at the sea" was clearly hyperbole, for although Beardsley preferred the café, the Casino or the bookshop to the beach, one of his most striking drawings, used in the first number of *The Savoy*, portrayed three women in modest mid-nineties' bathing dress, standing on the pebbled *plage* with the sea as a backdrop. Of such scenes as Beardsley drew, Symons—who could not have dreamed of French beaches dotted with bikini-clad (or unclad) females—wrote, "A sentimental sensualist should avoid the French seaside. He will be very pained at seeing how ridiculous a beautiful woman may look when she has very few clothes on."

Although Beardsley stored up most of his ideas for drawings he hoped to work on later in London, he had less difficulty attempting some literary experimentation. His morocco leather Louis XIV-period portfolio, with its gilt hinges, was his constant companion, a talisman he opened on impulse to set down penciled jottings of ideas and impressions for poems and stories (most of them never to be written), epithets, passages of dialogue, and newly coined words, agonizing over the right turn of a phrase, piecing together a puzzle of over-polished sentences, often making them fit where

Grotesque from *Bon-Mots of Smith and Sheridan*

*His mother made frequent trips back to London, while Mabel remained there either acting or seeking work.

they made the right verbal music to his ear, without worrying overmuch about making the sound match the sense. His major effort in Dieppe, worked at—in Symons's words—"with an almost pathetic tenacity," was "his story, never to be finished, the story which never could have been finished, *Under the Hill*, a new version, a parody (like Laforgue's parodies, but how unlike them, or anything!) of the story of Venus and Tannhäuser." He worked on it at the concerts, and in the "little, close writing-room" of the Casino where visitors wrote letters home extolling the bracing sea air.

 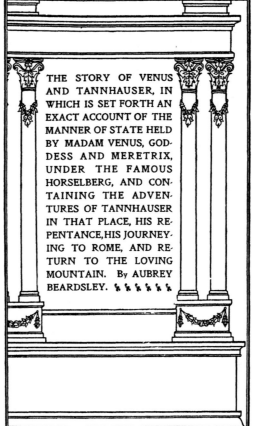

THE STORY OF VENUS AND TANNHAUSER, IN WHICH IS SET FORTH AN EXACT ACCOUNT OF THE MANNER OF STATE HELD BY MADAM VENUS, GODDESS AND MERETRIX, UNDER THE FAMOUS HORSELBERG, AND CONTAINING THE ADVENTURES OF TANNHAUSER IN THAT PLACE, HIS REPENTANCE, HIS JOURNEYING TO ROME, AND RETURN TO THE LOVING MOUNTAIN. By AUBREY BEARDSLEY.

Designs prepared for the frontispiece and title page of the never-finished *Venus and Tannhäuser* (1895)

ERDA

Erda, the fourth of a never-completed series of
illustrations for "The Comedy of the Rhinegold,"
reproduced in *The Savoy*, No. 8 (December,
1896)

Assuming for himself guardianship of the tone of the new periodical, Beardsley used part of his time at Dieppe to solicit potential art contributors, including Conder and Sickert, and literary contributors as well, although that was clearly Symons's responsibility. To another of their clan, Will Rothenstein, Conder reported, "There has been a great deal of excitement about the new quarterly here and discussion. Beardsley is very pompous about it all."*

Afterwards Conder wrote Rothenstein again from Dieppe to tempt him into the drawing for the new magazine and into joining him there. The sea was "like some drug," and life was "so beautiful that one thinks it must end soon," he enthused, "but ambition only comes in and interferes." Arthur Symons had taken rooms in the same *maison*, he added, and had "just written a poem as to the Dieppe sea being like absinthe—original n'est-ce pas?" In another letter to Rothenstein Conder noted that Symons, Beardsley and Smithers were all in Dieppe together, but he hoped that Smithers's imminent departure would induce Rothenstein to come. The publisher, he reported, was "too awful for words but very good hearted. He has decked himself out in a whole suit of French summer clothing from the *Belle Jardinière*, and although it suits his particular style very well one is not exactly proud of his companionship."

Far from looking forward to being seen with Smithers, Conder admitted to being particularly happy that day, probably because he had spent the day successfully "dodging" the bizarre publisher.[21] Smithers had come "in the company of a harlot or two—big, florid, noisy creatures were the kind he favoured—" and Conder had dreaded the occasion, although he had more than an aesthetic interest in women who were well-endowed. It was not that Smithers's conduct was more than he could stomach, but "more, rather, than he could stomach sober. . . . Drink in such company made Conder morose."[22] This Conder knew from experience, for in Smithers he had al-

*Barely a year later Beardsley and Conder were not on speaking terms, the clash of two such strong and widely different personalities resulting in Beardsley's rejecting a suggestion from Smithers that he do the cover for a book Conder had illustrated. "I feel that the relations that exist between us (humanly & artistically) stand very much in the way of any collaboration. . . . Whatever may be my private feelings against him, my artistic conscience forbids me to add any decoration to a book which he has illustrated." (Beardsley to Smithers, probably 29 October 1896.)

ready found a boon companion who encouraged in him excesses so severe that in the past they had brought on attacks of delirium tremens, which so frightened Conder that he would appeal to Will Rothenstein to sit up with him afterwards for most of the night: he was terrified of being left alone in that condition.[23]

Smithers and his companions had made the *petits chevaux* rooms "ring with their shouts and antics," compelling the distraught manager of the Casino to put up a notice in two languages: "Ladies and gentlemen are respectfully begged to keep a complete silence" — "*Prière aux joueurs d'observer le silence.*"[24] The incident, naturally, was not recorded in Symons's "Dieppe: 1895," but he did refer, patronizingly, to a "younger Englishman . . . [who] came into our society with a refreshing and troubling *bizarrerie*; all that feverish brilliance, the boyish defiance of things, the frail and intense vitality, how amusing and uncommon it was!" This, for the first *Savoy*, for which that "younger Englishman" was his co-editor. No wonder there was, almost from the start, an unspoken hostility between the ambitious Symons and the feverish young invalid he found upstaging him.

Unaware that Rothenstein found Smithers so unappetizing that he would cease contributing after *The Savoy*'s first issue, or that Conder would be writing in a far different tone, Beardsley wrote to Rothenstein about the delights in Dieppe and proselytized for *The Savoy*. "*Petits Chevaux* and everything most pretty and amusing," he observed. "Symons has written to Meredith to ask if he would sit to you for a portrait [for *The Savoy*]. . . ." Despite misgivings, Conder found it exhilarating to sit in on the planning sessions for the magazine while the unlikely triumvirate managing the enterprise aired their hopes and dreams, and he looked forward to *The Savoy* as a mighty gallery for the new art. But neither he nor Beardsley could stir Rothenstein, who preferred to keep his distance from Smithers. Yet Rothenstein agreed to make a set of etchings for a Smithers edition of Voltaire's *La Pucelle* and published one in the first number of *The Savoy*.

It was as far as he would go: "I disliked Smithers and his ways, and I withdrew from the contract. I thought Smithers had an evil influence on Beardsley, keeping him up late into the night, which was bad, too, for Beardsley's health." Although any exposure to Bohemia was hard on his health, he craved his chances to play truant from invalidism. "I remember," wrote Rothenstein, "Beardsley, Conder and Dowson starting off from The

Design for a catalogue cover, using the same placement of figures as in the final *Yellow Book* cover (p. 127)

Crown one night, wandering about London, and taking the early boat-train to Dieppe without any luggage—Beardsley and Dowson coming back a few days later looking the worse for wear. Conder stayed on. . . ."[25]

For Beardsley, August along the Channel coast did not always measure up to Conder's catalogue of delights. "Aubrey is feeling very tired," Mabel reported in an apologetic note to Blanche. "Dr. Caron, whom you so kindly recommended to mother, forbids him to go out—on account of the nasty north wind. Is it always as sharp at this time of the year in Dieppe?" It meant that Beardsley had to miss a meeting he had looked forward to with pioneer stream-of-consciousness novelist Édouard Dujardin.

When the weather drove him from the resort for the season, it was with a suddenness which Beardsley, inured to living with hemorrhages and exhaustion, could not have expected. The weeks at Dieppe had been among the happiest of his life, and in the cafés, hotels and promenades of the town he had often forgotten that he was slowly dying. The news came to Blanche, who had finished his portrait of Aubrey and was an arm—or a sleeve—from completing one of Mabel, in an urgent note from her on 2 September: "Mother determined to leave Dieppe for Paris and perhaps go south. Aubrey is too fragile. Doctor Caron pronounces . . . but I'd rather not write the word. In haste. We are packing."[26]

It was a false alarm. Beardsley remained, and even found the late September weather (in a letter to Smithers) "quite perfect so I shall linger a little while here." To Rothenstein in London he sent some lengths of string representing the dimensions of Blanche's portrait so that a frame could be made, but almost immediately afterward returned to "desolate" London, setting himself up at 10 St. James's Place, apparently to be near the offices of *The Savoy*—Smithers's shop just off the Strand.

From his new quarters Aubrey crowed to Smithers over a satirical fusillade against the future *Savoy*, in a November number of Henley's *National Observer*, and pressed hard to have sufficient copy of *Under the Hill* ready for publication. Assembling materials for the inaugural issue, he and Symons relied heavily on their own work and that of their mutual friend Yeats. The prospectus for the issue was dominated by a Beardsley drawing of a Pierrot stepping out on a footlighted stage to announce the new publication. One hand held a copy of *The Savoy* dated December, which made it clear that the intention of the editors was to produce an issue which would appear in

THE SAVOY

AUBREY BEARDSLEY. 1896.

Design for the front cover of *The Savoy*, No. 1 (January, 1896), in which a cherub in the foreground demonstrates Beardsley's feelings about *The Yellow Book* (see p. 155)

Design for the front cover of the prospectus for *The Savoy*, later used in No. 1 of *The Savoy* after evidences of John Bull's sexual excitation were expunged (see p. 156)

time for Christmas and gift-book purchasers. But Beardsley's cover design for the volume, in black on the pale pink paper of the boards, expressed his contempt for his former Bodley Head employer, and Smithers had mixed emotions about the touch of pique. He had no love for his rival John Lane, whose *Yellow Book* had then completed seven quarterly issues; still, the *Savoy* cover was not for a book to be sold over the counter. Beneath the outspread legs of a barebottomed cherubic figure in the foreground lay a copy of *The Yellow Book*.

Beardsley may have been overly proud of his malicious little touch, for word got round of it, and the matter quickly would have been taken out of Smithers's hands. Smithers ordered the nasty details expunged, and the artist removed *The Yellow Book* as well as the cherub's genitals (while carefully preserving his unemasculated original drawing). But the delay in revising the cover meant putting off the release of the first *Savoy* until after Christmas, and dating it with the new year. It was a pre-natal financial setback for the magazine, one from which it would never recover.

Just the fact of Beardsley's notoriety towards the end of 1895 would have been enough to set stories quickly circulating in literary and artistic London about the insinuations he would insert into his *Savoy* drawings. After the deaths of both Beardsley and *The Savoy*, Robert Ross suggested that "Quite wrongly, Beardsley's art had come to be regarded as the pictorial and sympathetic expression of an unfortunate tendency in English literature." As Ross knew, the unfortunate tendency had a very real existence, and Beardsley often—but not always—echoed it only to mock it.

The softening of his initial *Savoy* contributions had been spurred by an even earlier storm over the beleaguered first issue, for the drawing intended first for the prospectus and then for an inside cover had run into violent criticism from some of Smithers's writers. Earlier, Smithers had objected that the Pierrot who tripped onstage before the footlights suggested a flippancy uncharacteristic of the new publication's contents. It was only a familiar Beardsley device, influenced by the Brighton music-hall entertainments of his boyhood, but "John Bull," Smithers maintained, would undoubtedly prefer something more serious. Beardsley, who knew that the average Englishman would never be a *Savoy* reader, maliciously substituted a monumental John Bull figure for the unwanted Pierrot.

Although it slipped past Smithers, Beardsley failed to anticipate that the

A bookmark designed for Robert Ross

revised drawing, reproduced in black on pink paper, would undergo George Moore's scrutiny. When Moore detected in a strangely drawn bulge in the figure's breeches that John Bull was represented in a state of strained sexual excitement—Beardsley's over-playful revenge upon Smithers—he called for a protest meeting. Several prospective *Savoy* contributors, including Moore, met in Edgar Jepson's rooms in the King's Bench Walk to discuss what to do about what they considered to be Beardsley's self-defeating devilishness, and then went as a delegation to Smithers's office in Effingham House, Arundel Street, to demand that the offensive drawing be withdrawn. Smithers, the story goes, confessed that he was delighted with the drawing; but Bernard Shaw, Selwyn Image and Herbert Horne insisted that Smithers ask Beardsley to make his John Bull less objectionable by removing what Shaw called the "subtle stroke that emphasized the virility of John."

There was in Beardsley's work, Shaw realized, "an indescribable element even in its beauty which I can describe only as poisonous," and as one of the "intending contributors" to Smithers's magazine he "felt that this impish boy genius should be placed in the right hands: else he would inevitably be seized by the wrong ones."[28] "In this puerile mischievousness," Shaw saw dangers, for it was "exploitable by speculators in pornography." And the publisher of *The Savoy*, it was no secret, was one of them. Yet since Smithers had already circulated the prospectuses, the problem for him was happily academic. "Not having any of the 80,000 left, he agreed," Shaw remembered; "and peace was restored." Ironically, Jepson, who had made the most fuss, had contributed a story for *The Savoy* which was so indecent, he confessed, that he could not sign his name to it. After the battle over Beardsley's drawing it provided the excuse the editors needed to return it to him.

When the cleansed drawing reappeared as an elaborate title page for two additional pages of contents, John Bull was sensual-lipped, but nothing marred his profile other than a magnificently distended paunch.* Still, word of the battle, and imaginative glances at the black-and-pink circulars, only added to the rumors that *The Savoy* would be a very "advanced" publication.

*The "John Bull" incident had a predecessor a dozen years earlier when Mark Twain's nephew and business manager, C. L. Webster, discovered to his horror that one of the illustrations in the advance sheets of *Huckleberry Finn* had been altered in the engraving by an

AUBREY BEARDSLEY.

Panel design for front wrapper of *The Savoy*, No. 4 (August, 1896)

unknown prankster. The caption above the illustration read "In a Dilemma," and the indecent alteration of a figure's trousers left no doubt as to what the new dilemma was, jeopardizing the book's reputation and delaying its publication beyond the Christmas season of 1884. "The illustration showed Uncle Silas with his pelvis thrust forward, Aunt Sally looking sidewise at her spouse and grinning. The prankster with his awl or graver . . . drew a *penis erectus* (or was it a gosling with head and neck protruding from the man's fly?) at the appropriate place. J. J. Little told how his printing plant handled the problem: '. . . thousands of copies of the book were in the plant . . . a new sheet was run off with a re-engraved plate to eliminate the damage and . . . these sheets were tipped in, using a stub of the excised page. . . .' If taking these measures postponed publication in New York beyond the holiday period the huge size of the first printing must have been an important cause." (Walter Blair, *Mark Twain and Huck Finn* [Berkeley and Los Angeles, 1962], pp. 366-7.)

8

1896

The Savoy Ascendant

Release date for *The Savoy* was set by Leonard Smithers for Saturday, 5 January 1896. To celebrate its birth he gave a supper party in a private room at the New Lyric Club, and invited all the contributors to the first number. It was one of the rare occasions that his wife was permitted the society of Smithers's professional associates, and Max Beerbohm recalled that she was

small, buxom and self-possessed. She did the honours. She dropped little remarks. It did not seem that she was nervous; one only knew that she *was* nervous. . . . The walls of the little room in which we supped were lined with bamboo instead of wallpaper. "Quite original, is it not?" she said to Yeats. But Yeats had no ready reply for that; only a courteous, lugubrious murmur.

Max disliked Yeats, and what he thought were petty pomposities on the part of the young Irishman. And he disliked, too, Yeats's portentous dinner-table discussions about his favorite subject (and no one else's), Diabolism—"Dyahbolism" in the Yeatsian pronunciation. "He had made a profound study of it," Max wrote;

and he evidently guessed that Beardsley . . . was a confirmed worshipper in that line. So to Beardsley he talked, in deep, vibrant tones across the table, of the lore and the rites of Diabolism. . . . I daresay that Beardsley, who seemed to know by instinctive erudition all about everything, knew all about Dyahbolism. Anyhow, I could see that he, with that stony common-sense which always came upmost when anyone canvassed the fantastic in him, thought Dyahbolism rather silly. He was too polite not to go on saying at intervals, in his hard, quick voice, "Oh really? How perfectly entrancing!" and "Oh really? How perfectly sweet!"[1]

Like Max, Yeats considered his pornographer host a disreputable and scandalous person, and was reluctant to go; but Symons explained that after accepting one invitation from Smithers one need not go again. Various friends of some of the contributors had been protesting with moral earnestness about the questionable ethics of being in the pay of such a person as Smithers. In *The Trembling of the Veil* Yeats recalled getting a letter on the subject from fellow Irish poet "A.E." (George Russell). He had passed it, along with a similar one from T. W. Rolleston, to Symons, who read the one from A.E. under his breath as the guests stood about the supper table waiting for the signal to be seated. The new magazine, A.E. declared passionately, was the "Organ of the Incubi and the Succubi." Overhearing this, Smithers shouted, "Give me the letter, give me the letter, I will prosecute that man." Symons quickly waved Rolleston's letter out of reach, and tucked it into his pocket; but as a diversion he continued reading from the one he had begun, in which A.E. besought Yeats not to sell his poet's birthright for a mess of aesthete's pottage. "I [shall] never see *The Savoy*," A.E. added, "nor do I intend to touch it. I don't want to get allied with the currents of people with a sexual mania like Beardsley, Symons or that ruck. It is all 'mud from a muddy spring' and any pure stream of thought that mingles [with it] must lose its purity."

When Symons finished reading, Beardsley crossed over and confided, "Yeats, I am going to surprise you very much. I think your friend is right. All my life I have been fascinated by the spiritual life—when a child I saw a vision of a Bleeding Christ over the mantelpiece—but after all to do one's work when there are other things one wants to do so much more, is a kind of religion."*

Realizing that the remainder of his earthly passage would be brief, Beardsley had been drifting more and more in the direction of the Catholic Church. Some months before, in France, Beardsley had mentioned the boyhood vision to Symons. That summer they had spent two days at Arques-la-Bataille, Beardsley working on verses he later printed in *The Savoy* as "The Three Musicians." Afterwards, on the balcony of the Hôtel Henri IV at Arques, Symons had the only "serious, almost solemn" conver-

Design for a *Savoy* poster; also used as the first page of *The Savoy*, No. 8 (December, 1896)

---

*The version of this evening described by Yeats in his withheld *Memoirs* is slightly at variance in both quotations and details, but the two versions coincide at almost every point.

sation he had ever had with Beardsley. Looking up at the stars, they wondered "whether they were really the imprisoning worlds of other creatures like ourselves; the strange ways by which the soul might have come and must certainly go; death, and the future." And Beardsley spoke of his dream-vision, remembering waking up at night in the moonlight and seeing a great crucifix, with a bleeding Christ, falling off a wall where there was not and had never been a crucifix. He spoke of it in a tone of awe utterly unlike the irreverent young artist of the legend already created about him in his own young life, and his partner in the *Savoy* venture, who outlived him by nearly fifty years, never forgot it.

After the supper, Smithers invited his guests to join him in his rooms in Effingham House, above his business quarters in Arundel Street. Beardsley went, although the supper had been ordeal enough, while Yeats hung back, intending to retreat unobtrusively to Fountain Court. Symons stayed to persuade Yeats, and the debate delayed them long enough, so that by the time they arrived, Yeats recalled,

I found Beardsley propped up on a chair in the middle of the room, grey and exhausted, and as I came in he left the chair and went into another room to spit blood, but returned immediately. Our publisher, perspiration pouring from his face, was turning the handle of a hurdy gurdy piano—it worked by electricity, I was told, when the company did not cut off the supply—and very plainly had had enough of it, but Beardsley pressed him to labour on, "The tone is so beautiful," "It gives me such deep pleasure," etc., etc. It was his method of keeping our publisher at a distance.[2]

"After the supper we sat up rather late," Max recalled. Beardsley

was the life and soul of the party, till, quite suddenly, almost in the middle of a sentence, he fell asleep in his chair. He had overstrained his vitality, and it had all left him. I can see him now, as he sat there with his head sunk on his breast: the thin face, white as the gardenia in his coat, and the prominent, harshly-cut features; the hair, that always covered his whole forehead in a fringe and was of so curious a colour—a kind of tortoiseshell; the narrow, angular figure, and the long hands that were so full of power.[3]

Arthur Symons's editorial note which prefaced the January 1896 issue was reminiscent of the prospectus for *The Yellow Book* issued two years earlier, but at the same time it announced that the new magazine was counting on quality, rather than on name-dropping, for its success:

It is hoped that "THE SAVOY" will be a periodical of an exclusively literary and

THE SAVOY

AUBREY
BEARDSLEY.
1896.

Title page of *The Savoy*,
No. 1 (January, 1896)

Mrs. Pinchwife, from Wycherley's *The Country Wife*, from *The Savoy*, No. 8 (December, 1896)

artistic kind. To present Literature in the shape of its letter-press, Art in the form of its illustrations, will be its aim. For the attainment of that aim we can but rely on our best endeavours and on the logic of our belief that good writers and artists will care to see their work in company with the work of good writers and artists. Readers who look to a new periodical for only very well-known or only very obscure names must permit themselves to be disappointed. We have no objection to a celebrity who deserves to be celebrated, or to an unknown person who has not been seen often enough to be recognized in passing. All we ask from our contributors is good work, and good work is all we offer our readers. This we offer with some confidence. We have no formulas, and we desire no false unity of form or matter. We have not invented a new point of view. We are not Realists, or Romanticists, or Decadents. For us, all art is good which is good art. We hope to appeal to the tastes of the intelligent by not being original for originality's sake, or audacious for the sake of advertisement, or timid for the convenience of the elderly-minded. We intend to print no verse which has not some close relationship with poetry, no fiction which has not a certain sense of what is finest in living fact, no criticism which has not some knowledge, discernment, and sincerity in its judgement. We could scarcely say more, and we are content to think we can scarcely say less.

The magazine was immediately denounced in the expected quarters, *Punch* attacking it with the most ironic praise its editor could muster. "There is not an article in the volume which can be put down without feeling the better and purer for it . . . it should be on every school-room table; every mother should present it to her daughter, for it is bound to have an ennobling and purifying influence." The *Sketch* was equally sarcastic: "I am glad to notice . . . that Mr. Aubrey Beardsley has discovered a new type of woman. Unlike her predecessors in his artistic affections, she is almost pretty, and does not suggest that her nose is frequently in a trough." There was one point on which both advocates and detractors agreed: *The Savoy* was not an imitation of *The Yellow Book*. The *Sunday Times* thought it was "a 'Yellow Book' redeemed of its puerilities," and went on to praise much of its contents, balking only at the short fiction, which although respectable, "somehow after Guy de Maupassant and Catulle Mendès, one feels that the English short story is never quite a success."

The lead contribution was the one *The Times* singled out as the best, Bernard Shaw's "On Going to Church." It would remain the most personal statement of his feelings about religion, and his best-shaped essay, foreshadowing ideas he would later put into his plays. Shaw's eventual successor as *Saturday Review* drama critic, Max Beerbohm, who was contributing satires to *The Yellow Book*, made several token offerings to *The Savoy*, but found Smithers unpalatable, and remained loyal to the more respectable John Lane. The first *Savoy* contained his caricature of actor-manager Herbert Beerbohm-Tree, and a short mock-serious essay, "A Good Prince." The young prince was Edward of York ("Though it is no secret that he prefers the society of ladies, not one breath of scandal has ever touched his name"). In 1896 the future Prince of Wales, Edward VIII and Duke of Windsor was a toddler.

Symons published his own translation of a poem by Verlaine, an original poem, and the piece on Dieppe he had composed on the scene the summer before. His friend Yeats contributed two poems and a story, "The Binding of the Hair," an overheated piece of Celtic legendry. Another Symons crony, Ernest Dowson, was also represented by both verse and fiction, both clearly inspired by the author's failing health and failures in love. The poem bore the pompous title "Impenitentia Ultima," and the story, "The Eyes of Pride," was dedicated to "A.F." (Adelaide Foltinowicz, or "Missie"), for whom his love was as long standing as it was ineffectual. The double contribution, each work in a different medium, was the rule rather than the exception for the issue, for Beardsley's patron Joseph Pennell also appeared twice, with an impressive pen-and-ink evocation of Regent Street, and a piece of art criticism, "A Golden Decade in English Art." Havelock Ellis, another close friend of Symons, contributed a piece of literary criticism, "Zola: the Man and His Work," and there was art by Conder, Shannon, Rothenstein and—a surprising Beardsley coup—Whistler.*

Beardsley continued the pattern of complementary contributions, publishing not only the cover and title-page art, and illustrations for Symons's Dieppe piece, but striking illustrations for his own literary work, the first serious writing he had ever committed to print. Beardsley, Arthur Symons said condescendingly, wanted desperately to be a great writer, but "his plans for writing changed even more quickly than his plans for doing drawings, and with less profitable results in the meantime." Once Symons acted as his reference for admission to a library, and on the form Beardsley had to complete, he identified himself as a "man of letters." Almost literally, letters

*Not a new work, but a drawing dating back to 1861, suggesting some ambivalence on Whistler's part in being linked with the magazine.

Moska (the name of a dance referred to in the article), illustrating Symons's "Dieppe" in *The Savoy*, No. 1 (January, 1896)

Illustration to "The Three Musicians,"
The Savoy, No. 1 (January, 1896)

represent the bulk of his extant writing, for aside from his scanty correspondence he left little prose other than his novel fragment, and no mature verse but the three pieces published in *The Savoy*. Because he was so anxious to excel, wrote Symons with faint praise,

his patience over a medium so unfamiliar, and hence so difficult, to him as verse, was infinite. We spent two whole days on the grassy ramparts of the old castle at Arques-la-Bataille, near Dieppe; I working at something or other in one part, he working at "The Three Musicians" in another. The eight stanzas of that amusing piece of verse are really, in their own way, a *tour de force*; by sheer power of will, by deliberately saying to himself, "I will write a poem," and by working with such strenuous application that at last a certain result he had willed, did really come about, he succeeded in doing what he had certainly no aptitude for doing.

Beardsley's art was the result of similar pains, and the peevishness in Symons's reminiscence (written in 1898, close after the fact) may have reflected a little of his annoyance at his art editor's audacity in attempting to insinuate himself into the literary aspects of *The Savoy*. Literature was a dominant force in Beardsley's artistic inspiration, and this spill-over was almost inevitable. Although his drawing appeared to come more easily than his writing, his painstaking method was the same in each case. According to Robert Ross, Beardsley

sketched everything in pencil, at first covering the paper with apparent scrawls, constantly rubbed out and blocked in again, until the whole surface became raddled from pencil, india-rubber, and knife; over this incoherent surface he worked in Chinese ink with a gold pen, often ignoring the pencil lines, afterwards carefully removed. So every drawing was invented, built up, and completed on the same sheet of paper.

Beardsley, whose art training had consisted of a few months of intermittent night classes, continued to find that the only lasting influence upon his art was literature. His uses of language and line were from parallel perspectives, and the "hot-house growths of thought" Holbrook Jackson saw in his art seemed as visible in his writing as in his draftsmanship. It was, as Osbert Burdett (in *The Beardsley Period*) said of the latter,

as if the forms of nature in plant and spray had been given their revenge. Human imagination had evoked them for a delight of its own, for an alien purpose, and now it was to mete the same treatment to its kindred. If we possessed drawings of human beings, or any representation of them by flowers or beings of sub-human or superhuman life, we might expect something like Beardsley's vision of us.

Beardsley's verse and illustration (again a drawing rendered less offensive before publication) for "The Three Musicians" were, for him, only faintly naughty and relatively quiet in tone. The three were "a Polish pianist," a "soprano, lightly frocked,"* and "a slim, gracious boy" who worships her.

> The gracious boy is at her feet,
>   And weighs his courage with his chance;
> His fears soon melt in noonday heat.
>   The tourist gives a furious glance,
> Red as his guide-book grows, moves on, and offers up a prayer for France.

The most exotic of all Beardsley's hot-house growths was his *Venus and Tannhäuser*—its milder *Savoy* form finally titled *Under the Hill*. However unfinished and fragmentary, the combination of pictures and prose for the *Under the Hill* version represents one of the great creative achievements of the period. Not every critic has thought well of Beardsley's erotic tale. Haldane MacFall—Beardsley's own biographer—considered it "fantastic drivel, without cohesion, without sense, devoid of art as of meaning—a sheer laboured stupidity, revealing nothing—a posset, a poultice of affectations." To MacFall its opulently tortuous language was only "pedantic phrasing" combined with "housemaid's use of English," and it was gross error to call it satire: "A satirist does not gloat over evil, he lashes at it. Beardsley revelled in it." And it was true that in the lush artifice of the prose are descriptions which combine the sensual and the anatomical, [†] including a

A Snare of Vintage, illustration for *Lucian's True History*

* In a letter to his mother [c. April 1896] Beardsley referred to Austrian pianist Sophie Menter as "the heroine of the 3 musicians." The "Polish pianist" of his poem is male, and it is rather the poem's soprano who is patterned after the real-life pianist. Of her Bernard Shaw had written, several years earlier, "I confess to a weakness, not altogether musical, for Madame Sophie Menter. There is an enormous exhilaration and sense of enlarged life and freedom communicated to me by her . . . I expand in the reflection of her magnificent strength, her suppleness, her swiftness, her inexhaustible, indefatigable energy. . . ." (*London Music in 1888—1889.*)

† A medieval analogue which Beardsley knew, and referred to in an epigraph, was *The Romance of the Rose*, with its equally anatomical imagery. The great Old French narrative poem ends with the lover, his "staff unshod," entering "the sacred place"—a "sort of tower" supported by two limb-like ivory columns, a "sanctuary" hidden by "a shroud/That curtained the fair relics." (Translation from Jean de Meun by Harry W. Robbins [New York, 1962].)
Beardsley half-remembered in his title the home of art critic More Adey, a friend of Wilde's who later edited *The Burlington Magazine* and even later went mad and pulled his inherited

considerable literary acquaintance with what has since been called *pornotopia:*

> In the middle distance there looms a large irregular shape. On the horizon swell two immense snowy white hillocks; these are capped by pink . . . peaks or tips—as if the rosy-fingered dawn itself were playing just behind them. The landscape then undulates gently down to a broad, smooth, swelling plain, its soft, rolling curves broken only in the lower centre by a small volcanic crater or omphalos. Farther down, the scene narrows and changes perspective. Off to the right and left just two smooth snowy ridges. Between them, at their point of juncture, is a dark wood. . . . This dark wood—sometimes it is called a thicket—is triangular in shape . . . and in its midst is a dark romantic chasm. In this chasm the wonders of nature abound. From its top there depends a large, pink stalactite, which changes shape, size, and color in accord with the movement of the tides below and within. Within the chasm . . . there are caverns measureless to man, grottoes, hermits' caves, underground streams—a whole internal and subterranean landscape. The climate is warm but wet. Thunderstorms are frequent in this region, as are tremors and quakings of the earth. The walls of the cavern often heave and contract in rhythmic violence, and when they do the salty streams that run through it double its flow. The whole place is dark yet visible. . . .
>
> The essential imagination of nature in pornotopia, then, is this immense, supine, female form. . . .[4]

Imaginatively, Beardsley often dwelt in what has been called "a velvet underground tolerated by Victorians in literature and art as long as it wore the air of fantasy." His frontispiece for John Davidson's *The Wonderful Mission of Earl Lavender* (1895) depicted a blasé lady who, while with one hand holding up her gown, the shoulder straps of which have slipped down, exposing most of her bosom, with the other hand flagellates a stripped-to-the-waist male supplicant, "wielding the most fragile of whips as if it were a fan at high tea."[5] "Lovers of the birch . . ." one mid-Victorian pornographic novel claimed, "are almost as common as the lovers of Venus." Whether or not the claim was true, there was a vast sub-literature of flagellation produced during the Victorian period, often describing a well-bred young lady coolly brandishing an elegant rod over a bare and enraptured form. In the *Earl Lavender* drawing, on the mantelpiece behind the lady with the rod is a familiar (and fetishistic) three-branched candlestick—as much a Beardsley signature as his name below.

---

manor house down looking for hidden treasure. Adey lived in the Gloucestershire village of Wotton-on-Edge, which may have suggested the name of Dorian Gray's friend Sir Henry Wotton to Wilde. And the old family home there was Under-the-Hill.

AUBREY
BEARDSLEY.

Frontispiece to *A Full and True Account of the
Wonderful Mission of Earl Lavender* (1895), which
should be compared to the far less elegant reversal
of roles illustrated in the Juvenal drawing on p. 143

Pornotopia, writes Stephen Marcus,

could in fact only have been imagined by persons who have suffered extreme deprivation, and I do not by this mean sexual deprivation in the genital sense alone. One
gets the distinct impression . . . that it could only have been written by men who at
some point in their lives had been starved. The insatiability depicted in it seems to
me literal insatiability, and the orgies represented are the visions of permanently
hungry men . . . Inside of every pornographer there is an infant screaming for the
breast from which he has been torn. . . .[6]

One need not accept this premise; yet Beardsley was deprived of his
mother's breast by the puerperal fever she suffered after his birth, and his
illnesses as well as hers did keep them apart for large periods of his childhood. And Beardsley's work evidences from the beginning an obsession
with mammae, which appear both anatomically realistic and grotesquely
surrealistic, in shadowed or decorated borders, or hermaphroditic figures, in
symbolic shapes and curious multiples on dwarfs, fetuses and hunchbacks,
on trees and flowers, on pedestals and columns. As late as the drawings he
completed on his deathbed the obsession manifested itself, the "M" drawing
for *Volpone* portraying an angel-winged cherub reaching out its arms for a
bare-breasted mother figure framed by six-breasted female-shaped pedestals. He was still reaching for the withdrawn breast.

For Beardsley it was a double deprivation. A case study as a creator of a
literary and artistic *pornotopia,* he almost certainly suffered deprivation in
the genital sense as well. Almost every page he wrote or drew demonstrated
the intensity of his emotional hunger.

The legend of Tannhäuser which Beardsley intended to follow—at a
distance—in *Under the Hill* is that of the handsome knight who, after many
wanderings, finds the Venusberg. He enters the cave where the Lady Venus
(the Frau Hulda of German folklore) holds her court, and abandons himself
to a life of sensual pleasure. Eventually he is overcome by remorse and,
invoking the aid of the Virgin Mary, he obtains permission to return temporarily to the outer world. He then goes as a pilgrim to Rome and entreats
Pope Urban to secure for him the forgiveness of his sins. The Pope declares,
knowing the extent of the knight's sins, that it is as impossible for him to be
pardoned as it is for the staff he has in his hand to blossom. In despair,
Tannhäuser departs and returns to the Venusberg, beyond the reach of ordinary mortals. In three days the abandoned staff begins to put forth green

The Abbé, portrait of the Abbé Fanfreluche
(the Chevalier Tannhäuser in the original
version), illustrating *Under the Hill*, the sanitized
version of *Venus and Tannhäuser*, in *The
Savoy*, No. 1 (January, 1896)

leaves, and the Pope orders messengers to ride in all directions in search of the penitent, but the knight is never seen again.

Beardsley's aborted tale clearly had a long way to go, as the four early chapters show; for the part of *Under the Hill* we have indicates that the author intended numerous digressions and elaborate conceits in the form of footnotes, wherever his overheated fancy would take him. The story line, Haldane MacFall objected, "was without consequence, without cohesion, without unity; it was the laboured stringing together of little phrases, word pictures of moods, generally obscene moods and desires such as plague a certain type of consumptive whose life burns at fever heat in the troubled blood." Privately, he added, the *Venus and Tannhäuser* version was "the unashamed testament and revelation of the man that lurks behind the whole of his work—from youth to death."[7] There are passages, another critic observed, "which read like romanticized excerpts from the *Psychopathia Sexualis* of Krafft-Ebing." Yet *Under the Hill* opened deceptively with a lengthy Machiavellian pseudo-dedication to a fictitious Cardinal Pezzoli, a dedication, Osbert Burdett said, "[which] with its elaborate compliment and ornate grace, would have pleased Congreve and delighted Pope." The book, Beardsley explained in his epistle dedicatory, "will be found to contain matter of deeper import than mere venery, inasmuch as it treats of the great contrition of its chiefest character, and of canonical things in certain pages." Thus he was "not without hopes that your Eminence will pardon my writing of a loving Abbé, for which extravagance let my youth excuse me."

The line contained clues to Beardsley's own chief interests—amorous passion and religious ritual—but his own youthful extravagances were mainly on paper, and were verbal as well as linear. *Under the Hill's* rococo style is at least the equal of Wilde and Beerbohm. There is a pictorial glamor only a painter's eye could conceive. In "The Toilet of Helen" episode, for example, although there may be echoes of Max Beerbohm's "The Toilet of Sabina" in "The Perversion of Rouge" (the Oxford precursor of *The Yellow Book's* "A Defence of Cosmetics"), there is an economy of phrase amid the rococo. There is Helen "in a flutter of frilled things" at "taper-time" before her mirror; there is the "depraved" young Sporion, with his "slight stoop" and "a troubled walk." So the characters are realized. And the settings of the unfinished tale are, in Bernard Muddiman's phrase, "unrolled before us like priceless tapestries."

The pictorial texture of the prose can only be described as "a Beardsley drawing transfused into words." Muddiman found this equally true of the description of the woods of Auffray and "the wonderful supper served on the terrace to Helen and her guests" as of the toilet scene: "To find such another supper in literature one has to turn to some French author, or better still, to the 'Cena Trimalchonis' of Petronius himself. From this it will be seen that Beardsley's literary work, like his black-and-white, though the embodiment of the spirit of his age, is also of the noble order of the highest things in art." Yet *Under the Hill*, both in line and in letters, remains primarily a triumph in decoration. Beardsley, said Martin Birnbaum, "cultivated a magical technique which could convert the most repulsive ugliness into a strange, forbidding, fascinating beauty." But it was a limited achievement, one of cold artifice and icy eroticism, or icy eroticism and cold artifice (the emphasis alters from one version to the other).*

Pictorially and verbally, *Under the Hill*, even more than *Venus and Tannhäuser*, is a triumph of excess. In the original, "the keynote of text and illustration is profusion. The most typical feature, frequent enumerations in the text (of decorations, shoes, masks, names, and habits, etc.) reflects an attempt to grasp reality by the means of saturation and excess." In the *Savoy* version, *Under the Hill*, "Beardsley goes knowingly too far: the monstrous proliferation of rococo detail devours space, stifles the characters, rapturously exists for its own sake. There remain none now of the empty spaces

The Fourth Tableau of *Das Rheingold*, product of Beardsley's continuing obsession with Wagner, and part of the never-completed series, this drawing reproduced in *The Savoy*, No. 6 (October, 1896)

---

*Edmund Wilson was one of the earliest critics not only to refuse to become hysterical about the sinister side of Beardsley's tale but to see some positive values in it. "Who can read," he asked in 1923, "*Les Fleurs du Mal, A Rebours, The Picture of Dorian Gray* or Swinburne's *Poems and Ballads* with the enthusiasm of their contemporaries? The effectiveness of the subjects dealt with depends upon one's being shocked by them, and when the prejudices to be baited have been removed, the works of art are no longer exciting. I can think of only two writers of that period and school who escaped the moral confusion of the reaction against respectability: Aubrey Beardsley very often exploited in his drawings the fascination of Evil as evil; but he also wrote the opening chapters of rather a remarkable erotic romance called *Venus and Tannhäuser*, in which he does succeed in investing a sort of pagan world with the artificial graces of the nineties without allowing it to become darkened and tragic with the fumes of a burning orthodoxy; his Venus, unlike the Venus of Swinburne or the Harlot of Wilde, is not destructive and terrible, but girlish and agreeable. The grotesqueries and orgies of her court are to her all quite natural and harmless; she really approaches much nearer to the naïve naughtiness of the eighteenth century than anything to be found in Wilde . . . a neo-eighteenth century world, erotic, lighthearted and skeptical. . . ." ("Late Violets from the Nineties," reprinted in *The Shores of Light* [New York, 1952], p. 71.)

which so mysteriously acquired color and texture by juxtaposition; characters and planes are now only distinguished by a close weave of hatching and stipple."[8]

The French model for Beardsley's arabesque was clearly Laforgue, whose witty and bizarre preciosity in the *Moralités légendaires* the author of *Under the Hill* admired. Although the subject matter was not as important as its treatment, since Laforgue burlesqued Salomé, Lohengrin and Hamlet, Beardsley chose a parallel theme, and simultaneously played with language and with legend. He smuggled in foreign words and used them as if they were English; and he spoke the simplest trifles with portentous gravity. There are "little mutinies of cravat and ruffle," "intelligent curls," "blonde trousers," eyes "sated with perfection" and a "wan hill." Shoes are *pantoufles*, the ladies' maid (Mrs. Marsuple) who assists with the cosmetics is a *fardeuse*, and hair is *chevelure*. But all the borrowings are unitalicized and are used as matter-of-factly as the many incongruous details. The work is allusive with a vengeance, with references to obscure (and often non-existent) books, technical (and often invented) minutiae, fantastic (and sometimes accurate) knowledge. Beardsley's literary skill is Joycean in his use of common words in uncommon contexts, and of recondite words like *spellicans, pudic* or *vallance*. There are flashes of Wildean wit, as in the description of the banquet in which "mere hunger quickly gave place to those finer instincts of the pure gourmet," and in the footnote which explains why it was remarkable for St. Rose of Lima, at the age of four, to vow herself to perpetual virginity.

The footnotes themselves are as preciously pungent as the text, and almost as insubstantial. Imaginative references are invented, such as *A Plea for the Domestication of the Unicorn*. And the artificial texture of the language is complemented by Beardsley's drawings, similar in tone, meticulous in draftsmanship, detail-crowded with half-hidden, grotesque wit. The illustration for "The Toilet of Helen" has such density of detail and diversity of activity that Beardsley could have mined it for thousands of additional words for his text. And the servitors at the banquet fill another lush tapestry.

Not yet finished with Oscar Wilde, Beardsley even used the opportunity of "The Toilet of Helen" to add to the many caricatures of Oscar he had already concealed in earlier drawings, this time via an obese seated figure in the crowded foreground—Priapusa the manicurist. "Priapusa's voice," he wrote

The Toilet of Helen (Venus in the original story),
illustration to *Under the Hill, The Savoy*, No. 1
(January, 1896)

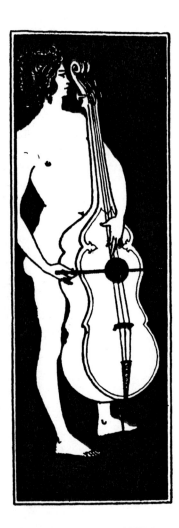

Title page ornament (ca. 1895) first published in John Lane's *The Early Work of Aubrey Beardsley* (1899), the symbolism of the nude male bowing and fingering a female-shaped instrument clearly intended as erotic

in *Under the Hill,* "was full of salacious unction; she had terrible little gestures with the hands, strange movements with the shoulders, a short respiration that made surprising wrinkles in her bodice, a corrupt skin, large horny eyes, a parrot's nose, a small, loose mouth, great flaccid cheeks and chin after chin." It was an aspect of Wilde before which Beardsley refused to shut his eyes, pursuing him by words as well as by line.

After the original three chapters of the entrance of the Abbé, the toilet of Helen [Venus], and her banquet, Beardsley continued with a single, footnote-embellished chapter in the second number of *The Savoy,* in which the Abbé awakens and prepares for his first full day in Helen's elaborate lair. There were also two weaker drawings accompanying it, one a Wagnerian illustration unrelated to the chapter but hurriedly thrown in as a filler. Unquestionably Beardsley had intended to develop the story further in that issue, and could not—something Smithers admitted in an appended publisher's note: "It is regretted that owing to Mr. Beardsley's illness he has been unable to finish one of his full-page drawings to Chapter IV of *Under the Hill,* i.e., 'The Bacchanals of Sporion,' and that its publication in consequence has to be postponed to No. 3 of *The Savoy.*"

The drawing never appeared, and there remain drawings of scenes never written, and announcements in Beardsley's letters of proposed drawings for which only the text survives. He even had the curious idea, described in one of his letters to Smithers, of a chapter consisting only of drawings. But when the third number of *The Savoy* was published in July 1896, there was no continuation of *Under the Hill,* but instead an editor's note: "In consequence of Mr. Beardsley's severe and continued illness, we have been compelled to discontinue the publication of 'Under the Hill,' which will be issued by the present publisher in book form, with numerous illustrations by the author, as soon as Mr. Beardsley is well enough to carry on the work to its conclusion." He was never able to, although during the spring he wrote twice to Smithers to promise more material for the novel. He had "a good idea for a story to be told by Mrs. Marsuple, in which Hop o' my thumb is the hero," he wrote on 26 April. And on 7 June he wrote that "the Juanesque continuation of Under the Hill begins to take form bootifully." This was more self-reassurance than anything else, and only indicated how far he had thought out the elaboration of his unfinished, and never-to-be-finished, novel.

Beardsley had gone slightly farther in *Venus and Tannhäuser,* the literarily undisciplined and Rabelaisian original. But the longer manuscript's first eight chapters had sufficed for only four refashioned chapters of the purified and playfully footnoted *Savoy* text; the author's health had halted the original near the close of the Dieppe-inspired tenth chapter, where Tannhäuser, touring Venus's domain, observes a game of *petits chevaux* at her casino, listens to Rossini's "Stabat Mater" at her opera house, and visits the studio of the artist De La Pine, who paints the pair and hosts them (as well as Cosmé the barber) at dinner that evening. Still, the *Venus and Tannhäuser* version was more *pornotopia* than literature, an amalgam of Beardsley's own erotic inventions with his borrowings from writings as disparate as Poliphilus's *Hypnerotomachia*[9] and Suetonius's *History of the Twelve Caesars*, where Nero is recorded as wallowing in depraved delights such as Beardsley's Tannhäuser is offered in Venus's pleasure dome by his "valets de bain, or pretty fish, as he called them. . . ."* Yet Beardsley's hero—first called "Abbé Aubrey," afterwards altered to "Abbé Franfreluche" for *Under the Hill*, but renamed "the Chevalier Tannhäuser" in Smithers's 1907 "unexpurgated" printing—is still heterosexually able to offer Venus "a thousand gracious things, tuning her body as a violinist before he plays upon it."

Inset from the frontispiece to the *Comedy of the Rhinegold*, reproduced in *The Savoy*, No. 8 (December, 1896)

Although it stopped after only sixty-seven manuscript leaves—and eighty-eight printed pages—Beardsley's narrative left few varieties of sexual experience undescribed. Later, Smithers's son Jack, perhaps confusing language with line, as well as reversing roles, complained that Beardsley was not content with fulfilling his commissions for *The Savoy* but

persisted in sending to London, or bringing them personally obscene drawings . . . begging my father to take them and sell them for him . . . I have seen some of these, and believe me, they could only have sold to the utterly depraved. Wishful of further continued work from Beardsley, Smithers accepted them and hid them away . . . I saw them, and if I refer those interested to Leviticus, ch. xviii, verse 23, it will not be necessary to say anything further.[10]

---

*"He devised in the woods . . . certaine places for lecherie and venereous Acts. . . . He incurred yet the infamie of greater and more shameful filthinesse . . . to wit, that hee should traine up and teach fine boyes the tenderest and daintiest that might be had (whom he called his little fishes) to converse and play between his thighes as he was swimming, and pretily with tongue and teeth seeme to make unto his secret parts, and there to nibble. . . ." (Trans. Philemon Holland [*a.* 1606], London, 1899, I, 204-5.)

The biblical reference was very likely a condemnation of the eighth chapter of *Venus and Tannhäuser*, with its episode of Venus and the ecstasy of Adolphe, the unicorn.*

The unicorn episode was Aubrey's most erudite irony in a work of acutely sophisticated malice. He may have seen the ornate fifteenth century tapestry, "The Lady and the Unicorn," in the Musée de Cluny in Paris, and knew the allegorized Christian medieval interpretations in which the unicorn was likened to Christ, who raised up a horn of salvation for mankind and dwelt in the womb of the Virgin Mary. (Aubrey had already produced an impish "Annunciation"—with a nude Virgin and the Archangel as pagan god.) And he probably knew the tradition of the unicorn as an animal which could only be trapped between the legs of a virgin. His perversion of the legends surrounding the unicorn thinly veils a view of the corruption of Christianity. All iconography becomes erotic for (in Yeats's description) "the first satirist of the soul English art has produced."

When Beardsley had moved from Chester Terrace late in 1895, he had abandoned some possessions there, writing to Smithers, "All the books I have left behind are at your disposal. Also a set of erotic Japanese prints." Very likely the prints were the same ones Will Rothenstein had bought in Paris and given to Beardsley several years before, but Jack Smithers—who was only five years old in the year of *The Savoy*—may not have realized this, as well as that the most "devilish" work Beardsley did was the unfinished novel. "Beardsley," Jack Smithers explained, nevertheless, "was an absolute gentleman and there is no need for me to laud his intellect and that nicety of culture which was peculiarly his . . . Beardsley was a chronic invalid, yet possessing intellectually just those desires which all men possess, he could not gratify them, and this inhibition was the cause of those Levitical drawings. I don't blame him for them. . . ."[11]

Perhaps, after all, the unfinished nature of Beardsley's tale has a symbolic quality, especially in its unexpurgated "Levitical" version, for pornography resists completion. "The ideal pornographic novel," Stephen Marcus writes, ". . . would go on forever; it would have no ending, just as in pornotopia there is ideally no such thing as time."[12]

---

*"Neither shalt thou lie with any beast to defile thyself therewith; neither shall any woman stand before a beast to lie down thereto: it is confusion." (The episode in Beardsley's tale is, almost literally, a masturbation fantasy.)

The Toilet, from *The Rape of the Lock*, published
by Leonard Smithers in 1896

The Rape of the Lock,
from the Smithers edition

Apart from the novel fragment, Beardsley's contributions to the second *Savoy*, published in April, were his cover and title-page drawings, and a pen-and-ink sketch destined to be one of nine illustrations for a Smithers edition of Pope's *The Rape of the Lock*. *The Rape* was one of Beardsley's most distinguished achievements, one he had completed before he had had to leave England for his health the previous winter. It had even earned the approbation of the acerbic Whistler. Like many others, Whistler had transferred his distaste for Wilde to Beardsley, and publicly announced his dislike for *Yellow Book* art during Beardsley's editorship. With Whistler there was often something personal about his artistic tastes which had little to do with objective criticism, and in Beardsley's case it was not only the brief *Salome* connection with Oscar, but such facts as that the upstart young artist had drawn caricatures of both Whistler and Mrs. Whistler. But one night when Whistler was visiting Elizabeth and Joseph Pennell (as they relate in their *Life* of the painter) Beardsley turned up, as usual with his portfolio under his arm. When he opened it, apparently unabashed at the great man's presence, and began to show them his new drawings illustrating *The Rape of the Lock*, "Whistler looked at them at first indifferently, then with interest, then with delight. And then he said slowly: 'Aubrey, I have made a very great mistake—you are a very great artist.' And the boy burst out crying. All Whistler could say, when he could say anything, was 'I mean it—I mean it—I mean it.' "

For a man of genius, who was at the same time an expert self-publicist, Beardsley was often paradoxically diffident about showing off his work in progress, or even admitting that there was any in progress. When he was at home in London, and alone, he must have labored on his drawing until he had worked himself into the easy exhaustion of the near-invalid;* for almost without exception his visitors now rarely found him at work, nor saw any of his rough sketches, or even any evidence of pen, ink and paper. But there were always books. It was his pose to appear as the gentleman dwelling

---

*Beardsley gives himself away on a page in one of his sketchbooks, which, in its entirety, reads

I
A M
T I R E
D

AB.

The New Star,
cul-de-lampe from *The Rape of the Lock*

amongst his books, and his conversation had the charm, but not the affectation, of scholarship. In the few years when his illness was—however debilitating—relatively stable, and jointly with his mother and sister he held a weekly Thursday-afternoon *salon*, three or four of his newest drawings would pass from hand to hand, while his pale, thin face creased with delight each time a friend praised one of his sketches. Arrogance and diffidence about his own accomplishments were inextricably mixed in Beardsley, probably because instant, early fame had simultaneously brought with it such heaping measures of opprobrium.

Although Beardsley was in London while the second *Savoy* was being prepared for the printer, before he had finished the cover he was again abroad for his health, this time in Paris and Brussels. Before he left London he had been busy with plans which both included and excluded Smithers, despite his exclusive-services agreement with his publisher. One proposal, outlined to William Heinemann, was for an edition of the Perrault version of the Cinderella story, with twelve illustrations, one for each month of the year, including the heroine attiring her sisters for the dance, her being "left disconsolate in the kitchen," "the fitting of the slipper," the marriage of Cinderella to the Prince, and a concluding "they lived happily ever afterwards."[13] Apparently nothing came of it.

He was again seriously ill, having over-extended himself in helping to launch *The Savoy*. In addition, with the rehabilitation of his reputation had come more social engagements than he could handle, and new friendships. One young man about town, the hedonistic and wealthy Jocelyn Persse, was far from being either artistic or literary, but liked to be on the fringes of such activity, and tried to cultivate Beardsley. It was not a success, Beardsley having to put him off with "I am afraid I shall have to break my promise to dine with you to night. I have had another attack of blood spitting. So must stay within doors to-day."[14] The attempt at friendship faded. Seven years later Persse became one of the consolations of Henry James's declining years.

In Paris Aubrey showed signs of improvement, hobnobbing briefly with Toulouse-Lautrec, Smithers and Dowson, even going with Dowson to the first performance of Wilde's *Salome*, produced by Lugne-Poe at the Théâtre de L'Oeuvre on 11 February. Wilde's sexual heresies and imprisonment had, if anything, increased the size and enthusiasm of the audience, and after Dowson left Beardsley he wrote a long account of the event to Mrs. Wilde, in the innocent assumption that she would be pleased. On one visit to Lautrec with the inevitable Dowson and Smithers, Beardsley was talked into experimenting with hashish for the first time. No result was apparent, and the Englishmen left puzzled and disappointed. Hours later, when the three were dining at Margery's, the narcotic took effect with a vengeance. "Luckily," Dowson wrote a friend, "we were in a *cabinet* or I think we would have been turned out—for Beardsley's laughter was so tumultuous that it infected the rest of us—who had *not* taken haschish & we all behaved like imbeciles."[15]

There were no ill effects, and Aubrey complained only of being "hideously overcharged" at his rooms in the Rue St. Roch, where—when he was not working at a table in his favorite place in Paris, the Café Anglais, he had begun what he proposed would be nine drawings for a Smithers edition of *The Rape of the Lock*. And he also continued to collect promises of art work for *The Savoy*.

From whatever venue he operated, he drew with a meticulous concentration that shut out all distracting influences. (His inwardness as he worked once prompted an onlooker to ask him whether he ever saw visions. "No," he answered. "I do not allow myself to see them except on paper."[16]) Pleased with his work in Paris, he wrote to Smithers, "The meticulous precision & almost indecent speed with which I have produced the drawing I send you by this post will prove that I have been nowhere near the Rue Monge.* I remain the same old hardworking solotaire you know & love so well. The drawing is one of the best I have done for the Rape." (The use of the "rare noun" has been suggested as a clue to his inexperience of sex, for in *Under the Hill* he wrote of one of its characters, "What were his amatory tastes, no one could tell. He generally passed for a virgin, and Cathos had nicknamed him 'The Solitaire.'"[17] Smithers liked the drawing, and said so in a letter which also included a check. Responding from his portable studio in the Café Anglais, Beardsley announced that his last drawing for *The Rape*, "The battle of the beaux & belles," would be dispatched in a day or two. "Regular March weather here," he added, and used the second page

Front cover design for *The Rape of the Lock*

---

*¹The Rue Monge connected the Quartier Latin, of easy morals, with the Quartier Mouffetard, with its reputation for more serious debauchery.

The Battle of the Beaux and the Belles, from *The Rape of the Lock*

of his letter for a top-hatted and cloaked Beardsley huddled against the chill winds which had followed him south.[18]

He had no idea when he would return to London—"filthy hole where I get nothing but snubs and the cold shoulder," he wrote Mabel,[19] still bitter at the literary and artistic establishment which had seemingly punished him for Wilde's débacle. His sister, who had been performing in Arthur Bourchier's company at the Royalty Theatre in *A Chili Widow*, had also been taking instruction in order to be received into the Roman Catholic Church; and Aubrey on her formal conversion sent her a correct rather than affectionate acknowledgment of the fact—a prayer book he had picked up for the purpose. "I am sending you," he postscripted, "a little parossien which I hope is the right thing."

In mid-March he moved to Brussels, where he expected to be joined in discussions on *Savoy* business by Smithers. From the Hôtel de Saxe he wrote his publisher that the "celestial" weather was wasted on him, as he never crossed the hotel threshhold, being too busy with both literary and art contributions for the April issue. He had completed another part of *Under the Hill* as well, and promised that the next chapter "will consist of pictures." When April came, and his publisher had not yet arrived (although Mabel visited briefly to determine for their mother how far Aubrey had run down), he appealed to have him send a suit of warm-weather clothes, as he had arrived from Paris unprepared. Shortly after the suit—which would make him feel like a "beastly toff," Beardsley predicted—came the young expatriate American poet Vincent O'Sullivan, who wrote for Smithers, and then Smithers himself. Inviting Beardsley and O'Sullivan to the Théâtre de la Monnaie to hear *Carmen*, he surprised them both by bringing along

as his travelling companion Alice his wife, whom he generally left to amuse herself as best she could in London. That night Alice surpassed herself, shewing, like Madame de Staël, her advantages where she had them. And a man alone in a box, who looked like an important personage, and perhaps was, fell for her. . . .

I was sitting next to Alice and called her attention discreetly to her conquest. She played it up in a way I should never have supposed she had it in her to do.

Afterwards, in a restaurant, there was the man again at an opposite table . . . and Smithers, who had at length become aware—he could scarcely help it—suddenly turned sarcastic and peevish.

How the comedy developed I do not know, for Beardsley in his half-invalid state had to go back to his hotel, and I went with him. . . .[20]

Usually Smithers found more exotic companionship than his wife, once—according to O'Sullivan—turning up in Paris with "some appalling Venus—sagging breasts, pouched jaws, varicosed legs, rheumatic ankles, wall-eyed—hideous to the point that one wondered in what suburb of Houndsditch he could have gone to seek her." It was a female of this type that Oscar Wilde met with Smithers, who announced that she was a Belgian, although he had brought her over from London.*2 In French, she explained to Oscar when presented to him, "*Monsieur Wilde, je suis la femme la plus laide de Londres.*" "*Du monde, Madame,*" Oscar replied, "*du monde.*"[21]

Neither the picturesque women nor the picturesque scenery of Brussels had any attraction for Beardsley. "The Hotel," he wrote Smithers early in April,

is of an abysmal dulness just now. I am about the only person stopping on. Weather filthy. I am taking creosote pills & am not allowed to eat fish &c., nor wine yet. I have tried to amuse myself by writing limericks on my troubles but have gotten no further than

> There once was an young invalid
> Whose lung would do nothing but bleed.

Symons shall finish it if he is a good boy.[22]

The crack about Symons as a critic of poetry resulted from Beardsley's second effort as a poet, "The Ballad of a Barber," about Carrousel, the barber of Meridian Street, who could "curl wit into the dullest face"—at least until something happened to cause his fingers to lose their cunning. The something was the golden-haired daughter of the King, "thirteen years old, or thereabout," and entrancing as "one of Schubert's melodies."

> Three times the barber curled a lock,
> And thrice he straightened it again;

*2"He surprised one of my friends by taking him for a long walk through London streets. Neither of them had noticed where they were going and as night closed in they found themselves, say, in Dalston. '*Tiens!*' said Smithers, if he had any French, or 'Don't worry!' if he had only English—'I have a mistress here. We'll go and have tea with her—no, we'll take some beer with us. . . .' On inquiry my friend discovered that Smithers had mistresses all over London. He chose them for the neighbourhoods in which they lived, that, wherever he was, he might always find company—in much the same spirit as that in which the Postmaster-General sprinkles post offices throughout the length and breadth of London. . . ." (Grant Richards, in *Author Hunting*, p. 34.)

Two Athenian Women in Distress, from Leonard
Smithers's edition of *Lysistrata* (1896)

And twice the irons scorched her frock,
And twice he stumbled in her train.

His fingers lost their cunning quite,
His ivory combs obeyed no more;
Something or other dimmed his sight,
And moved mysteriously the floor.

He leant upon the toilet table,
His fingers fumbled in his breast;
He felt as foolish as a fable,
As feeble as a pointless jest.

He snatched a bottle of Cologne,
And broke the neck between his hands;
He felt as if he was alone,
And mighty as a king's commands.

The Princess gave a little scream,
Carrousel's cut was sharp and deep;
He left her softly as a dream
That leaves a sleeper to his sleep.

He left the room on pointed feet;
Smiling that things had gone so well.
They hanged him in Meridian Street,
You pray in vain for Carrousel.[23]

Although the poem on first glance seemed inspired by the ballad of
Sweeney Todd, the demon barber of Fleet Street, it hardly aimed at the
comic horror of a barber who cut his victims' throats in order to supply his
mistress with the wherewithal for her succulent meat pies; and Symons may
have seen more in it himself. He told Smithers that it was too poor for *The
Savoy*, yet perhaps the trouble with the poem was that it was too effective.*
"The Barber" complemented Beardsley's *Under the Hill* perhaps even more
than he knew. All he told Smithers was that he thought it was "rather interesting," and suggested that if Symons thought it would embarrass his art
editor it could be printed under a pseudonym. "What do you think," he

---

The Rape of the Lock was still fresh in Beardsley's mind, and the barber of his poem also
commits an act of symbolic rape. (Beardsley may also have recalled John Gray's poem "The
Barber," published in 1893 in *Silverpoints*, a sexual fantasy in which the poet dreams he is a
barber coiffing—and otherwise fondling—his young girl clients.)

The Coiffing, illustrating Beardsley's "The Ballad of a Barber," *The Savoy*, No. 3 (July, 1896)

inquired, "of 'Symons' as a nom de plume?" More seriously, he suggested that any signature would do, and proposed "Arthur Malyon." But Symons still objected, drawing from Beardsley a firm reply to his publisher, for not only did he have a literary effort at stake, but an illustration for it which has since been classified as among his finest achievements:

> I am very disappointed at what you tell me about the Ballad and its illustration. The picture is such a good one & its withdrawal leaves me rather thinly represented in the number. You see the writing of the poem & the illustration took nearly five days out of my time for the preparation of work for the Savoy & I could have been doing other things if I had known that Symons would have made arrangements to keep things of mine out of the magazine. Surely as lit. Ed. he could have written to me earlier saying that the last verses must be re-written—you know how willing I am always to make alterations & listen to suggestions. Of course it is too late now to revise the poem. I will never get work ready for the Savoy again away from London.[24]

The "Ballad" went to press, but barbering remained on Beardsley's mind, for he informed Smithers that he was going to take the "daring step" of having his tortoiseshell locks, now thick as a sheep dog's, trimmed—although not without first offering up a little prayer:

> Oh Lord who art never unmindful of the prayers of thy faithful people, & whose loving kindness is so particular that thou hast not disdained to number the hairs of our heads, grant I beseech thee that in the difficult ordeal (through which it has pleased thee I shall presently pass) some *few* hairs may be left to be numbered, & to be an everlasting annoyance unto thy people Philistia.

On the second page of the letter he drew a shaggy-haired caricature of himself.[25]

Grotesque from *Bon-Mots of Smith and Sheridan*

9

The Savoy in extremis   *1896*

Towards the end of April, after Beardsley had completed a cover for the third *Savoy*, and some additional drawings for it, and was arranging for other art work in future issues, he had a relapse, and—as he put it— "stained many a fair handkerchief red with blood." Belatedly, *The Times* carried the news in a dispatch from Brussels dated 6 May.*¹ "Aubrey Beardsley, the English artist," it reported, "is in this city suffering from a pulmonary complaint, which his physicians fear may terminate fatally. Friends are constantly watching at his bedside." An obituary-like biographical sketch followed, and after it a comment which proved its own point: "Aubrey Beardsley is not a man of genius, but he is attacked as if he were."

As with previous setbacks since he had arrived in Brussels in February, Beardsley improved enough to move about painfully while gasping for each breath, propped at each step by a walking stick, hurling unspoken imprecations against his local doctor for incompetence. "Of course I am damned civil to the doctor," he admitted to Smithers, "or else he will stick it on his bill."

To his mother he reported, finally, that the doctor intended permitting him to leave for London early in May. "My spirits have gone up at the prospect of wiping Brussels dust from my shoes." If André Raffalovich had not come over to visit Beardsley, and then insisted on taking him to lunch, Beardsley might have left Brussels on the day he planned; but the delay left him with-

---

*¹Beardsley had actually left Brussels for London on 4 May.

out help to pack, for Raffalovich's good intentions dragged out Aubrey's stay into a week when the hotel servants were preoccupied with the marriage of a child of the proprietor, and could not be spared to speed the departing guest. On the evening of 2 May, while the wedding guests danced and drank, he wired Mabel to come "pilot" him over the Channel; but Mabel could not leave her play. Mrs. Beardsley had to go herself, although she was ill, and when she arrived the next day was "so knocked up" (Aubrey wrote Smithers) that they had to remain another day for her recuperation. "Deep-felt grief at my departure is noticeable all over the hotel," he wrote Smithers ironically. "What a thing it is to be loved!" Almost certainly his departure was little-noticed: the hotel personnel were still recovering from the wedding.

Raffalovich appears to have been of little if any real help, although he was always full of good intentions. More a camp follower than a man of letters,*[2] he was bent on directing Beardsley towards the faith to which he was a convert himself, Roman Catholicism. "Poor André!" Oscar Wilde once mocked; "He came to London with the intention of founding a *salon*, and has succeeded only in opening a saloon."

"André," Ada Leverson cattily wrote a friend in *Yellow Book* days, "is hard at work furnishing [his town house]. Aubrey says he has a little steeper [*sic*] staircase leading into a tiny garden where he will give garden parties—never more than two people, including the host."[1] At Raffalovich's request Beardsley had agreed to design a frontispiece for a book of verses the young poet was publishing, *The Thread and the Path* (1895). Eventually Beardsley wrote him, "I am beginning the frontispiece—a literal rendering of the first line." The line was "Set in a heart as in a frame love liveth," and Beardsley translated it into his pen-and-ink drawing "The Mirror of Love (Love Enshrined in a Heart in the Shape of a Mirror)." Although Raffalovich acquired the design, the book was published before Beardsley had managed to complete the assignment. A year later, Raffalovich was beginning to assume for himself a crucial place in Beardsley's life.

Vignette from *Bon-Mots of Foote and Hook*

---

*[2]Yet he published two playlets (with John Gray), five slim books of poetry and a treatise on homosexuality called *Uranisme et Unisexualité: Étude sur différentes manifestations de l'instinct sexuel* (1896).

A thin unhandsome man in his early thirties, with manners as impeccable as his clothes, and seemingly inexhaustible amounts of spending money, Marc-André Raffalovich had left Paris, where his father, a Russian-Jewish émigré, was a prosperous banker, to seek his literary fortunes in England, but his successes were primarily extra-literary, chief among them his homoerotic—and lifelong—friendship with poet (later Father) John Gray. Raffalovich had been baptized just a few months before, in February 1896, at the church of the Jesuit fathers in Farm Street, Mayfair, and was certain he had a candidate for conversion in Beardsley, if he were only sufficiently patient. Although his admiration for Beardsley apparently remained platonic, and his aims spiritual, he pressed money on the ailing artist, assuring him that as long as illness prevented him from being self-supporting he need only call on his friend. Yet Raffalovich seldom waited for the call, sending money, books, gifts—and priests. Since payments from Smithers came erratically, Beardsley was usually careful not to offend Raffalovich; but he was already considering doing for Smithers a series of drawings for a translation of Aristophanes' bawdy anti-war comedy *Lysistrata*. Not only was it remunerative labor—it was potentially scandalous besides. As a result Beardsley prudently waited until the job was done, then tucked a mention of it into a letter to his benefactor. "In a letter to Raffalovich today," he wrote Smithers (several months later), "I told him that I had completed a set of illustrations to Lysistrata. I wonder if he will take any notice of it."[2]

By the time Beardsley returned to London from Brussels the second *Savoy* had appeared, and the third quarterly number was in press. Symons had published a prefatory editorial note in the second issue which indicated in its smugness that the initial number had been a popular, if not critical, success. "In presenting to the public the second number of 'The Savoy,' " he wrote,

I wish to thank the critics of the press for the flattering reception which they have given to No. 1. That reception has been none the less flattering because it has been for the most part unfavourable. Any new endeavour lends itself, alike by its merits and by its defects, to the disapproval of the larger number of people. And it is always possible to learn from any vigorously expressed denunciation, not, perhaps, what the utterer of that denunciation intended should be learnt. I confess cheerfully that I have learnt much from the newspaper criticisms of the first number of "The Savoy." It is with confidence that I anticipate no less instruction from the criticisms which I shall have the pleasure of reading on the number now issued.

Vignette from *Bon-Mots of Lamb and Jerrold*

Choosing the New Hat, design for front cover of *The Savoy*, No. 2 (April, 1896), which continued Beardsley's preoccupation with eighteenth-century French prints (although the women's clothes are of later date)

For the most part the literary establishment did not disappoint Symons, and similarly condemned the new number, forcing the editor to ransack the columns of Glasgow newspapers in order to find a group of favorable press notices to quote for the next issue. The Glasgow *Evening News* had praised the triptych of pieces on Paul Verlaine, one by Edmund Gosse on tracking down Verlaine, another by Yeats on meeting the poet for tea, and a third by Verlaine himself, telling about his 1893 visit to London, and reproducing a lecture he gave. The Glasgow *Record* and the Glasgow *Quiz* both compared the current number of *The Yellow Book* unfavorably ("stale and humdrum") with *The Savoy*. But another Scottish paper, the *Scotsman*, considered *The Savoy* "most entertaining when taken least seriously." Yet even the *Scotsman* found the draftsmanship of Beardsley worth serious praise:

His drawings are a never-ending source of pleasure and admiration . . . extraordinary in the daring with which they sail so near the grotesque without ever stepping across the line of beauty. Perhaps the most noticeable of them is "The Rape of the Lock," a subject which gives Mr. Beardsley a good opportunity of showing his peculiar power of putting romance into the stiffness and stateliness of the artificial politeness of the eighteenth century.

Beardsley had also solicited some of the material for the second number. He had written to John Gray the previous summer asking for a contribution to *The Savoy*: "I look to you for a fine essay on archery after your summer exploits with the bow and shaft, for it will seem quite fit that a member of the 'Société des Enfants d'Apollon' is also an archer." "La Société" was probably a Parisian group of symbolist poets, but Beardsley's hint about the subject matter—possibly he had ideas about sketches for such an essay—failed. Instead, Gray submitted a Hopkins-like poem, "The Forge," its subject matter as far removed from the way he spent his days as could be imagined.

Yeats contributed "Rosa Alchemica," a mystical story, to the second issue, as well as his Verlaine reminiscence and two poems, while Symons published a poem and a story of his own. Havelock Ellis added an article on Nietzsche and a translation from Cesare Lombroso, thus representing Germany and Italy as well as France in the issue. But Verlaine remained the patron saint of *The Savoy*. In addition to other fiction and verse, there was a witty article by Vincent O'Sullivan, "On the Kind of Fiction Called Morbid,"

which in its challenging conclusion sounded a keynote of the *Savoy* group: "Let us cling by all means to our George Meredith, our Henry James—our Miss Rhoda Broughton, if you will; but then let us try, if we cannot be towards others, unlike these, if not encouraging, at the least not actively hostile and harassing, when they go out into the black night to follow their own sullen will-o'-the-wisps."

Frankness in literature and art was not then defended on legal grounds but on scientific grounds, but it took writers like Havelock Ellis to carry the war into the enemy's camp. The new fiction (as well as art of the Beardsley school) had been called "morbid," "neurotic," and "diseased," but Ellis made the point that the more accurate a writer's perspectives were, the more profound was his art as an instrument of morality, for the chief enemy to civilized behavior was ignorance, not knowledge. O'Sullivan found wit a better weapon than Ellis's high seriousness, and made fun of the philosophy of fiction for which preachers and purveyors of three-volume novels were beginning to fight a losing rear-guard action. Hilariously summarizing their idea of a novel plot—which he titled "the history of Miss Perfect"—he found that such fiction was nourishing our morals on "the thinnest milk and water, with a good dose of sugar added, and not a suspicion of lemon at all."

The financial success of the first two numbers prompted Smithers to take a risk which Symons announced for him in an editorial note in the third issue:

A new volume of "The Savoy" commences with the July number, and it has been decided, in consequence of the interest which has been taken in the two numbers already issued, to make the Magazine a Monthly instead of a Quarterly.

The policy of "The Savoy" will remain precisely what it has hitherto been, but the opportunities of monthly publication will permit the issue of a serial, and arrangements are being made with Mr. George Moore for the serial publication of his new novel, "Evelyn Innes."

It is not unreasonably assumed that those who have welcomed "The Savoy" as a Quarterly will welcome it with at least equal interest as a Monthly, and it is confidently hoped that the large public, to which a quarterly comes with too occasional an appeal, will appreciate the monthly publication of a Periodical whose only aim is to offer its readers letterpress which is literature, and illustrations which are art.

The move was disastrously timed, although neither Smithers nor Symons realized it early in June 1896, when it was made. Initially there was enthusiasm from some of the contributors, Dowson, for example, writing from Brittany that *The Savoy* had become "a great & admirable institution," and adding the wish, "May the hair of John Lane grow green with Envy!" George Moore's *Evelyn Innes* was a novel good enough possibly to have prolonged *The Savoy's* life when Beardsley's health cut off his crucial contributions. But Moore's only effort for the magazine would be a brief translation from Mallarmé he produced for the third number. After the great success of *Esther Waters* in 1894, he hardly needed the shop window of *The Savoy*, and the over-hasty promise of *Evelyn Innes* remained unfulfilled.

There was still another blow, as *Savoy* readers discovered from Smithers's note which brought up the rear of the issue. Beardsley had written to Smithers that his own contributions to the magazine would have to be suspended indefinitely. Dr. Symes Thompson "had pronounced very unfavourably" on his condition, and had ordered absolute rest and quiet, and removal from London.

C. Lewis Hind had just visited Beardsley, realizing as soon as he saw him that it was probably for the last time. It was a day of brilliant summer sunshine, yet as usual the curtains in the ground-floor flat were drawn, and the room lit by tall ormolu candles. On the walls hung framed reproductions of Mantegna drawings. It was a Beardsley sketch come to life. In the room the artist sat in a yellow dressing-gown, wearing red slippers turned up at the toes; and, as Hind entered, Beardsley lifted a hand in a wan gesture of welcome and laughed his gay laugh—which turned into a terrible cough. Hind forced himself to laugh back. "It's a great game!" Beardsley cried. Then he seated himself in front of his drawing-board, and his face became tense again. "He was in high spirits during our meeting," Hind thought, "and seemed as brisk and cheerful as he had ever been." But Hind knew, and Beardsley knew about himself, that he was "seriously ill, indeed not expected to live. . . ."[3]

Beardsley was frightened, whatever his outward reaction, and began his last restless journeys in search of health. By the time the third *Savoy* was released, he was at the Spread Eagle Hotel in Epsom, snatching at moments of strength between hemorrhages to work at illustrations for *Lysistrata*. His condition seemed belied by his contributions to the July number, but they

Opposite: *Atalanta in Calydon*, illustrating Swinburne's poem and intended for Vol. V of *The Yellow Book*, but not used when Beardsley was sacked

Illustration to Justin Huntly McCarthy's poem "At a Distance," in *A London Garland*, edited by W. E. Henley with art by members of the Society of Illustrators (1895)

had been produced long before. He had done the drawings for the paper cover and the title page, and illustrated the sprightliest piece in the issue, his own "The Ballad of a Barber."*

His London doctor had ordered such drastic measures that Beardsley confessed, "I am beginning to be really depressed and frightened about myself." But late in May, once he arrived for what proved to be a brief stay in Twyford, Sussex (before going on to Epsom), he could write bravely to Smithers, "As to my health I think it will improve very quickly here & perhaps I yet may be strong enough to kick Symons's little . . ."—and he appended a drawing of a backside.

The auguries of disaster—but for Smithers's postscript—were still invisible in the third number, and there was fulfillment as well as promise. The realistic "Anthony Garstin's Courtship," one of Hubert Crackanthorpe's best short stories, was the chief prose fiction; and there was the first of three articles by Yeats on "William Blake and His Illustrations to the Divine Comedy," which provided—through the reproductions of Blake's drawings—a means of filling the art gap left by Beardsley.

Ironically, it was the long-dead Blake whose drawings were to create even more distribution problems for *The Savoy* than the dying Beardsley. For once Beardsley was not at the center of the storm although, thanks to a case of mistaken identity, he was indirectly the cause of it. The bookselling firm of W. H. Smith had long been behind the effort to protect the growing public being educated to read from such books as, in their opinion, might injure its moral or its religious beliefs; and Smith's controlled the bookstalls at the railway stations, a proliferating and profitable octopus. The refusal of the railway bookstalls to display *The Savoy* came as an economic thunderclap, and Symons rushed to the office of Smith's manager.

According to Yeats,

The bookseller's manager, no doubt looking for a design of Beardsley's, pitched upon Blake's *Anteus setting Virgil and Dante upon the verge of Cocytus* as grounds for refusal, and when Arthur Symons pointed out that Blake was considered "a very spiritual artist," replied, "Oh, Mr. Symons, you must remember that we have an

*Teasingly, he then wrote Smithers, well aware of Symons's hostility towards his "Ballad": "Sequel to Barber nearly finished. The first ten verses give a very spirited description of the post mortem examination of the princess." (Postmarked 1 July 1896.)

audience of young ladies as well as an audience of agnostics." However he called Symons back from the door to say, "If contrary to our expectations the *Savoy* should have a large sale, we should be very glad to see you again."

The hypocrisy dumbfounded, then enraged, Yeats, whose article was illustrated by the offending drawing of Blake's. He wrote a letter to the editor of "a principal daily newspaper" reporting the "remarkable saying" of the bookseller. But in his letter Yeats mentioned the notorious Beardsley, and was told "that the editor had made it a rule that his paper was never to mention Beardsley's name." Later Yeats met the gentleman and asked him, "Would you have made the same rule in the case of Hogarth?" The editor, realizing that the same objections made about Beardsley *could* have been made about Hogarth, replied with "a dreamy look, as though suddenly reminded of a lost opportunity—'Ah, there was no popular press in Hogarth's day.' "[4]

The new number suffered also from a poor press, although Gelett Burgess (of "Purple Cow" fame) would soon be writing in his alphabetical guide to the nineties,

> B is for Beardsley, the idol supreme,
> Whose drawings are not half so bad as they seem.[5]

The best encomium Symons could locate for *Savoy* self-advertising was the faint praise of the *Saturday Review*, which reflected, "We do not know that 'The Savoy' can claim any extraordinary merit except on the score of Mr. Beardsley's drawings; but his coiffeur in this issue, and three at least of his contributions to the last, must clear away any doubts there may have been as to his supreme position as a draughtsman." A private note agreed. From Paris, a young woman whose thin figure in a yellow dress and long black gloves appeared on Toulouse-Lautrec posters about the city, and who sang to rapt audiences of heartbreak and cruelty, wrote to Symons, "The more I see what does Aubrey Beardsley the more I am in love with him! What a talent of conception he has! et quelle élégance, quelle *distinction* dans les lignes de ses dessins c'est admirable!"[6]

Beardsley was missing entirely from the fourth number (August), except for the use of *Lysistrata*-influenced designs for cover and title-page art; and *The Savoy* was clearly faltering from his absence. "I *like* this number of the Savoy vastly," he diplomatically wrote Smithers, "but should have *loved* it

Cover design for *The Savoy*, No. 5 (September, 1896), the purported artist's signature one of Beardsley's jokes, his sense of humor belying the fact that he drew the cover while ill at Bournemouth

Lysistrata Defending the Acropolis, from
Smithers's edition of *Lysistrata* (1896)

had there been an Aubrey or so within its covers." Still, his hand remained unfaltering, for through July, while languishing in his two rooms at the Spread Eagle Hotel in Epsom, he had completed his eight Greek-vase-inspired drawings for *Lysistrata*.[7] "The pisspots is turning out a pretty thing," he confided to his publisher, indicating by his uneuphemistic code name for the project his awareness of its impossibility for trade publication. More carefully to John Gray, who—with Raffalovich—was trying to make a Roman Catholic of Beardsley, the artist wrote that the *Lysistrata* illustrations were "in a way the best things I have ever done."[8] And they were, for their lines were strong and simple, and they communicated a satiric power which placed them beyond decoration. Yet Beardsley knew as he worked on them that there were elements in the drawings which would classify them as "obscene" and limit their distribution—not so much nudity as a liberal (rather than literal) and stylized representation of female pubic hair. "If there are no cunts in the picture," he explained to Smithers, "Aristophanes is to blame, and not your humble servant." But he failed to explain to Smithers why the proliferation of fifth century B.C. erect penises, however Brobdingnagian and grotesque, were circumcized, although for Smithers there were clearly enough of them for his purposes, whatever the state of the foreskin. He planned to offer one hundred copies "for private distribution."[*1]

While Beardsley was working on his *Lysistrata* drawings, and beginning his never-to-be-completed series for *Ali Baba and the Forty Thieves*, Smithers paid several visits to Epsom to see how his most important investment was faring. Between inspections he sent weekly checks, at first in £10 amounts and later in £12 amounts, to maintain Beardsley in board, doctors, and medicines. One "wondrous medicine" which left his head aching Beardsley described as containing, among its "simplest" ingredients, "Ammonia, Potassium, Belladonna [and] chloroform." Still, the hemorrhages regularly returned, and spurts of blood bore a direct relationship to his spurts

---

[*1]As recently as 10 August 1966 reproductions of Beardsley's *Lysistrata* drawings—and more modest Beardsleys—in reproductions selling for twelve and a half pence were seized by Scotland Yard detectives from a shop in Regent Street, less than two miles from the Victoria and Albert Museum, where the originals were on reverent display. The seizure was made under the Obscene Publications Act of 1959, under which drawings can be confiscated and their publisher, seller or distributor prosecuted. "I suppose the police never go into the Victoria and Albert," said an official of the firm which supplied the reproductions.

of creative energy, both in cause and effect. He worked with the intensity of a condemned man—as he literally was—and paid the price with each setback. Each relapse would inspire a new creative burst, for each project was one he knew he might never complete. Thus in the last week of July 1896 he could write Smithers, "I am feeling wonderfully well, considering my little set back. The last of the Lysistrata drawings is finished. Surely it is the occasion for a little prayer and praise."

Smithers was prospering, although the faltering *Savoy* was not, and he celebrated his shaky prosperity by moving his business quarters from Arundel Street to the Royal Arcade in Old Bond Street—which Beardsley promptly suggested should be christened "The Sodley Bed."*² But the wit failed to conceal Beardsley's increasing enfeeblement. The bones of his face were more pronounced, and his prominent ribs and gaunt arms and legs showed how little weight he had left to lose. Forbidden by both his doctors to go to Brighton, he had to settle for a move in mid-August to a more distant—and more sheltered—seaside location, Bournemouth. Journeys by rail were always hard on Beardsley, and the one to London to change trains was nearly fatal, resulting in such severe bleeding that once he arrived in Boscombe (Bournemouth) he was marooned in his room for weeks. Nothing seemed to help. "Tonics, milk, retirement, & Boscombe air, seem to avail nothing in keeping back the blood, which like murder *will* out. Yesterday," he wrote Smithers bitterly toward the end of the summer,

I was laid out like a corpse with a haemmorhage [sic]. For me and my lung there seems to be little hope. . . . Everyone here is very kind flowers & fruit galore which give me not the slightest satisfaction. It is a month now since I left my room & I fear it will be some time yet before I can even get down to meals. I suppose it is a special providence that has sent this spell of damp and damnable weather, I write sitting clammy from head to foot.⁹

Meanwhile the fifth (September) *Savoy* was released, with a Beardsley cover drawing signed "Giulio Floriani" to tease the critics, and a long-

---

*²In October, Smithers made a second move, taking up residence at 6a Bedford Square, once the town house of the Dukes of Bedford and later the Spanish Embassy. Before his bankruptcy, he lived there in grand style, and invited many of the leading literary and artistic figures there—a few of whom came. His son Jack "recalled" meeting Beardsley there, among others, but this is unlikely—although not nearly so unlikely as his recollection of Wilde there at a time when Oscar was either in prison or in exile. (Jack Smithers, *The Early Life and Vicissitudes of Jack Smithers*, p. 17.)

Lysistrata Haranguing the Athenian Women, from *Lysistrata*

The Lacadaemonian Ambassadors, from Lysistrata

completed sketch borrowed from Frederick H. Evans, "The Woman in White," in order to give some Beardsley tone to the "illustrated monthly." There were the inevitable poems by Symons and Yeats, the third of Yeats's Blake series and short fiction by Ernest Rhys and Theodore Wratislaw, both more romantic than "decadent." The sixth issue—in the use of a Beardsley cover drawing once meant to illustrate *Under the Hill*—again maintained the facade of Beardsley's art editorship of *The Savoy*. There was also a second Beardsley, the dramatic and suddenly timely "Death of Pierrot," done several months before, which the artist had captioned, "*As the dawn broke, Pierrot fell into his last sleep. Then upon tip-toe, silently up the stairs, came the comedians Arlecchino, Pantaleone, il Dottore, and Columbina, who with much love carried away upon their shoulders, the white frocked clown of Bergamo; whither, we know not.*"

Death further stalked the pages of the failing *Savoy*, although the artistic standard remained high. There was the strikingly illustrated Villon "Epitaphe in Form of a Ballade," in Wratislaw's translation, and a poem by Edith Thomas, "A Soul at Lethe's Brink." There were also substantial prose pieces, among them Havelock Ellis's "Concerning *Jude the Obscure*." Hardy, wrote Ellis about this disturbing and controversial novel, "was less a story-teller than an artist who has faithfully studied certain phases of passion, and brings us a simple and faithful report of what he has found." The charge against *Jude*, Ellis said, was not that it was bad art as that it was a book with suspect moral purposes, and "It would not be pleasant to admit that a book you thought bad morality is good art. . . . So are most of our great novels." It was a deliberately hasty generalization, but there were enough shockers he could name (*Tom Jones, Madame Bovary, Les Liaisons Dangereuses*—and even *Jane Eyre*) to make the reader think about reassessing his critical criteria.

One of the major works of fiction to appear in the entire run of *The Savoy* was the leading contribution in the sixth number, Joseph Conrad's long short story "The Idiots," a brooding Hardyesque tale. Its bleak realism was as typical of *The Savoy* as was—in contrasting contributions—the sickly-sweet atmosphere of decay. Symons paid forty guineas for it—two guineas a page—and it became one of the few times before 1912 that Conrad earned a respectable fee for a piece of fiction. Yet the price suggested an erroneously optimistic view of *The Savoy*. By the time the October number went to press, the magazine's fate had been decided.

"By the way," Beardsley had wondered to Smithers that September, "what about Lysistrata? When may I hug to my withered bosom a copy of it[?]" But Smithers was having difficulties, including the major one of arranging for *The Savoy*'s demise—news he broke with great care to Beardsley, who responded realistically, "Nothing else could I fear be done with The Savoy. . . . I shall do you some scortching [*sic*] drawings for No. 8. . . ." The magazine, which had meant so much to Beardsley the year before, was something he could quickly think of in the past tense. With little future, he lived utterly in the present—as long as his hand did not fail him. "My genius for work," he wrote his publisher, "possesses me in an extraordinary degree just now. Pray God it continue to do so. It is so important to turn out stuff. Down here there is nothing else to do; the heavens be praised."

As far as Beardsley was concerned, his claim to some measure of posthumous significance would lie in a substantial volume of collected work, and the establishment through it of his artistic development. "It's all nonsense what they say about my early work," he explained to Smithers. "Just compare the drawing of the nude [in a bookplate he had made] with the nudes in the Morte; and the drawing of the trees and general handling of line." Despite his contention, as he worked into the early autumn arranging for release of some of his past work for the publication—which became *A Book of Fifty Drawings* (1897)—he chose a disproportionate nineteen illustrations from the *Morte d'Arthur* for it. On receiving J. M. Dent's permission for their use, he acknowledged his gratitude by sending him "The Return of Tannhäuser to Venusberg," a drawing he had intended for a never-written section of his novel. Aware of Beardsley's condition, Dent was so moved by the gift that he replied with an emotional letter:

Sept 21st 1896

My dear Beardsley

I am inexpressibly touched by this beautiful gift of yours from your sick bed—it shall be kept as one of my great treasures and handed down to my children after me. It has all the old power—and suggests to me wonderful things which may God bring to pass.

There is only one Aubrey Beardsley and they cant hurt his work with all their imitation.

Cinesias Entreating Myrrhina to Coition, from *Lysistrata*

God bless you and make you well again.

There is one great book which you should turn your attention to if your strength comes back—that is the "Pilgrim's Progress," don't laugh! just take it up and read it. If you could do it I believe it would be your monument for ever. . . .

Is there anything that I can do that will give you pleasure? Have you plenty of books—would you like one or two of my Balzac translations? . . . You know you urged me to publish this great master.

Don't try to write. I shall be glad if you will thro your Mother let me have a line now and then as to your continued progress to health.

God bless you once more this little picture speaks wonders to me—that bit of clear white sky out of all that Blackness of Despair—and the eyes of Tannhäuser are opening to it—yes, Humanity will come back from Hades some day—it is coming already.

Yours very sincerely,
J. M. Dent[10]

On 30 October 1896, when the November number was in press, Hubert Crackanthorpe wrote to Grant Richards, "I have just heard from Arthur Symons that the *Savoy* is to cease in December." If Richards would take over the publication from the unsavory Smithers, and he replace Symons as editor, the magazine might be saved. Further, he suggested, because Beardsley was already in effect out of the picture, there was a chance to "break away from the "Beardsley tradition" and have . . . a very fair chance of success." Since Symons would be out of a job anyway when *The Savoy* foundered, Crackanthorpe felt no sense of immorality in proposing himself,* but Richards cautiously rejected the idea. The "reaction" against what the reading public associated with Wilde and his disciples "had not spent itself," he thought. Back in Fountain Court, Symons and Yeats, who were closer to the situation, had similarly grim impressions.

In an opening editorial note in the seventh issue, dated November, Symons announced the forthcoming death of *The Savoy*. It was far from a whimpering, defeatist valedictory:

I have to announce that with the next number, completing a year's existence, the present issue of "The Savoy" will come to an end. It has done something of what I intended it should do: it has made warm friends and heated enemies: and I am

Opposite: *The Return of Tannhäuser to the Venusberg*, one of the hoped-for two dozen illustrations for *Venus and Tannhäuser*, neither the illustrations nor the text ever completed (ca. 1896)

---

*Less than two months later Beardsley was writing, ironically, to Smithers, "I hear tragic things of Hubert Crackanthorpe." An apparent suicide, he was found drowned in the Seine on 23 December 1896.

THE SAVOY

AN ILLUSTRATED MONTHLY

No. 7   November 1896   Price 2/-

EDITED BY ARTHUR SYMONS

Title page of *The Savoy*'s penultimate issue, both figures showing Beardsley's continuing fascination with the pierrot

equally content with both. It has, in the main, conquered the prejudices of the press; and I offer the most cordial thanks to those newspaper critics who have had the honesty and the courtesy to allow their prejudices to be conquered. But it has not conquered the general public, and without the florins of the general public, no magazine such as "The Savoy," issued at so low a price, without the aid of advertisements can be expected to pay its way. We therefore retire from the arena, not entirely dissatisfied, if not a trifle disappointed, leaving to those who care for it our year's work, which will be presented to you in three volumes, in a cover of Mr. Beardsley's designing. . . .

In the issue Beardsley returned not only with a cover drawing of spectacled old age being snubbed by youth, but with a brief written contribution accompanied by an illustration. The artist's literary offering was a striking translation of Catullus: "Carmen CI," in which the poet announced that he had come to the "sad grave-side" so that he could "give the last gifts to the dead." It was, actually, his literary hail-and-farewell to *The Savoy*. As Beardsley had matured, according to Max, he had "gradually" (although *gradually* hardly fits the compression of Beardsley's development) become "more human, less curious of horrible things." Of this tendency, Max thought, the best example was this "Ave atque Vale": "Nothing could be more dramatic, more moving and simple, than the figure of that Roman who mourns his friend. . . . These lines . . . seem to me no less beautiful than the drawing itself. . . ."[11]

The poem "Epilogue," in the same penultimate number, was Dowson's last contribution. Perhaps it was only coincidentally applicable to the imminent death of the magazine and so many of its ill-starred contributors, but certain lines seem almost like a judgment upon the literary set who represented so large a part of the pages of *The Savoy*:

> . . . vain things alone
> Have driven our perverse and aimless band.

Not everything in this number was valedictory, nor was there a slackening-off in anything but the issue's thickness. Although Symons was responsible for at least a quarter of the contents himself, indicating both editorial frugality and the diminishing manuscript submissions inevitably following diminishing appeal and rumors of approaching death, the quality of the literary contributions remained high. The prose included tales of Scotland and of Ireland by "Fiona Macleod" and Yeats, and an essay on

AVE ATQVE VALE

Ave Atque Vale (see p. 209), Beardsley's "hail and farewell" to *The Savoy* as well as an illustration to his translation of Catullus

Casanova by Ellis. ("Fiona Macleod" was the pseudonym of William Sharp, whose relationship to the publicity-shy "Scottish authoress" only became known after his death in 1905.)

Number eight, dated December 1896, brought the venture to a close. More out of Symons's stubborn pride than because there were few contributions to the dying journal left on his desk, he and his art editor played the roles of captains going down with their ship: the whole of the literary contents was by Symons, and the art—all fourteen drawings—supplied by Beardsley, mostly from long-completed work—from *The Rhinegold* and other works he had been illustrating. Boldly, Symons used the occasion of the last issue for a demonstration of his literary range, publishing a poem of his own, a translation of a Mallarmé poem, a short story, a critical article and a travel essay. His final "Literary Causerie" piece was his epilogue, ascribing *The Savoy*'s demise not to an unfavorable press—for he believed that the critics were being won over—but to the "too meagre support of our friends." The expected rationalizations might have reasonably been given for burying *The Savoy*, its first and last editor thought, but none of them were really crucial. It had been a mistake to give "so much for so little money," and to abandon the quarterly for monthly publication. It had been a misfortune that Messrs. Smith and Son—out of hostility to Beardsley— had turned *The Savoy* out of its bookstalls. Still, it had been a miscalculation on the part of the editors and publisher when they had assumed nevertheless "that there were very many people in the world who really cared for art, and really for art's sake." This last error was the blow to *The Savoy* which really killed it, Symons concluded, the assumption that a broad base of artistic appeal would bring popularity and sales, for "Comparatively few people care for art at all, and most of them care for it because they mistake it for something else." The half-crown charged for each issue was well within the range of a numerous cultured class, but there was no public whose purse strings *The Savoy* could seize, at least partly because its criteria for acceptability of contributions did not go beyond artistic merit to the issues which touched a broad base of buyers. It espoused no religion or party, took no stand on war, peace, taxation, socialism, imperialism, suffrage or other problems directly meaningful to a public; nor did it print reviews of current books, plays or concerts or appeal to other tastes which formed a public for a periodical. Neither was its appeal to decadence, or naturalism, or aesthet-

THE
SAVOY

EDITED BY ARTHUR SYMONS

No. 8 and last
December
1896

LEONARD SMITHERS
4 & 5 ROYAL ARCADE, OLD BOND STREET
LONDON W

icism, for *The Savoy* published many writers who could be modern without being decadent or otherwise restrictive—Bernard Shaw, Joseph Conrad, Havelock Ellis, Edmund Gosse among them. Artistic merit has no public. Despite some assertions since, neither was *The Savoy* the organ of Symbolism, although Symons was hospitable to French writers he later classified as Symbolist; for the only unequivocally doctrinal pieces were Yeats's development of a canon of Symbolist painting based upon Blake's distinction between Symbol and Allegory. Beardsley himself had been unaffected, except as the Blake drawings provoked the fatal confrontation with the censorship of W. H. Smith.

Logically then, *The Savoy* had to fail, yet the experiment might have been commercially successful for the wrong reasons. For the one appeal *The Savoy* did make, perhaps unwittingly, was to the cult of personality, and the magnetic Beardsley attracted as well as repelled. If there was one thing about which critics and readers agreed, it was the excellence and the drawing power of Beardsley's contributions, and the popular interest in the artist as a personality. The public might have bought a Beardsley, but lost interest in a *Savoy* with an ever-thinning Beardsley façade. He was the base of popular appeal as well as the magnet which drew many of its top contributors. As Hesketh Pearson so neatly put it, *The Savoy* "might just as well have been called *The Beardsley*, for he was, if not the life and soul, at least the body and death of it."[12]

The Fall of the House of Usher, third of four Beardsley illustrations to Poe (1895), the melancholy figure based on an earlier drawing of Chopin

10

Retreat

From Pier View in Bournemouth at the end of October 1896, Beardsley mailed to Smithers "the last of No. 8"—his final contributions for *The Savoy*. He was in an "agony of depression," intensified by his isolation from London and his realization that at best he was painfully dragging out his life day by day. To André Raffalovich he admitted that he was "paralysed with fear." The *Book of Fifty Drawings*—to be dedicated to Joseph Pennell—began to seem his last testament, and he worked carefully over a cover for the book, as well as over additions and corrections to the iconography Aymer Vallance had prepared for it—another symbol of finality. Nearly two months passed before he was even strong enough to leave his room—not that there was anything in the Bournemouth area worth leaving it for. The sun appeared only intermittently, and a tenacious mist clung to the sea coast, saturating everything with damp, including Beardsley's books and papers. Even the ink bled.

As much as he wanted to write, drawing left him no strength for it, and he abandoned thoughts of working in both media. In an agony of frustration and suffering he wrote bitterly to Raffalovich of his wretched state, then hoped that it was "pardonable" that he had done so. As his condition temporarily stabilized again at walking invalidism he chafed more about his enforced exile than about the weather or his recurrent hemorrhages. "Bournemouth is at the world's end," he complained to Smithers; and in another letter, "The distance between London and Bournemouth is driving me crazy. We shall have to establish a half way house on the line."

When he was able to sit up he not only worked on the *Book of Fifty Drawings* but on what he called "rather a pretty set of drawings for a foolish playlet of Ernest Dowson's, *The Pierrot of the Minute*," which Smithers was to publish in 1897. The frontispiece drawing, with its dotted tracery demanding great control of hand and pen, remains one of Beardsley's most famous works, yet it was accomplished, along with its accompanying headpiece, initial letter and tailpiece for the book while he was too ill to leave his room. Worried as he was about money, he still had protested his assignment to "Dowson's filthy little play"—filthy being used only as his criticism of the work's low literary qualities. Smithers had also got Beardsley to design the cover for a book of Dowson's poems, and the artist drew two curves, which—he explained to Vincent O'Sullivan, who visited him in Boscombe—represented the letter Y: "Why was this book ever written?"* Yet if he really despised both books as much as he affected to do, O'Sullivan thought, he would not have done the art work for them at all: "Whatever Smithers may have thought of the rest of his young team, Beardsley he sincerely admired and, I think, under his cynical skin, even loved. I find it hard to imagine him forcing Beardsley to do anything which Beardsley did not want to do."[1]

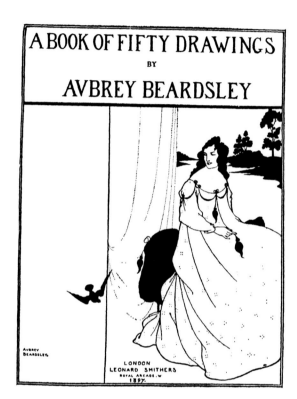

A series of illustrations he *was* eager to do was projected for Yeats's play *A Tower of Polished Black Stones* (afterwards revised and retitled *The Shadowy Waters*), and the poet even prepared a detailed synopsis for the six pictures Beardsley planned. One was even begun, a double-page picture Beardsley cheerily described to Smithers as "a young man on horseback following the young woman on horseback," with the man "vastly beau," the woman "vastly belle," and the artist all the while "drinking beaune." † But there the project ended, although with an apparently forced gaiety going beyond his French pun Beardsley declared that the pictures for Yeats "will be amusing." If they had been amusing they would have belied the somber nature of the play. But Beardsley was not up to completing any extended work, although in the desperate loneliness of Pier View he needed the sense of a future which planning ahead partly satisfied.[2]

* *The Verses* included Dowson's most famous line, "I have been faithful to thee, Cynara, in my fashion."

† A wine from Beaune in Burgundy.

Although he was grateful for visitors to counterbalance the dreary isolation of Bournemouth, Beardsley was not particularly happy to see O'Sullivan, for whose current tome, a collection of macabre short stories titled modestly *A Book of Bargains*, he had little admiration. Reluctantly he had designed the frontispiece for it, then cautioned Smithers, "I want you *particularly not* to put my name on the title page. . . ." He was then planning elaborate (and never-completed) designs for a translation of Laclos's *Les Liaisons Dangereuses* Smithers had commissioned the inevitable Dowson to do, but he was cool to this project as well, much as he admired the original. The translation, he told Smithers more diplomatically than was his wont when Dowson was concerned, "will want a good deal of touching up, at least it seems so to me." In the past, when Smithers had entertained Dowson, he had often brought along a sometimes reluctant Beardsley—an experience the artist had found difficult afterwards to shut out of his mind, Vincent O'Sullivan recalled, for

in sight of Dowson's appearance and way of life, Beardsley lost all patience and tolerance, of which he had not a large stock. He knew he had only a few years to live, but he loved life, was interested in lots of things, was not in the least morbid, and if he had been able, would have taken part in all the manifestations of life where were to be found brightness, music, comely women, beautiful dresses. The spectacle of a man slowly killing himself, not with radiance, still less with decorum, but in a mumped and sordid way, with no decoration in the process, but mean drinkshops, poisonous liquor, filth and malady, for all accompaniment to the march down under—that, when he saw it in Dowson, irritated Beardsley beyond control.

Design for front cover of *Salome* (1894)

To Beardsley it was inconsiderate of Smithers to bring a man like Dowson to fashionable restaurants and clubs, among "well-dressed people who paid a good sum of money for the pleasure of dining in clean and wholesome surroundings," for Dowson often looked—and perhaps smelled—"as if he had slept in the gutter and, what was more, had a very visible malady. . . ." On the rare occasions when Beardsley had permitted Smithers to take him off for an evening in Dowson's company he had found it difficult to hold his temper except through falling into prolonged silences, and then would answer only in fretful retorts. One night at Bullier's in Paris, the dance hall in the Latin Quarter frequented mostly by students, Dowson had pointed out Julien Leclerq, a young poet: "He looks as if he had just stepped out of one of your pictures."

"Then," said Beardsley, getting up to walk out, "the best thing he can do is to step in again."

When any of Dowson's writings were pressed on Beardsley, the image of the dissipated derelict came between him and the text. "But Dowson is a great poet," Smithers would protest.

"I don't care. No man is great enough to excuse behaviour like that."[3]

Unless he were in someone else's company, Ellen Beardsley now remained close to her son, for life was no longer possible for him unassisted, however he might intermittently joke about his fragility. From Pier View in mid-December Aubrey decided to walk with his mother to the Boscombe Winter Gardens. The modest climb was too much. "You might have tracked our path down, the bleeding was so profuse," Ellen Beardsley wrote to Robert Ross.[4] To Smithers Aubrey confided that he "expected to make an 'al fresco' croak of it," but "struggled péniblement to where I expected to find a drinking fountain. There *was* one there, & so the pretty creature drank."* A man and woman nearby offered to watch over him while Mrs. Beardsley went for help, which came in the form of a bath chair in which he was wheeled home. "There seems to be no end to the chapter of blood," he wrote his publisher dishearteningly.[5] It would be a grim winter.

Traveling in Dorset, one cold, cheerless afternoon, the Pennells, with Whistler in tow, stopped at a small inn at Poole, near Bournemouth. The landlady watched Whistler sip his hot whisky-and-water, convinced by his manner that he was an important personage, but unable to place him. "And who do you suppose I am?" he finally asked her. "I can't exactly say, sir," she declared, "but I should fancy you was from the 'Alls!" Nearby at Boscombe, they knew, was Beardsley, but Whistler shrank from the sight of suffering. The Pennells went without him. When the Pennells had Christmas dinner with Whistler, he kept the subject off Beardsley, lamenting instead "the sad British substitute for the good wine in his Rue du Bac cellar. . . ."[6]

To Elizabeth Pennell, Beardsley appeared "quite paralysed with fear" but would only admit that life in Boscombe was "ignominiously dull." How dull

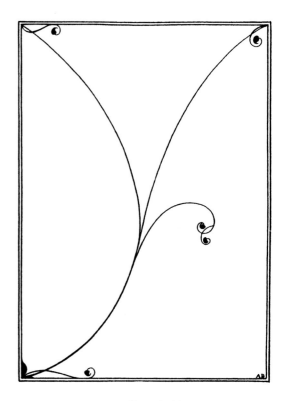

Design for front cover of *Verses* by Ernest Dowson (1896), perhaps meant to be a stylized *V*, perhaps meant to mean nothing at all

---

*Inevitably full of literary allusions, Beardsley was quoting Wordsworth:
    The dew was falling fast, the stars began to blink;
    I heard a voice: it said, "Drink, pretty creature, drink!"

Boscombe watering-place life was in the off-season Beardsley's publisher knew at first hand, for he had visited just before Christmas, and Beardsley wrote him afterwards, "Conversation at table is much the same; two more old women have arrived, one of them *owning* to 83."[7]

Punctuating the end-of-the-world aspect of life at Boscombe was the obituary-like nature of both public and private reaction to Beardsley that Christmas season. Toulouse-Lautrec wrote to ask for a recent book of Beardsley's pictures for an article he intended to write summing up the artist's work. And Edmund Gosse, to whom Beardsley had dedicated his edition of *The Rape of the Lock* that spring, wrote, just before New Year's Day:

How much beautiful work you have done in 1896! I quite marvel to think of your energy in wrestling so bravely with ill-health. I see no traces of it in your drawings, so characteristic of your genius. You have put your stamp on the age. If you were to do no more, your name could never be forgotten: you are a part of the art-history of the century.

I am afraid you have had a great deal of pain and *longeur*. You do not know how often my sympathy has gone out to you in silence. But I confidently hope for better things [for you] in 1897. . . .[8]

One Sunday afternoon that December Beardsley submitted to an interview—more of a self-interview—which, in the form it was later published in the *Idler*,[9] again struck an obituary-like note. "Although, according to medical opinion, he has not long to live," the interviewer began,

Mr. Aubrey Beardsley is yet but twenty-three years of age, and it is doubtful whether in such a short period of time as five years any artist has ever succeeded in obtaining so much public attention. Whether the public be a good, bad, or indifferent judge is a debatable matter, but certain it is that in no series of articles dealing with the black-and-white work of the past half-dozen years could Mr. Aubrey Beardsley's work be safely ignored. When an artist succeeds in an amazingly short space of time in catching the public eye, he is reckoned as having achieved something; and it may be safely assumed with regard to Mr. Beardsley's work that, even if it does not represent genius it at least represents something more than the spoiling of paper; while, if it be true that imitation is the sincerest form of flattery, a walk down the street and a glance at the hoardings, or a cursory inspection of the illustrated periodical press will serve to convince one that—however unfortunate it may seem to us—Mr. Beardsley has founded a school, and has been blessed for some time by that superlative form of flattery which unoriginal artists are ever ready to supply.

Mr. Aubrey Beardsley is, at present, staying—his mother with him—at a south of England seaside resort. He has the young man's natural preference for life in London or Paris; but the air of these cities is not considered by the faculty as being

The Billet-Doux, from *The Rape of the Lock* (1896)

The Baron's Prayer, from *The Rape of the Lock* (1896)

Apollo pursuing Daphne (ca. 1896),
an unfinished drawing first reproduced
in R. A. Walker's *Some Unknown
Drawings of Aubrey Beardsley* (1923)

conducive to the cure of haemorrhage of the lungs in an advanced stage, and in Mr. Beardsley's case medical orders are strict. Accordingly, it was on a cold and wet winter's afternoon that I presented myself at his house, and, after a tiring journey by train, I must admit that though an optimistic interviewer, I felt inclined to look on the bad side of everything. Questions of art did not appeal to me; and grotesque art, or decadent art, least of all. When, however, I found myself sitting and chatting with the invalid in his combined sitting- and work-room my spirits gradually rose, for although he looked haggard and pale, as victims of consumption generally do, I found in Mr. Beardsley an excellent talker, concise and to the point, interested in everything, listening eagerly, and, although his slight stoop and frail physique betrayed the invalid, entering into every point with considerable keenness.

Mr. Beardsley, when I saw him, was faultlessly dressed; and I suddenly remembered that a candid friend of his had told me that "Beardsley had two grand passions in life. One was for Wagner's music, and the other," which he thought surpassed in intensity his love for music, "was for fine raiment."

His charming study overlooks the sea. Before we commence chatting I glance at his library, with its rare copies of last century *livres à vignettes*, and various presentation copies of valuable books, and he points, with considerable pride, to his numerous pictures, engravings from Watteau, Lancret Pater, Prud'hon, and so on.

"Yes, this is my studio," Mr. Beardsley explains. "It is made up of a table and those two old Empire ormolu candlesticks. Without those two candlesticks I never work, and they go with me everywhere."

"But is it true that you always work by candlelight?"

"I suppose I ought to express some apology for its being the truth; but I admit that I can't work by daylight. I am happiest when the lamps of the town have been lit, and I am so used to working by artificial light that if I want to work in the daytime I have to pull the blind down and get my candles in order before I begin. . . ."

Considering Beardsley's frail health, the interview reflected more his general methods of work than any current spate of drawing, yet it described well Beardsley's life in exile, for—wherever he could—he carried with him his symbolic studio: the pair of candlesticks and favorite pieces of furniture, the rare books and favorite framed drawings.

"I don't really know," remarks Mr. Beardsley, in reply to another question, "whether I am a quick worker or not. I have got through as many as twenty chapter headings in an afternoon, but this particular sketch," showing me a drawing with a great deal of fine work in it, "took me nearly a fortnight to do."

"This interviewing is a wonderful and terrible business," my host exclaims suddenly, "and I suppose I ought to make something in the nature of a confession. Well, I think I am about equally fond of good books, good furniture, and good claret. By-the-way, I have got hold of a claret which you must sample, and I think you will act

Cover design for Vincent O'Sullivan's *The Houses of Sin*, published by Smithers in an edition of 400 copies (1897)

on my advice and lay down a few dozen of it while there is a chance of getting hold of it," Mr. Beardsley interjects with a childlike heedlessness of the fact that interviewers do not, as a rule, receive princely salaries from publishers, while very often their credit is none of the best. But Mr. Beardsley is not to be denied on these matters, and refuses to say anything more about himself until I have sufficiently admired a goodly collection of Chippendale furniture—two rare old settees in particular, which he assures me are almost priceless—while he rapidly goes over the titles and dates of some of his rare editions, making up a collection sufficient to cause a bibliophile's eyes to bulge with envy.

"My opinion on my own work?" my host exclaims, as I bring him back to the main point of our chat. "Well, I don't know in what sort of way you want me to answer a question so inane—I mean so comprehensive. Of course, I think it's marvellously good; but if you won't think me beating about the bush, I may claim it as a proud boast that, although I have had to earn my bread and cheese by my work"—("together with the Château Latour of 1865," I murmured)—"I have always done my sketches, as people would say, 'for the fun of the thing.' No one had prescribed the lines on which I should work, or set any sort of limits on what I should do. I have worked to amuse myself, and if it has amused the public as well, so much the better for me! Of course, I have one aim—the grotesque. If I am not grotesque I am nothing. Apart from the grotesque I suppose I may say that people like my decorative work, and that I may claim to have some command of line. I try to get as much as possible out of a single curve or straight line."

Then Mr. Beardsley goes on to tell me, amongst other things, how much he loves the big cities, and smilingly points out, that when a year ago his doctor ordered him to the Ardennes, he had obeyed his directions by going over to Brussels, following his stay there by a sojourn in Paris. "How can a man die better than by doing just what he wants to do most!" he adds with a laugh. "It is bad enough to be an invalid, but to be a slave to one's lungs and to be found wintering in some unearthly place and sniffing seabreezes or pine-breezes, with the mistaken idea that it will prolong one's existence, seems to me utter foolishness."

A well-known publisher having described Mr. Beardsley to me as "the most widely-read man" he had ever met, I questioned my host on the subject. "I am an omnivorous reader," he replies, modestly, "but I have no respect for classics as classics. My reading has been mainly confined to English, French, and Latin literature. I am very interested just now in the works of French Catholic divines, and have just received a copy of Bourdaloue's sermons from my publisher. I suppose my favourite authors are Balzac, Voltaire, and Beardsley. By the way," he continues, "the goody-goody taste of the British public is somewhat peculiar. The very work that they expect from a French artist or author will only excite indignation if it emanates from the pencil or pen of an Englishman."

"But in matters of taste we go to extremes," I suggest.

"Yes, you are right," my host replies. "We first of all reach the high-water mark of narrow-minded bigotry, and then follows the reaction. Rabid Puritanism comes in like a high wave and is immediately followed by a steady ebb-tide of brutal coarseness. This again is succeeded by the finicking censorship of the present day which I hope will be followed by a little more tolerance and breadth of opinion. . . ."

Adept at intolerance himself, Beardsley made sure that the interview did not come to an end without his slap at William Morris (unmentioned by name), and a curt dismissal of the greatest English painter of the nineteenth century, J. M. W. Turner:

"Do you know, I think that the attempts of modern artists to go back to the methods and formulae of the primitive workmen are as foolish as would be the attempts of a fully-matured man to go back to the dress, manner, and infantile conversation of his babyhood. To my mind," Mr. Beardsley remarks confidentially, "there is nothing so depressing as a Gothic cathedral. I hate to have the sun shut out by saints."

. . . To my intense horror, my host remarks of Turner that "he is only a rhetorician in paint. That is why Ruskin understood and liked him."

"I love decorative work," Mr. Beardsley tells me, as I glance at the hour indicated by a Louis Quatorze clock on the mantelpiece and determine to wind up my merciless interrogatories; "and wherever I have gone I have always brought away some little decorative scheme with me. In fact, I think you could always guess where I am working from the work in my sketches. But have you never noticed that it is the realism of one age which becomes the decorative work of the next?"

As the old year ended, with its hopelessly clear indications to Beardsley that the next would probably be his last, the subtle pressure of his friends Raffalovich and Gray began to take effect. He had told Symons earlier that he had always been fascinated by the spiritual life, and it was already a fact of nineties' life that literary and artistic "decadents" found in the texture of Catholic ritual and belief a sense of protective stability. Now emotionally vulnerable as well as desperate for the £100 a quarter that had been offered by Raffalovich, Beardsley, at least half-sincerely at first, began to take Roman Catholic instruction at Boscombe. Maintaining the pressure, Raffalovich and Gray consoled him with "spiritual" letters, visited Bournemouth regularly, and sent priests to proxy for them when they could not. (Gray was himself already inclining towards the priesthood, and was eventually ordained in 1901, after which he studied theology in Rome and Switzerland. It was said later "that during the 'nineties there had been so many scandals over so-called 'decadents' becoming converts to Catholicism that the Pope had decreed that John Gray, on receiving holy orders, must not remain in Eng-

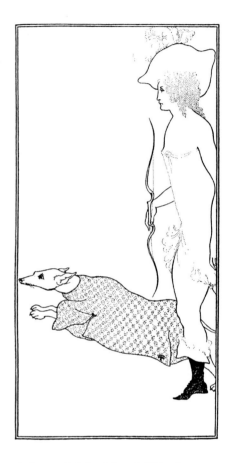

Atalanta in Calydon (also titled *Diane*), published in *The Idler* (March, 1897) and in Smithers's *A Book of Fifty Drawings* (1897), and demonstrating, like the drawing for *The Houses of Sin*, Beardsley's mastery of the disbalanced design

land!"[10] When Gray did return, it was to a diocese in Scotland, where Raffalovich, to be near him, also moved in 1905 and supplied the funds for the erection of St. Peter's Roman Catholic Church, Edinburgh, where Gray then served.)

Raffalovich even did literary research for Beardsley, looking up biographical details on Laclos in the *Biographie Universelle*; the fact that Beardsley continued to plan his edition of Laclos, whose epistolary *Liaisons* is one of the great erotic novels,* was only one of many evidences of his ambivalence towards Rome. "Blessings be upon you for Xmas & new year," he wrote wryly to Smithers several days before Christmas 1896, enclosing a card imprinted with a holy portrait and matching sentiments. "The enclosed lady is I believe a most effective medium through which to obtain all worldly & spiritual benefits. Quite the most potent virgin & martyr on the calendar." And as a new year's greeting—further evidence that his vulnerability to Rome had more to do with pounds than with passions—he told Smithers about a lady who had written to ask him for verses on a picture of his. He wired a "chaste thing"—as he put it—about his "St. Rose of Lima," an impious, masturbatory limerick in which

> She played dirty tricks
> With a large crucifix. . . .[10]

Hope, and an undefeated sense of humor, kept him going. He snatched at alternatives. London might again be possible, especially if Mabel were back. She had not been happy touring from New York to Toronto to Chicago, but had to seize theatrical work where it was offered. Aubrey thought that when she returned, they might "set up temporary house together. I feel that we shall be better friends than ever after such a long separation, and six months of this horrid place will have made me abjectly thankful for the smallest gaieties and pleasures in town."[11]

On New Year's Day 1897 there was a "grand specialist's consultation" at Pier View to determine whether Beardsley was able to return to London. He was counting on London to relieve his depression, and his doctors admitted that his will to live was sufficiently weak that Boscombe might do him in,

---

*His ambitious scheme was for initial letters to be drawn for each of the 170 letters in the fictional correspondence, for ten full-page illustrations and a frontispiece to each of the two planned volumes.

The Ascension of Saint Rose of Lima, illustration
to a passage in *Under the Hill*, published in
The Savoy, No. 2 (April, 1896)

while London was a lesser risk. Still, he was too "shaky [and] feverish" for the trip, and the medical consensus was to provide him with the worst of both worlds, moving him inland from the ocean—but only as far as Exeter Road in Bournemouth.

It snowed the week he moved, but that was not the worst of his horrors. For a week his departure was postponed day by day as his condition deteriorated, for no one wanted to have the carriage become a hearse. Finally he was carried downstairs and into a heated conveyance to outwit the "filthy frost." He arrived alive at his new quarters, where the address offered him an opportunity to clutch at a revealing bit of whimsy. "Muriel" was the name of the house as well as its address. "I suffer a little from the name of this house," he wrote; "I feel as shy of my address as a boy at school is of his Christian name when it is Ebenezer or Aubrey." To a London friend, Julian Sampson, he complained from Bournemouth with apparently equal whimsy, "Chastity has become almost a habit with me now, but . . . it will never become a taste."[12] Intellectually it had never been to Beardsley's taste.

A change of scene usually rallied him, and the move to Muriel repeated the pattern. But the mood faded quickly. Early in February he was confiding despondently to Smithers that he had "of course long lost anything in the nature of hopefulness. Whom the sods love etc. —" His life's work was over, he was sure; and he was surprised to remember suddenly that he had drawings for Dowson's play soon to be published: "It seemed so funny to me that there was still something more of mine to appear."

Once, in February, when he was briefly able to totter unaided, he cajoled his physicians—and his mother—into letting him go to a concert in Bournemouth. Beethoven's rarely performed Fourth Symphony was scheduled, a work Beardsley had never heard. A doctor accompanied him—"ready to feel my pulse, & help me in case of calamity," he wrote Raffalovich. To everyone's surprise, there was no calamity, and for Beardsley it was "a great treat after my long exile from music." Still, it marked no passage of the crisis, for there was no prospect that far-advanced pulmonary tuberculosis would heal itself. New and severe hemorrhages followed, and with them new and agonizing secondary ailments: Beardsley was sure that he would never see the city again. There was good reason. His physician's ministrations were only exacerbating his physical horrors. "I am only a poor shadow of the gay rococo thing I was," he would write in better moods, while in

Count Valmont, probably intended as design for cover or title page of a Smithers translation of *Les Liaisons Dangereuses* but first published in *The Savoy*, No. 8 (December, 1896)

worse ones despair was unleavened by wit. A medicine prescribed for him frighteningly blackened his bowel movements, and a "turpentine Bath" of dubious relevance to tuberculosis provoked a "magnificent rash" which served only to take his mind off his continuing hemorrhages.

"London will never see me again," he told Sampson, "for bacilli flourish rather too vigorously in its giddy atmosphere." "London I fear," he wrote his publisher, "will be too great a risk. You see I may not have many months now to live, & I must arrange my future for some definitely settled spot. God only knows where that will be. My doctor today speaks of Normandy and Brittany, he is frightened to let me go further." Ironically, the *Idler* for March had just then appeared, with the Beardsley interview that began in so lugubrious a fashion. For its subject, it would be like reading one's own obituary. Perhaps fortunately, by the time Beardsley sent for a copy in Bournemouth, they had all been sold out. Belatedly he did acquire a copy, determining on reading that he had "not long to live" that he would try "to make out twelve more months before I go away altogether."[13]

The sense of being among the unburied dead persisted, although he began to feel stronger, enjoying visits from Smithers as well as the inevitable Gray and Raffalovich ("the Russian prince"). "Dodo" (E. F.) Benson's newest novel, *The Babe, B. A.*, appeared with three "immortal" references to Beardsley in it. "There will be a statue yet," he joked to Smithers. The central character of *The Babe* —a satire on Cambridge—was palpably modeled upon the smooth-faced and well-to-do Herbert Charles Pollitt, who had bought some of Beardsley's work, but who was nevertheless to the irreverent artist "pretty Pollitt."* In the novel, the hero, a Trinity undergraduate, possesses "several of Mr. Aubrey Beardsley's illustrations from the Yellow Book, clustering round a large photograph of Botticelli's Primavera," while in his bookcase are several numbers of the magazine, "which the Babe declared bitterly had turned grey in a single night since [Beardsley] had ceased to draw for it."

Unable even to travel to London, he wearily answered a suggestion from Pollitt that he visit the United States with "America will never see me in this incarnation. I have been ill beyond expression, and nearly went away al-

Design for Beardsley's own bookplate, but which became the bookplate instead of his friend H. C. Pollitt

---

*Wilde during his post-prison exile once referred to Pollitt as "a gilt sunbeam masquerading in clothes," which suggests something about Wilde's interest if not Pollitt's sexuality.

together."[14] Debts oppressed him, and hints to Smithers resulted in no significant relief. "I am being pursued with a bill for 11/3. Christian martyrs not in it with me," he wrote; and two days later, "Now I have another bill—for 6d. Exciting work clearing off these debts of mine. Sir Walter Scott not in it with me."* His debts became more exciting in March, however, and Beardsley, unwilling to appeal for help to Raffalovich if he could avoid it, wrote urgently to Pollitt:

> I have been fussed lately beyond all words. Not this time mere pulmonary irritations, but assaults from the vulgar world without. Imagine me being served suddenly with a horrid writ for a bill which I have owed long enough to be forgotten by everyone concerned with it. Hence many tears, and the imminent levying of an execution upon my goods & chattels. Oh mon cher ami, if you could but lend me twenty sovereigns . . . I am in a deuce of a hole. You see my state of health (much improved of late, by the way) will not yet allow me to make an impromptu flitting. . . .

Two days later he wrote to Pollitt with relief, ". . . You are the great enchanter who has dispersed Bailiffs with a stroke of your pen. . . ."[15] To Smithers he announced, "I fear no longer for my shirts and my socks."

When March turned springlike, Beardsley showed signs of improvement, although he was still "a prisoner in bed" and confessed (to Raffalovich), "Oh how tired I am of hearing my lungs creak all day like a badly made pair of boots." Drawing, he told Raffalovich, now tired him because of the physical effort needed to bring a work to completion; thus he intended to work on "some small contes." He actually did begin one he called "The Celestial Lover":

> The Café Strélitz was almost empty.
>
> Upon a hot midday in July, Don Juan wandered into the Café Strélitz for his breakfast. I know not by what chance he had left the rest of the world to go that day to the Valdau races with[out] him. Whether in the search of some adventure. . . .
>
> The most fashionable of Restaurants was white with empty tables for the prix d'honneur was being run that afternoon at Valdau. Magnificent waiters sat about in magnificent unruffled expectation of the telegrams from the . . . .[16]

Don Juan, Sganarelle, and the Beggar, illustration to Moliere's *Don Juan*, published in *The Savoy*, No. 8 (December, 1896)

*In 1826, as a result of improvident borrowings, and the mismanagement of James Ballantyne, his business partner, Scott found himself involved in the bankruptcy of Ballantyne and of his publisher, Constable, and liable for £130,000. Afterwards he struggled heroically to pay his debts by his writing efforts, shortening his life and ironically thus paying off his creditors with sums realized by the posthumous sale of his copyrights.

His notes for his story went no further, although he had also begun an illustration for it. "'The Celestial Lover,'" he told Smithers cryptically, "is the person who occupies the unoccupied chair at the table in my picture, in the end he makes short work of an intruding & uncelestial *amant*, who pays far too much attention to the lady with the petit banc."[17]

When the March weather turned raw again, his condition matched the climate. "I grind my rotten teeth," he confessed with frustration. "March," he told Smithers, "is a fiendish month & must settle scores of people. May I not be one of them." With his hemorrhages unrelenting, and his religious instruction continuing, he had an unlikely suggestion for his publisher. "When you pray," he wrote, "Pray for me, at the top of your voice."

Working for Smithers until the last moment, Beardsley redrew with a still-disciplined hand an illustration the publisher had seen in an earlier form on a visit to Bournemouth, the "Lady and the déjeuner"—which the artist, as usual, thought "delicious." It was the drawing later reproduced as "The Lady at the Dressing Table," the fourth of six illustrations to Théophile Gautier's *Mademoiselle de Maupin.** Whatever his state of physical decay, he was still striking out in new—although eighteenth-century derived— artistic directions, the frontispiece for the set done in water-color and the five accompanying drawings in subtle tones achieved through India ink and wash. The last of the six, and perhaps the most famous, was still to be done—"The Lady and the Monkey." In the respites between coughing and gasping, the Smithers industry would go on.

In the first days of April Beardsley ended a letter to his publisher with "Je suis catholique & ever yours." His final medical examination in Bournemouth had resulted in urgent instructions for him to retreat to the South of France. It meant winding up his affairs in England, and hastening the

---

*It is easy to see why *Mademoiselle de Maupin* (1835) would have appealed to Beardsley. Called by Mario Praz "the apologia of lesbian love" and "the Bible of the Decadence," it preached the philosophy that nothing is truly beautiful unless it is also useless, for the useful expresses a need, "and the needs of man are ignoble and disgusting, like his poor weak nature. The most useful place in a house is the lavatory." Like Huysmans' Des Esseintes, in *A Rebours*, Gautier's hero d'Albert craves sensual satiation, and d'Albert even yearns to be a woman in order to fulfill that untasted aspect of his experience. In this he is less successful than the ambisextrous beauty with whom he falls in love, the lady of the title. Mademoiselle de Maupin eventually gives herself to d'Albert for a night, but only after enjoying his mistress as an appetizer.

conversion which had by then become inevitable. On 31 March, he made his first confession, and was received into the Church. He was not well enough to go to church, let alone go to Menton, and plans were made to bring the Sacrament to him before he was assisted to leave Bournemouth. Raffalovich delightedly took over all the travel and ritual arrangements, having achieved one of the great ambitions of his life; and Beardsley, his stoical gaiety gone, confided to him sentiments the "Russian prince" had long waited to hear. "I feel now," he wrote, ". . . like some one who has been standing waiting on the doorstep of a house upon a cold day, & who cannot make up his mind to knock for a long while. At last the door is thrown open & all the warmth of kind hospitality makes glad the frozen traveller."[18]

He seldom had such kind words for Rome, and seldom would again, except to Raffalovich; but the conversion was on the level of feeling rather than intellect. All through the few years of his career he had drawn and written what the Church could only have considered sacrilege or (at the least) blasphemy. When he had drawn an "Ascension of St. Rose of Lima" to accompany his facetious note on her in *Under the Hill*, Yeats read it mildly as a charming blasphemy because the saint's face expressed a love of a kind not usually associated with sanctity. Earlier, for *The Yellow Book* he had drawn another of his pictures which could only have troubled the faithful:

"The Mysterious Rose Garden" shows as background a rose-trellis; in front of this a tall male figure in lavish flowered draperies, carrying a slender rod with a lantern hanging from it, bends over and whispers behind his raised right hand to a slender nude girl. We do not need much knowledge of traditional iconography to read this drawing correctly. The male figure is a divine messenger, for he has Mercury's winged slippers (as well as the rod, whose top we cannot see). The rose hedge goes with the Virgin. The drawing then is a version of the Annunciation—the messenger's lantern may be a variant of Beardsley's familiar street lamp, a travesty of the angel's glory, or an allusion to the parable of the wise and foolish virgins. Beardsley's friends knew that *Annunciation* was the title he intended; he is said to have been surprised and annoyed the drawing might give offence.[19]

There was an additional irony in his skirting the edges of pornography and blasphemy in his art, for, as Roger Fry once pointed out, Beardsley had "all the stigmata of the religious artist—the love of pure decoration, the patient elaboration and enrichment of surface, the predilection for flat tones and precision of contour, the want of the sense of mass and relief, the ex-

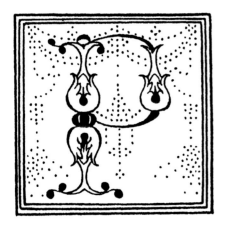

Initial letter *P* for Dowson's *The Pierrot of the Minute* (1897)

travagant richness of invention."[20] Ritual, religious and otherwise, had always pervaded his life as well as his art: as dandy, as artist-by-candlelight, as writer, as Catholic convert. Without ritual there were no rites for him to parody.

Polarized between Smithers and Raffalovich, Beardsley had tried to survive while surviving as an artist. To his religious mentor, who had told him about a Jesuit who managed to acquire a reputation as a painter, he frankly countered, "But what a stumbling block such pious men must find in the practice of their art." And, discussing the impact of conversion upon creativity, he observed, "Heine certainly cuts a poor figure beside Pascal. If Heine is the great warning, Pascal is the great example to all artists and thinkers. He understood that to become a Christian, the man of letters must sacrifice his gifts, just as Magdalen must sacrifice her beauty."[21]

Unquestionably, the conversion initiated with obvious skepticism (ten days afterwards he was pleased with himself that he had not been baptized in the process) had some real and lasting emotional impact, but the terminal consolations the adopted faith offered were still at variance with Beardsley's unsuppressed desire to survive and create. As Brian Reade has provocatively phrased it, "kindly talons . . . closed in upon him," while the internal conflicts which conversion could not stifle continued—conflicts "suggested by the piety of the letters he sent to Raffalovich and the cynicism of others he wrote to Leonard Smithers."[22]

To Smithers, Beardsley reported that their "tender tearful meeting & farewell" would soon take place in London. En route to France he did stop in London for the last time, after his departure from Bournemouth was delayed two days by a severe new hemorrhage. Gray met him with a carriage at Waterloo Station late in the afternoon of Wednesday 7 April, and took him to the Windsor Hotel in Victoria Street, for changing trains and continuing on the same day was beyond Beardsley's strength. The rooms, as well as everything else involved in the journey, were "en Prince," who also provided a stack of art books to keep his charge occupied while in the hotel. Gray and Raffalovich also supplied Father Bampton, who visited and expressed sorrow that Beardsley could only stay another day, for it would have taken longer than that to arrange for a private visit from Cardinal Vaughan to confirm him. Diplomatically, Beardsley offered regrets.

With his mother, and a doctor provided by Raffalovich, Beardsley

Frontispiece for *An Evil Motherhood*, by Walt Ruding, published by Elkin Matthews (1896), although it could easily have served as illustration for Shaw's *Mrs. Warren's Profession*, which Beardsley may have read

boarded the boat train to Dover (the doctor a wise precaution, as he was again sick on the train). Receding in the rectangle of his window was his final glimpse of London.

Headpiece for Dowson's *The Pierrot of the Minute* (1897)

11

Exile   *1897*

Crossing the Channel to France had the effect of crossing the River Styx in the reverse direction. "Here I am & as right as ninepence . . .," Beardsley wrote Pollitt. "A perfect resurrection. . . ." He had borne the crossing well, and in Paris found that for the first time in four months he could walk unaided. The Hôtel Voltaire had no elevator, but arrangements had been made to carry him up and down the stairs to his room.

Beardsley's room overlooked the Quai Voltaire, and provided a view down to the Louvre; next to the hotel—an easy walk for him in the cold Paris sunshine—was a bookshop. Although he could get no sitting-room adjoining his bedroom, his room at least furnished the effect of what he had wanted, for his bed was in an alcove which could be curtained off during the day, lessening the hospital look his quarters usually had. The cafés were cheerful and accessible, too. Because they were in the playhouse district, he could saturate himself in the theatre atmosphere he loved merely by being inside a *bistro* when it would fill with the playgoers who poured out of the theatres between the acts. "Such a blessed treat to be here again," he wrote, almost incredulously, to Smithers. "Imagine me letter writing in a café, with sun blinds drawn all round, & a theatre entr'acte bell ringing, & people clamouring for bocks. I shall drop into a Symonsy mood if I don't take care. . . ."[1]

Print shops were nearby, and Beardsley did more than browse, having discovered that it was possible to cash a Smithers check in Paris—a feat not always possible even in London. To Mabel, who had not yet returned to

THE
PIERROT
OF
THE
MINVTE.

Design for the front cover
of *The Pierrot of the Minute*

London, he wrote that he had two "delicious dix huitième engravings from the Goncourt sale. 'Toilette du Bal' 'Retour du Bal' engraved after Troy. Dreadfully depraved things."[2]

In Dieppe, Will Rothenstein had heard from Charles Conder that Beardsley was "very bad in Paris as he caught cold on arriving." It was rumor rather than fact. As soon as Rothenstein arrived in Paris to look up friends in the artist colony he went to see Aubrey at the Voltaire. Aware of his friend's conversion, he was disposed to accept it as Beardsley's making peace with his God; and in their reunion he found no reason to change his mind.

All artifice had gone; he was gentle and affectionate, and I realized now how much I cared for him. He had found peace, he said; but how rudderless he had been, how vain; and he spoke with regret, too, of many drawings he had done, and of his anxiety to efface the traces of a self that was now no more . . . I had done well to come; but for this, I had never known the Aubrey whom I now loved, and would have continued to love, had he been spared. Perhaps some would say the old Beardsley was the true Beardsley. True as he had been to a former self, the new Aubrey would have been true to a finer self.

Rothenstein had captured his friend in a reflective mood induced by conversion and new thoughts of mortality. It was a new Beardsley, although not the only Beardsley; and certainly not the Beardsley just come from the Parisian print shop. Impressed by the "new beauty . . . new gentleness . . .,"[3] Rothenstein opened his sketch-pad and drew, while his subject sat pensively at the window of his room and looked out on to the Quai Voltaire. Afterwards Rothenstein sent him an inscribed proof, which Beardsley told Smithers was "a very distinguished affair," one he liked "immensely."

Before the end of April Raffalovich and Gray had also been over to see him, and to introduce him not only to the inevitable priests, but also to the literary celebrities they knew in Paris, such as Alfred Vallette, editor of the *Mercure de France*, and the circle of writers and critics who frequented the regular Tuesday receptions the *Mercure* had established. Vallette quickly arranged for an article about Beardsley to appear in his magazine; his wife, the fecund novelist Rachilde, even more quickly took over the job of seeing to it that he met everyone of artistic consequence. At first Beardsley affected to be more amused than impressed, for handsome and energetic Madame Rachilde had a reputation for assuming guardian-angel roles, having already taken over—as much as was possible—the mad young genius Alfred Jarry, author of *Ubu Roi*. "Yesterday," Aubrey wrote Mabel, "we had a charming lunch party at Lapérouse. Rachilde & some long haired monsters of the Quartier [Latin] were with us. They all presented me with their books (which are quite unreadable). . . . It's quite wonderful the way I have recovered; everyone says I dont look a bit malade. . . ."[4]

Another long article on Beardsley appeared in April 1897, in the Parisian journal *L'Ermitage*, and he wrote its author, Henry D. Davray, a young but already influential translator, editor and critic, to acknowledge a copy. "I hardly know how to thank you sufficiently for so generous & sympathetic an article. It has given me the greatest pleasure." To Davray's invitation to visit he added, "I should be so glad to come up & see you one evening but I dare not yet venture out at night." Instead, he suggested lunch at his hotel at noon on the fourth of May, and added the news that his publisher would be dining with them.[5] Smithers was delayed, but Davray and Beardsley met for luncheon anyway. As a result both missed an event which otherwise would have been *de rigueur*.

The annual Charity Bazaar was a grandly fashionable occasion, in the cause of which the great ladies of Paris served as saleswomen and waitresses at the booths and counters. That year the bazaar was set up in a temporary wood-and-canvas structure near the Place des Vosges in the rue Juan Goujon, with a décor representing the narrow, twisting lanes of medieval Paris. Amid the banners and the bunting, the chief novelty and most popular attraction was a primitive motion-picture exhibition—so crude that it needed an ether-activated projector. A spark from the grinding projector exploded the ether, sending flames up the buntings and ribbons, and on to straw hats and taffeta capes. There was panic, and in thirty minutes one hundred and twenty-seven people were burned or trampled to death, few of them the young dandies and clubmen who had been so conspicuous before the fire. They had run like rats: only five of the dead were men.

Beardsley had not heard of the fire until later that afternoon, when he was visiting Madame Rachilde. Paris was quiet after the first consternation, mourning its injured and dead. Among the people he knew, he wrote Raffalovich, "Everybody has lost somebody." That night the cafés and theatres were empty. The following day Jacques Blanche canceled his luncheon date with Beardsley; Blanche had lost several friends in the fire.

Flosshilde, illustration intended for *The Comedy of the Rhinegold* but first published in *The Savoy,* No. 8 (December, 1896)

The catastrophe and its aftermath, remote though Beardsley had been from it, exhausted him. He was beginning to wear down physically after the early exhilaration of Paris had given way to new traces of blood on his handkerchiefs; and well-meaning friends had begun suggesting that Egypt—Luxor or Cairo—was a better place for him to protect what was left of his lungs than was Paris. How he would continue to live—whether in France or elsewhere—set him brooding too. Paris was expensive, even when the excellent Pauillac at Lapérouse was only two francs a bottle. In Egypt, he was told, one could live on ten shillings a day—if one could afford the journey. Miserable again, he wrote to Smithers, who had just sent him a check, "I live on thorns because I am more or less in the mortal funk of the pauper's life—& death. Would to God I had done even *one* piece of black and white work—transcendental or otherwise. Whilst my present filthy life goes on I shall do nothing."[6] The cry sounded a deathbed note, but Beardsley was suffering as much from frayed nerves as from pulmonary troubles, the sense of hopelessness which followed too much hope. Actually, Paris had been the scene of his belated acquaintance with the *Thousand and One Nights*—his current bedtime reading. Inspired by it, he drew for Smithers (who owned the rights to the Burton translation) "quite a sumptuous design"—his "Cover for Ali Baba," intended for an edition of *Ali Baba and the Forty Thieves.* It was as sumptuous as he had boasted, and portrayed an oily, obese minor Eastern potentate, his fingers and wrists encircled with rings and bracelets, his figure and clothing resplendent with jewels.

Before the end of May, Beardsley had accepted one of the less extreme suggestions from the great fund of gratuitous lay-medical advice proffered him in Paris, and gone with his mother to sample the country air at Saint Germain-en-Laye, a half-hour's rail journey from the city. A sour chord punctuated his departure—as he was making ready to leave his hotel, he was relieved by someone of a hundred-franc note. He had left Paris none too soon, yet arrived at Saint Germain before the "season" had opened, and was nearly the first guest at his hotel, the Pavilion Louis XIV. Again the new surroundings had their tonic effect, and he walked with apparent ease through the park and the terrace (from which one had a panoramic view of Paris) and breathed the atmosphere of his beloved eighteenth century. A Jesuit priest was staying in Saint Germain, one of the few early visitors. To

Opposite: Drawing for the front cover design of a never-produced Smithers publication of *The Forty Thieves,* first printed in his *A Second Book of Fifty Drawings* (1899)

make conversation, Beardsley displayed some of his newly acquired religious knowledge—he had been reading saints' lives sent him by Gray and Raffalovich together with a collection of collotypes and crucifixes meant to keep Beardsley's hotel rooms sufficiently spiritual. His lungs creaked as he talked, yet the French cleric, used to a country where conscription was a way of life, obtusely asked the gaunt, dying man whether he had completed his military service yet in England. "I felt quite ashamed to confess," Beardsley wrote Raffalovich, "that we were not expected ever to do anything at all for our country."[7]

Of all the medical cranks and quacks Beardsley suffered, perhaps the worst plied his grim trade in Saint Germain. He was Dr. Edouard Louvet Lamarre, who was, Beardsley told Smithers, "learned, famous, and décoré." The learned physician probed the patient's rack of ribs and offered what could only have been a minority opinion on the state of Beardsley's lungs. He could scarcely be called a consumptive at all, Lamarre told Beardsley. All he needed to cure his "weakness" was the special Lamarre treatment. To Raffalovich, Beardsley explained that the doctor had told him

that with care there is not the faintest doubt of my entire recovery. He raised his hands in horror when he was told that I had spent a year at Bournemouth. Nothing he exclaimed could have been much worse for my case, unless it had been the south of France.

Mountain air is apparently what I require. He spoke very hopefully of my chances here, & told me of a number [of] cures effected by Forest air. The terrace he will not allow me to approach. He has ordered me to get up every morning at 4 o'cl. & take two hours airing in the Bois, then to come home, rest & sleep; & continue the promenades at my pleasure during the day. I am never to be out after 5 o'clk. & am to retire to bed early in the evening. I begin the treatment tomorrow. Dr. Lamarre inspires the greatest confidence in me. . . .[8]

The beginning of the new treatment had to be postponed until the next day, for a few hours after Beardsley left the doctor's office he had a violent attack of bleeding from the lungs. Still, he began the drastic regimen, his doctor having advised him that his "grand attack of bleeding" did him worlds of good. Grasping at hope in whatever unlikely place it was proffered, he accepted the idea that he was quite curable, rising before cockcrow to walk in the chill damp of the woods. But after a week he found that he had had more than enough of the vigorous life. "I have found," he reported to his friends in London, "that I sleep better between four & six in the

MESSALINA.

Messalina returning from the bath,
intended as illustration to the *Sixth
Satire of Juvenal*, and based upon an
1894 *Yellow Book* drawing, but redrawn
in 1897 (first published in *A Second
Book* . . ., 1899)

morning than at any other time, so I have had to rearrange Doctor L's programme. I found that rumours of my early walks had reached my barber this morning, & all present—including M. Bertrand, congratulated me warmly on having staid in bed." Rebuffed, Dr. Lamarre agreed to substitute a less Spartan discipline. His patient's hotel room, he rationalized, was near enough to the Bois to permit all the healthful morning air Beardsley needed to seep in through an open window.

Weary and depressed, Beardsley could not lose himself in drawing or composition, and even found most of the books he had dragged with him to Saint Germain unpalatable. "I would forgive this abject sort of life," he wrote Smithers, "if I only made rapid progress towards recovery, but to go on month after month unable to turn my hand to anything is quite loathsome." Yet his reserves of wit were still available to be drawn upon in moments of direst depression. Queen Victoria, he knew, was scheduled to make a state procession through London late that June as part of the celebration of her Diamond Jubilee. "Why," he inquired of his scandalous publisher, "does not the Queen stop at the Royal Arcade on the 22nd to receive congratulations & a privately printed copy of something or other[?]"[9]

Mabel suggested Germany as a possible retreat for her brother in the autumn, and Aubrey, taking the idea of a German spa or mountain resort seriously, began (with his mother) taking German lessons three times a week. Although he found the language of his beloved Wagner aesthetically repugnant, and its grammar "inaccessible," he persisted, until another doctor (he had abandoned Lamarre), whom he made a special trip to Paris to see, advised him that the worst thing for his shattered lungs was the mountain air Dr. Lamarre had insisted was so beneficial. The sea coast of a hot country such as Egypt would be best, he suggested; but if there was no chance of this, Beardsley should at least remove himself to the relatively near Channel coast. It was more easily advised than accomplished, for he was feeble, but his sister—who had visited briefly after returning to England—insisted that they go. Early in July, Aubrey and his mother boarded a morning train going north to Dieppe.

No sooner had the pair placed their hand baggage on the train than the conductor shunted them off, insisting that only London-bound passengers could depart on the boat train. Minutes before the train was due to leave Paris they were still arguing their case, obstinately refusing to wait seven

Ali Baba in the wood,
from the abortive *Forty Thieves* (1897)

hours for the next Dieppe-bound train. Finally, the *chef de la gare* agreed to rescind the rules in their favor, but only if they left the major portion of their baggage behind, to be dispatched on the later train. On 12 July Beardsley checked in at the Hôtel Sandwich in the rue Halle au Blé.

Dieppe, as usual, was crowded with English summer visitors, including the perennial artist colony. But there was more than the usual excitement during the summer of 1897, for "Sebastian Melmoth" had arrived, and was staying more or less discreetly apart from the colony, at the Hôtel de la Plage in Berneval-sur-Mer, nine miles away. The "Melmoth" name* deceived no one. Late in May, just about everyone knew, Oscar Wilde had been released from Reading Prison into exile. Unable to remain either distant or discreet, he had already dismayed the proprietors of Dieppe cafés. When he would walk in, respectable tourists—and even members of the traditionally unconventional artists' and writers' colony—would walk out. Sometimes Oscar would bring his own crowd, mainly students and other young admirers who had entrained from Paris to see him; and the youths, who lived cheaply and noisily, were no less an embarrassment to the café proprietors who survived on the English tourist trade.

For a while the Channel weather was mild, and Beardsley would sit over a glass of milk at one of the quieter cafés, or at the Casino. He read, wrote letters, and—intermittently—began drawing again. He took short walks along the quay, sometimes with his mother, often with his friends, once— when with Conder and Blanche—seeing the hulking figure of Oscar Wilde approaching in the distance. Instinctively, the two Englishmen took hold of Beardsley's elbows and steered him into a side street. Beardsley never saw Wilde again.

Conder had previously snubbed Oscar in Dieppe, but Beardsley's reaction was the more shocking. His relationship to Wilde had always been uncomfortable, yet it had—at first—survived Wilde's imprisonment. Later, in Paris, reflecting on the incident with Vincent O'Sullivan, Wilde suddenly became indignant. "It was *lâche* of Aubrey," he said, his voice and hands trembling. "If it had been one of my own class I might perhaps have understood it. I don't know whether I respect most the people who see me or those who don't. But a boy like that, whom I made! No, it was too *lâche* of Aubrey."[10]

*"Sebastian O'Scar" was Aubrey's version of the alias.

Frontispiece to Vincent O'Sullivan's *A Book of Bargains*, intended to illustrate the short story "The Business of Madame Jahn" (1896), in which the lady is an apparition (hence the dotted and disembodied lower figure)

On the surface at least, Beardsley at the beginning had been friendly to Wilde in Dieppe. They had met on Saturday 24 July, Oscar wrote Robbie Ross, adding that "Aubrey . . . was looking very well, and in good spirits. I hope he is coming out here [to Berneval] tomorrow to dine. Smithers, the publisher, was with him: very intoxicated but amusing."[11] On 3 August Wilde wrote Reggie Turner that he had "made Aubrey buy a hat more silver than silver. He is quite wonderful in it." Had Beardsley, then, avoided Wilde? He may have, in the end, either to safeguard the remittances from Raffalovich, or to evade being dragged into any plans which Smithers and Wilde may have had for him—which again might have jeopardized the remittances. Wilde was nearly finished with his *Ballad of Reading Gaol*, which he wanted Smithers (the publisher of literary untouchables) to print and Beardsley to design. There was a long delay while Beardsley pondered the project, a period which apparently included listening to his mother's moral objections to Wilde, and Smithers's personal entreaties (he had just returned from yet another trip to Dieppe to work on the artist) to do, at the least, a frontispiece. Finally Smithers answered Wilde apologetically from London:

I yesterday sent you back your poem. I showed it to Aubrey and he seemed to be much struck by it. He promised at once to do a frontispiece for it—in a manner which immediately convinced me that he will never do it. He has got tired already of *Mlle de Maupin* and talks of *Casanova* instead. It seems hopeless to try and get any connected work out of him of any kind.

I left Conder on Tuesday night in a worse state than I have ever yet seen him. He got a small cheque on Tuesday morning and we devoted the whole of Tuesday to spending it. His bill at the [Hotel] Sandwich Bar is now colossal. . . .[12]

By not mentioning the obvious fact that Beardsley was too ill to take on new work, Smithers had made Beardsley's reluctance seem a snub—as in part it may have been. The only time the artist had added his work to a book of Wilde's—*Salome*—the result had been admittedly useful notoriety followed by nearly inextricable disaster. Aubrey—already little more than a thinly clad skeleton—had no need for further notoriety, and no time left to struggle out from under a new catastrophe. Yet Oscar sincerely wanted his collaboration, although even more than that he wanted his poem printed and offered for sale as quickly as possible. He wanted a great artistic success with the *Ballad*, but he needed ready money. "As regards Aubrey," he answered Smithers, "I wish you could get him to make a definite reply; there is no use his hedging. If he will do it, it will be a great thing, if not, why not try some of the *jeunes Belges.* . . .'' And Wilde suggested the name of a Belgian artist much influenced by the Pre-Raphaelite painters.[13] Afterwards, Beardsley may well have felt sufficiently uncomfortable about meeting Wilde to duck into a side street to avoid being confronted by him. Besides, prison had not dimmed Oscar's gift for glib talk, and in person he might have turned the decision his way.

Wilde's admiration for Beardsley's genius remained undiminished,[14] yet a few months later, when Smithers proposed a new magazine to replace the dead *Savoy,* the dying Beardsley's hostility to Wilde had only increased. "I will contribute cover & what you will, & also be Editor," he wrote, "that is if it is *quite agreed that Oscar Wilde contributes nothing to the magazine, anonymously, pseudonymously or otherwise.*"[15] It was his final imprecation upon the man whose fall had cost him the editorship of *The Yellow Book,* and so much else.*

The coolness which was setting in between Conder and Beardsley produced another uncomfortable situation in Dieppe. It mirrored the late-summer Channel weather, which had turned raw late in August, and was followed by a wet and cold September. Beardsley found the Sandwich uncomfortably exposed to the chill sea wind, and after his mother returned from a visit to relatives in Brighton she had him moved to more sheltered lodgings in the Hôtel des Étrangers in the rue d'Aguado. On the rare sunny mornings he would emerge from the white façade of his hotel to walk slowly along the waterfront to the Casino, where he would sit for hours with a book and a glass of the now-inevitable milk. And, often, there too would be Conder, jaunty after a night's dissipation. Each could sense in the other the awareness of the paradox in the pairing, and their mutual professional admiration and affectionate comradeship waned.

To the invalid . . . attired in tidy black, or sometimes discreetly debonair grey, the spectacle of the other, lounging in . . . check coat, riding breeches, boots and spurs . . . with the sea for background, seemed tasteless, and tastelessness he found the least forgivable of sins. And in the eyes of the adventurous lover, the invalid's literary obscenities were mere schoolboy nastiness, which not even their ingenuity and dazzling polish redeemed.

Vignette suggesting Oscar Wilde, from *Bon-Mots of Foote and Hook*

---

*Beardsley's hostility to John Lane, who actually fired him, had receded by then, and from Dieppe on 29 July 1897 he wrote Lane to offer "heartiest congratulations and best wishes" to him on his forthcoming marriage. (Ms. Oxford.)

Even their states of health were so mutually repellent that Beardsley once exclaimed impulsively to Conder, "I'm going to die, with all I might have done left undone, and you're going to live on and on—it's an intolerable thought." And, at luncheon with the faithful Jacques Blanche, Beardsley once drank accidentally from Conder's glass; and Conder, "with an involuntary gesture of revulsion that shocked the party, carefully wiped the rim."[16]

In mid-August, Beardsley quietly watched his twenty-fifth birthday pass. Cautiously, he kept to his routine through the first days of September, seeing few people except at the Casino or on the promenades, and retiring early, before cold breezes swept in. Although his health remained frail, it had at least remained stable; but rumors outside Dieppe persisted that he was dying; and from Pont Aven, on the rugged Brittany coast, one veteran of *The Savoy*, Ernest Dowson, set off to see him. "Your poet," novelist Gertrude Atherton heard from a friend, "left today to pay a farewell visit to Aubrey Beardsley, who is said to be dying. His only luggage was an extra sweater, which he carried under his arm. He may have had a toothbrush in his pocket, but I doubt it."[17] Arriving in Dieppe, too, were the Pennells, with Whistler and the then-popular painter Boldini in tow. As soon as they had checked into their hotel, Whistler unpacked his paint box and brushes, and set out for a shop front in a narrow street he knew. But then he remembered that he could hardly begin painting until he found another shop where he could buy a rosette of the Légion d'Honneur, for his had been mislaid, and he considered it wanting in respect to reappear without it in France. The shopkeeper to whom he explained his plight listened skeptically and then answered, "All right, *monsieur*, here is the rosette, but I have heard that story before." Whistler was torn between embarrassment and fury, but then broke down and laughed. More embarrassing, and no laughing matter, was the fact that the group, without at first knowing it, passed under Beardsley's hotel-room window, and Beardsley saw them go by without pause. Afterwards the Pennells discovered what they had done, and called on their old friend. Still dreading any contact with illness, Whistler refused to accompany them.[18] The rosette of the Légion d'Honneur remained uncontaminated.

When Beardsley's Paris doctor came to Dieppe early in September, he suggested that before autumn weather set in his patient return south to Paris. Encouragingly, he pointed to Beardsley's having survived without any

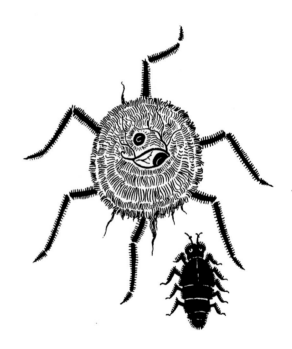

Grotesque from *Bon-Mots of Smith and Sheridan*

serious setback through an unfavorable summer, and suggested that with proper care in Paris there might even be some improvement. Beardsley had long expected the order. Late in July he had written John Lane that he had hoped to stay all summer but already found the sea air "terribly trying," and anticipated having to move to Paris "& then into winter quarters as soon as possible."[19] He had somehow delayed the inevitable into September.

"So sad to leave Dieppe," he wrote Smithers. The regret was unfeigned: he had grown to love the town in the two years since he had first gone there to plan *The Savoy* and complained that he was unable to work outside of London. On the night of 14 September he was back in Paris, hoping to set to work on his drawing again. His *A Book of Fifty Drawings* had been released in England, and it was a spur to renewed activity, although the critical reception had been one of respectful hostility. The collection, the *Athenaeum* complained in a representative condemnation, "comprises a number of Mr. Beardsley's drawings which have previously served as cuts in books and wall posters, and are remarkable for the pains the draughtsman has expended in the search for ugliness and deformities. . . ." Loyally, Max Beerbohm insisted otherwise, pointing to the adverse notices as a second stage in the critics' progress through

insult, doubt and servility. At present, these dull dogs are in the doubtful stage. They have taken their teeth out of Mr. Beardsley's calves, but they have not yet fastened them in his coat-tails. They soon will. For Mr. Beardsley's genius is so swift that . . . when most artists are still throwing about for ideals, and cursing their ineffectual fingers, he is —Aubrey Beardsley. . . .*

The Hôtel Foyot, in the rue Tournon, was his newest residence. He had a room facing the Luxembourg Gardens, but for the first few days could only gaze at the gardens from above, as colds and neuralgia kept him in; yet his doctor was full of optimistic predictions, leading him to write Raffalovich that he expected that he might not merely have "several years of life" before him, "but perhaps even a long one." The optimism survived as far as his work on the fourth of the *Mademoiselle de Maupin* drawings, by which time he realized that his generally weakening condition was irreversible, and that he could not survive a winter in the city. Money worries obsessed and de-

Cul-de-lampe illustrating Beardsley's "The Ballad of a Barber," *The Savoy*, No. 3 (July, 1896)

---

*Beerbohm's review —a brilliant summing-up of his friends's accomplishment as an artist—is reprinted in full as an Appendix to this book.

pressed Beardsley, too; and while his room was "littered with guide books to Menton, Cannes, Biarritz, etc . . ." he had no certainty that he could afford the Riviera cost of living, however modest his personal scale of comforts would be. Not only were checks from Smithers now rare, but he wondered whether his publisher, now drinking heavily and backsliding, had the resources to reproduce further work for him. In a letter to his sister Beardsley attempted some self-encouragement. "I have really got into a chronic state of worry—so thats nothing," he wrote her. "Really nothing but work amuses me at all. I am at work again & I hope on some very good drawings. I cant help feeling Smithers has honourable intentions, I dont think it would be to his advantage to ill treat me. Unless he is possessed by the devil. . . ."[20]

Now overwhelmed by gloom, his jaunty façade collapsed when he wrote to Smithers late in October, "I am utterly cast down and wretched. I have asked my sister to come & see you & have a talk with you. I must leave Paris. Heaven only knows how things are to be managed." But, once the first panic had subsided, he explained matters to his sister in a way which attempted to allay some of her worries about him:

It isn't money so much, by the way, that frets me, but being away from England & having to arrange everything by letter. It's the annoyance of sitting down to a drawing & not knowing if it will ever get published or paid for. I fancy that not only does Smithers find it almost impossible to pay one for work, but also that he cannot meet the expenses of block making printing & binding. Which means that my drawings will hang about hidden in his shop till Doomsday perhaps. I *have* got into a mess over it all. If I only dared offer my new drawings straight off to someone else. I dont even trust Smithers to bring out books nicely even if he does bring them out.[21]

To Smithers, Beardsley wrote a long, careful letter which explained his doubts about his publisher, and conveyed a suggested program of work within their mutual means:

I will try & collect my brains & write you a less silly reply than usual. I have been thinking a great deal about the Maupin & the reproduction of the drawings. I quite understand what a burden the expense of block making will be to you in such a large undertaking, & just now you are not over anxious to be burdened with expenses. Is not that so? Next year perhaps the difficulty will be less. In the meantime would it not be better for me to let you have a small series of line drawings for which you could find immediate use? You now have 4 wash drawings of mine, & a little one, for the Maupin 3 of which are eminently salable & in part payment of which you have

Vignette from *Bon-Mots of Smith and Sheridan*

already paid me £15. According to our contract for the Mdlle de Maupin about £15 more would be owing for this work.

I should suggest that any further payments from you should be for fresh drawings of mine for some smaller work that could appear complete in the immediate future, & which would mean far less outlay. Of course if you should sell the wash drawings you would let me have a share in the profits.

Among other things, the letter implied an end to Beardsley's long-abandoned dreams of completing his *Venus and Tannhäuser*, and provided an informal basis for continuing their relationship:

The question then is what work shall we choose? I am most anxious to produce something soon, so the book must be fairly short & not demand more than 5 or 6 pictures. Also it must be possibly popular. I have a very fine line drawing in hand & half way through for the legend of Tannhäuser. May I finish it & send it [to] you to look at[?] If you liked it I should propose that you get someone to translate the old ballad of Tannhäuser into English, or else print a translation of Wagner's libretto. Either would be attractive. The legend would be best.... It would make a very pretty little large picture book, & should sell.

To exert some pressure on his publisher, he confided that an American magazine, the *Century*, had approached him but knew that he did not have the strength to serve more than one master. "I would much rather work exclusively for you," he concluded to Smithers, "as long as you care to take my drawings & publish them."[22]

As soberly as he could, Smithers promised to fulfill his obligations as friend and publisher, and Beardsley solemnly promised to honor his artistic commitments by finishing the *Maupin* drawings and doing "some small and quite possible work." Smithers could guess one idea Beardsley had in mind by the request for his copy (Smithers was storing most of Aubrey's library) of the Mermaid Edition of Ben Jonson's *The Alchemist* and *Volpone*. "I ask for nothing better," he wrote, "than to send you chefs d'oeuvres, to have them published soon, printed well, & to toucher as often as can be a modest cheque or two."

With all his problems with Smithers, it was difficult for Beardsley to realize that his publisher was being true to him in his fashion, and in fact had been sending him checks—a number of them, it was true, drawn on insufficient funds—when Smithers was not even offering to pay anyone else. Smithers had created *The Savoy* and *The Savoy* had meant everything to Beardsley. It had restored and increased his reputation after Wilde and the *Yellow Book*

Cover design for *Ben Jonson His Volpone*, published by Smithers (1898)

débâcle had nearly ended it, and it had provided a public for his pictures and a chance to test his awakening literary talent.

In a review of *Le Mouvement Esthétique et Décadent en Angleterre*, Vincent O'Sullivan recalled an incident of Beardsley's last autumn in Paris which revealed to him what Smithers's *Savoy* had meant to its art editor. One evening Beardsley, frail and wan, was sitting in the restaurant of his hotel, the Foyot, with O'Sullivan. It was very quiet, and they were all alone but for a drowsy waiter

when the door opened and a little woman came in and sat down at a table facing us. She was dressed in the style of 1850. Out of a huge reticule she drew a snuff-box, took a pinch of snuff and set herself to examining a bunch of papers by the aid of a candle in a silver candlestick which she had told the waiter to set on the table. Beardsley could not keep his eyes away from her; he said she had come walking out of a book by Balzac. "Now if *The Savoy* were going," he added wistfully, "there would be a picture."

In November he was still in Paris because he was too weak to travel anywhere else. Blanche saw him at the Hôtel Foyot, and never forgot a wild drawing Beardsley made, taking a stick of charcoal and sketching on a pastel canvas a conductor, beating time, cutting off poppyheads, the heads of players in the orchestra. Deliriously, he announced in a loud voice that this was to be his masterpiece, and struck the canvas with his charcoal with such force that the easel tottered. Suddenly he sank back in his chair and blood poured from his mouth. "This field of poppies is the field you have sown," he cried out to no one in particular; "it is like an orchestra in which the players take no notice of their conductor. Am I raving?"[23]

The weather having turned cold and often foggy, Beardsley was finding it difficult to breathe. "If I don't take a decided turn for the better now," he wrote Raffalovich with foreboding just before he left Paris for the south, "I shall go down hill rather quickly." His doctor forbade them to take a night train, which delayed their departure from the Foyot yet another raw day; but Aubrey and his mother finally left for Marseilles on Friday morning, 19 November. As usual, the journey by rail nearly did Beardsley in: at Dijon he hemorrhaged, and was terrified, and arrived "shattered." Yet at Menton, their destination, the weather was bright and warm, and all was soon optimism again. Before he had left Paris he had promised himself that he would "settle down comfortably . . . & work famously in front of open windows & the

Grotesque from *Bon-Mots of Smith and Sheridan*

Mediterranean." When he settled in at the Hôtel Cosmopolitan, it was with a will to do more than survive. "*Such* sun," he wrote Smithers. "I must prosper."

Menton proved not to be the "loathsome" place Beardsley expected. It was picturesque and gay, and he could be outdoors without his breathing becoming labored and painful. People there at first were affable, and claimed—although none of them had seen him before—that he looked improved. A new location often rallied him, and he was full of plans "to develop a new style" for the edition of *Volpone* he promised himself he would do for Smithers. Warily, he asked his sister to keep an eye on the Royal Arcade, and to "put up prayers & candles" for the success of his new project. With new ambition, he sent Smithers a list of twenty-four proposed drawings for *Volpone*, and suggested the wording for an announcement in the *Athenaeum* of the forthcoming publication. It was important for him that the public be aware that he was still artistically alive.

Soon afterwards Beardsley had a photograph taken of himself in his bed-sitting room in the Cosmopolitan. As usual, it showed that he had moved a few symbolic objects with him to furnish the place in which he lived, objects which became fewer and fewer as he grew weary with moving. On the wall were reproductions of Mantegna prints, and on a bookcase a photograph of his benefactor Raffalovich—which made his comment to his sister, "I shouldnt like it to get round to André that I had been photoed," a strange one. On his bureau was a crucifix, and on either side of it his beloved ormolu candlesticks.

For two weeks he carried his text of *Volpone* with him "from dawn to down," assimilating ideas for his drawings, working on a preface to the volume and drawing the designs for a prospectus and a cover. It was the most intensive period of work he had managed in months, and he would keep going, he vowed to his publisher, as long as he was cheered by the evidence of returned proofs. Beardsley was concerned with the proofs not so much as evidences of good faith as of the fact that Smithers had the continuing means to have blocks made from the drawings. He was also disturbed by the ambitions Smithers had for a new periodical to be called *The Peacock*, although he agreed immediately (and conditionally) to be its editor. Referring to his *Volpone* project, he wrote Smithers,

I fear with all the work necessary to bringing out a magazine that you will give it [*Volpone*] second place in your plans. I beg of you not to allow it to be delayed. It will be an *important book* as you will see from the drawings I am soon sending you. It's [*sic*] marked departure as illustrative & decorative work from any other arty book published for many years *must create some attention*. I have definitely left behind me all my former methods . . . I want Volpone to appear well this side of June 1st 1898. You shall have all work done in time to make this possible. . . .

If only I can be spared from worry I shall send you good work, the best I have ever done & I know it will be worth your while to bring it out.[24]

Although Beardsley offered to draw "a resplendent peacock" for the proposed magazine's cover, and offered, too, his now-completed preface to *Volpone* as an article for the inaugural issue (if Wilde were barred from it), what he wanted most was to see *Volpone* published before his death. He looked on the work—which he still expected to complete—as the climax to his artistic achievement. Yet Smithers ambitiously pressed him for editorial plans for *The Peacock*, and Beardsley eventually sent a reply clearly based on his experiences with *The Yellow Book* and *The Savoy*. It was a considered judgment all the more pathetic in his inability ever to be able to carry any of it out.

As to the Peacock do you not think that the question of who *shall* write for it is far more important than the question of who shall *not* unless you have piles of stuff up your editorial sleeves. . . . The thing must be edited with a savage strictness, & very definite ideas about everything [must] get aired in it. Let us give birth to no more little backboneless babies. A little well-directed talent is in a periodical infinitely more effective than any amount of sporadic & desultory genius (especially when there is no genius to be got).

On the art side I suggest that it should attack *untiringly & unflinchingly* the Burne Jones & Morrisian medaeval [*sic*] business, & set up a wholesome 17th & 18th century standard of what picture making should be.

On the literary side, impressionistic criticism & poetry, & cheap short storyness should be gone for. I think the critical element should be paramount. Let verse be printed very sparingly. . . . Try to get together a staff. Oh for a Jeffreys or a Gifford, or anybody with something to say.

Have you settled definitely on calling it the Peacock?

As a title I rather fancy "Books & Pictures.". . .[25]

Turning on the old gods was to be expected. He had done it before. It is difficult to find a parallel in art for the pace of Beardsley's development from the *Morte* to *Lysistrata* and beyond. In four years, during which he was

Grotesque from *Bon-Mots of Smith and Sheridan*

often disabled and bedridden, he had absorbed the essentials, and discarded the paraphernalia, of Burne-Jones, Mantegna, Whistler, Morris, Lautrec, Japanese printmakers, Greek vase-painters and eighteenth-century French artists, and synthesized from these influences a series of distinctive styles, from a spiky, linear approach to form, to a mode characterized by simplicity and abstraction. And the elements of the earliest work show that the later was lurking within it all the time.

That Beardsley—and Smithers—still fancied the dying artist as a future editor is a reason for pause. One can understand the refusal of the victim to face his mortality, but one wonders whether Smithers's proposal was realistic (as far as he could conceive it), blindly selfish, or kindly consolation to the dying. Beardsley took it seriously. *

Christmas 1897 came to Menton, and Beardsley complained of the "horrid pseudo-Christmas gaiety spread over this un-French town." As a contrast to the dullness and silence it was both grotesque and depressing: for after having been greeted warmly as a new arrival he had been left alone, as people probably thought the wan young man with ever-present book and drawing-portfolio wanted to be. A rare party of visitors was Constance Wilde, Oscar's estranged wife, and their two sons, Cyril and Vyvyan. Beardsley "spoke with great affection of my father," Vyvyan recalled many years later. But to Smithers, Beardsley had just reiterated his refusal to be professionally associated with Wilde. Sympathy and art had to be rigidly separated.

Christmas Day itself was wet and cold, and Beardsley prudently remained in his room all day. Vincent O'Sullivan visited, suffering from a heavy cold, which is hardly what Beardsley, in his frail condition, needed to be exposed to. Once he was left alone he read in a volume of Racine his publisher had sent him. To Raffalovich he mentioned neither his visitors nor his reading, thanking him for his prayers and waxing optimistic about the healthful properties of Menton's climate. "An Abbé Luzzani who has a villa here," he added, "brought me the Blesséd Sacrament this Christmas & will do so regularly for me. . . ."[26] "I long for the new year," he wrote Smithers. "'98 will either see my death or chef d'oeuvres. Be it the latter."

Grotesque from *Bon-Mots of Smith and Sheridan*

---

*Since Smithers fancied *The Peacock* as a Beardsley vehicle, it was doomed never to appear.

Through December into early January, he worked on two versions of a preface to *Volpone* meant for the prospectus Smithers was to prepare. Brief as they were, they became his lone venture into a form he longed to explore, literary criticism. They provided some insight into Beardsley's artistic motives, for what he admired about Ben Jonson's grotesque comedy were qualities which, on the smaller scale of his medium, were characteristic of his own work.

The whole of Juvenal's satires are not more full of scorn and indignation than this one play, and the portraits which the Latin poet has given us of the letchers, dotards, pimps and parasites of Rome are not drawn with a more passionate virulence than the English dramatist has displayed in the portrayal of the Venetian magnifico, his creatures and his gulls. Like Le Misanthrope, Le Festin de Pierre, like L'Avare, Volpone might more fitly be styled a tragedy, for the pitiless unmasking of the fox at the conclusion of the play is terrible rather than sufficient. Volpone is a splendid sinner and compels our admiration by the fineness and very excess of his wickedness. We are scarcely shocked by his lust, so magnificent is the vehemence of his passion, and we marvel and are aghast rather than disgusted at his cunning and audacity . . . .

Volpone's capacity for pleasure is even greater than his capacity for crime, and Ben Jonson has added to these salient characteristics a third, which is equally dominant in the Italian—the passion for the theatre. Disguise, costume, and the [theatrical] attitude have an irresistible attraction for him, the blood of the mime is in his veins. To be effective, to be imposing, to play a part magnificently, are as much a joy to him as the consciousness of the most real qualities and powers; and how perfectly Volpone acts, how marvellously he improvises! He takes up a role with as much gusto and sureness as a finished comedian for whom the stage has not yet lost its glamour, and each new part gives him the huge pleasure of developing and accentuating some characteristic of his inexhaustibly rich nature, and of exercising his immensely fertile brain.

One of the most striking features in Elizabethan and Jacobean drama is the wonderful knowledge which our poets possess of the Italian nature, but it is generally upon the more gloomy side of that nature that they have dwelt with the greatest success . . . The qualities which Latin nations admire most are beauty, strength, cunning and versatility, and Volpone is Latin to the finger tips. He is as perfect an epitome of the Southern races as Hamlet is of the Northern. . . .[27]

"Please use them anyhow & just as you like," Beardsley wrote Smithers. "They are unconnected utterly."

Early in the new year, realizing that his time was getting short, he scaled down his ambitious intentions for *Volpone*, using as rationalization that he had intended all the drawings to be in pure line, but had made the ones he had already done—cover, frontispiece (prospectus) and initials—more elaborate. "I do not want to be longer than 12 weeks at the utmost on Volpone. . . ." When he wrote the letter on 1 January 1898 he had in fact less than twelve weeks to live.

Volpone Adoring His Treasure, frontispiece to *Ben Jonson His Volpone* (1898), Beardsley's last major drawing

12

Menton   *1898*

By the beginning of 1898 any optimism Beardsley had about his chances of recovery—or survival—could only have taken a grotesque turn, yet he tried every means of public, if not private, self-delusion. "There is a famous egyptologist here," he wrote Raffalovich, ". . . who looks like a corpse, has looked like one for fourteen years, who is much worse than I am, & yet lives on and does things. My spirits have gone up immensely since I have known him."[1] To Raffalovich he wrote of anything but his work, although his drawing remained his life. He did not want to mention his work in letters to "A," he told Mabel, for "He will only scold me. But of course I must if it is absolutely necessary. When I was in Paris I told him I drew a little." Since Raffalovich was providing him with an allowance partly on the grounds that he was a complete invalid—an accurate description of the patient but for his fierce will to draw—Beardsley kept worrying over the possibility that the allowance might be withdrawn, and how in such a circumstance he would then manage the day-to-day expenses of keeping his mother and himself in Menton. In hopes of reconciling his urge to draw with his urgent need of remittances from "A" he even toyed with the idea of editing a Catholic quarterly for Smithers. In his desperation the grotesque paradox of publisher and pietism escaped him. But by the end of January he had little reason to be concerned over any possible distress to the "Russian Prince." His tuberculosis was reaching out a little farther, and what he thought was only rheumatism had lamed the only effective part of his anatomy—his right arm.

Et in Arcadia Ego, the inscription from Vergil
and the drawing reproduced in *The Savoy*, No.
8 (December, 1896)

By the end of January, Beardsley was in bed much of the time, dozing and daydreaming between seizures of pain. Writing with great difficulty, he transformed one reverie afterwards into the beginnings of a poem he titled "The Ivory Piece" and identified (the word was then crossed out) as a "daydream":

> Carelessly coiffed, with sash half slipping down
> Cravat mis-tied, & tassels left to stream,
> I walked haphazard through the early town
> Teased with the memory of a charming dream.
>
> I recollected a great room. The day
> Half dead lit faintly on the walls the pale
> And sudden dyes that showed the formal play
> Of woven actors in some curious tale.
>
> In fabulous gardens, where romantic trees
> Perched on their branches without a name. . . .[2]

Incomplete and incoherent, it stopped, a wistful, morphine-inspired flight of the patient, dishevelled and in dressing-gown, from the prison of his last hotel room.

Beardsley could not, at the end of January, admit to himself that *Volpone*, incomplete, would be his last work. Instead he was briefly buoyed up by its first fruits. A proof of the cover had arrived from Smithers, and the artist could pronounce it "a great success." His line-and-wash drawings for *Mademoiselle de Maupin*, and cover, frontispiece and initial drawings for *Volpone*, with their echoes of seventeenth-century engravings, showed surprising strength and assurance in his art—masterworks from the unfailing hand of a dying man. But in his final drawings for *Volpone* he had to fall back on pencil. He knew how difficult the block-maker's task would be, but working in line-and-wash was beyond his reduced possibilities.

Possibly to improve his morale, Mabel wrote him that she was to contribute to an "Idler's Club" symposium (in the *Idler*) on the question, "Is Bohemianism Extinct?" and needed his expert advice. He strained for some helpful observations in his literarily allusive way:

Dearest Mabel

I feel dreadfully incapable & couldn't be sparkling to save my life. Does the Idler expect you to be funny?

Browning has some rather charming things about Gypsies & Bohemians at the beginning of Fifine at the Fair, so you might refer airily to his surmises as to the charms of a life freed from the ordinary social restraints.

The more society relaxes the less charm & point there is in Bohemianism.

Flourishes in France because society is so rigid. Will never quite die in England as it is the refuge & consolation of the unsuccessful. Young writers painters etc in England are in such a hurry to "épater" the bourgeois & to "arrive," to separate themselves from one another rather than to herd together, & to appear quite "sérieux."

They've come for the post

A³

When Lent came, he envied Mabel a "cosy little church" nearby, for he had been bedridden most of February. For the first time he cared little about his appearance, and when his Egyptologist friend came to his room to visit he found Beardsley with a stubble of a beard and "an extremely composite costume." On the twenty-second he was able to write to Pollitt that he had spent the previous three weeks in bed because of

a vile attack of congestion of the lungs. . . . It has left me an utter wreck and quite incapable of work. . . . Pray breathe not a word of this to *anyone*. I have told people in town that I have had a touch of rheumatism. However I shall set to work & get something written whilst I am in this state of exile from design. Such splendid things I had planned out too. The dear saints are my only comfort, & give me patience.⁴

The tug of the holy was becoming stronger as Beardsley weakened.*¹ He could do little more than read, and found consolation in saints' lives. Early in the month he had written Smithers to sell most of his books in order to raise ready cash, and specified among them "All french novels" as well as his beloved Racine (six volumes), Balzac (twenty volumes) and Voltaire (thirty volumes). Two weeks later he realized that among the books inadvertently consigned for sale was John Gray's *Spiritual Poems*. He appealed to Smithers not to sell it. "En revanche," he suggested piously, "get rid of the

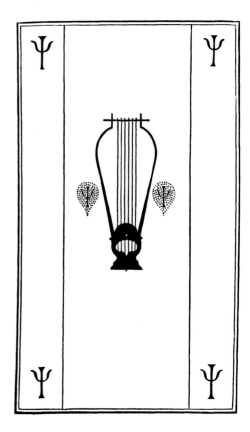

Cover design for *Sappho*,
published by John Lane (1895)

---

*¹Father John Gray afterwards reflected, "Aubrey Beardsley might, had he lived, have risen, whether through his art or otherwise, spiritually, to a height from which he could command the horizon he was created to scan. As it was, the long anguish, the increasing bodily helplessness, the extreme necessity in which someone else raises one's hand, turns one's head, showed the dying man things he had not seen before. He came face to face with the old riddle of life and death; the accustomed supports and resources of his being were removed; his soul thus denuded, discovered needs [which] unstable desires had hitherto obscured; he submitted . . . to the Catholic Church." (Introduction to *The Last Letters of Aubrey Beardsley*.)

3 vol Rabelais." Further making his peace, he reminded Smithers, "Dont by *any mischance*" sell his two-volume *Lives of the Saints*. He read a three-volume *Oeuvres de S. Térèse*, and urged it on his sister. And he still expected to struggle through the winter, and—perhaps when the Mediterranean sun became too hot—to retreat north to Lucerne.

Towards the end of February another proof of a *Volpone* drawing came in the mail. He approved of it happily, and admired, too, a proof of a preface Vincent O'Sullivan had written for the book. It meant that there was still something more of his to appear.

After the twenty-sixth he neither left his room nor dressed completely. To Robert U. Johnson, assistant editor of the *Century Magazine*, who had asked Beardsley to contribute the year before, Mrs. Beardsley afterwards wrote, "He used to be better some days & able to move about his room a little, & read a little, & then the haemorrhages would recur . . . one bad attack 10 days before his death. . . . The disease had touched an artery and it was tragic. . . . I wired for Mabel. . . ."[5] There was still one letter Beardsley wanted to write. No addressee's name appeared in the scrawl,[6] but he indicated that it was meant for Leonard Smithers:

Menton

Jesus is our Lord & Judge
Dear Friend
　　I implore you to destroy *all* copies of Lysistrata & bad drawings. Show this to Pollitt & conjure him to do same. By all that is holy—*all* obscene drawings.

Aubrey Beardsley

In my death agony

"He died as a saint," Mabel wrote Robert Ross.[7] "Nothing could be done to save him," Mrs. Beardsley wrote Johnson, ". . . his marvellous patience and courage amid very great suffering . . . touched all who were near him. . . . [Towards the end] morphia had frequently to be administered."[8] On 16 March 1898, at twenty-five years and seven months, he died. While his mother and sister had briefly left the room he had tried to grasp his favorite gold drawing pen. They found it by his bed, impaled in the floor.[9]

The Death of Pierrot, from *The Savoy*, No. 6
(October, 1896)

Years later, when Mabel Beardsley lay dying, bravely and in prolonged agony, she said to Yeats,* "I wonder who will introduce me in heaven. It should be my brother but then they might not appreciate the introduction. They might not have good taste."[10]

Solemn Requiem Mass was celebrated in the cathedral at Menton. Under a blue, cloudless sky Beardsley's wasted body was borne up a steep hill to a cemetery above the town, in sight of the sea. Nearly all the hotel guests followed in a modest procession: it was at the end of the season; and the resort had been emptying. Nevertheless, it was a magnificence denied his publisher less than a decade later.

Smithers had managed to publish the *Volpone* late in 1898, with cover design, frontispiece and five initial letters by Beardsley—all he had managed to draw. Soon he was reduced to selling forgeries of Beardsley's deathbed letter to him. He had been "the owner of Beardsley," but he was nothing without Beardsley. Before long, his career as a publisher would end in dissipation and bankruptcy. †

When Smithers died on 19 December 1907, there was no furniture in his house in the Fulham district of London aside from the bed in which he expired, and two empty hampers. In the days of *The Savoy* he had once (something Beardsley never knew) kept the faltering magazine going by raising money on his furniture. Clearly it had not been the last time for that expedient. The only ones at his funeral were the parish authorities. They buried the former owner of Beardsley in an unmarked grave in the Fulham Palace Road Cemetery.

Cover design for *The Souvenirs of Leonard,* published by Smithers (1897)

* In her honor Yeats wrote his verses "To a Lady Dying," and Ezra Pound, at the time a young newcomer to London, put his admiration of her into his *Pisan Cantos*:

> . . . The proud shall not lie by the proud
> amid dim green lighted with candles
> Mabel Beardsley's red head for a glory. . . .

† Beardsley, on the other hand, left an estate valued at £ 1015.17.10 on probate. Its net was 836.17.10.

13

The Long Shadow

Roger Fry once prophesied that Beardsley would be known as "the Fra Angelico of Satanism." While it is true that his subject matter was seldom innocent, his persistent influence has had little connection with the shock value of his art, for what scandalizes one age often leaves succeeding ages yawning. Beardsley himself had observed, "Have you never noticed that it is the realism of one age which becomes the decorative art of the next?" As he predicted, his chief effect would be a decorative rather than a diabolic one; but what he could not have anticipated was that the effect would be visible afterwards in literature and theatre as well as in pictorial art.

When in 1898 Serge Diaghilev and some of his friends founded a Russian review of the arts, *Mir Isskustva* (*The World of Art*), to "liberate" Russian art from stagnation, the journal began under heavy "decadent" influence. Diaghilev had met Wilde, Conder and French *fin de siècle* artists but was most impressed by Beardsley, whom he encountered in Dieppe in 1897; and after Beardsley's death the most important thing to Diaghilev about the new journal was that its inaugural number had to feature Beardsley drawings as well as an authoritative article to accompany them. He offered D. S. MacColl the commission:

> Being myself one of his greatest admirers and wishing to reproduce some of his works I should like them to be accompanied by an article acquainting our public with that refined and exquisite artist's meaning, with the causes of the apparition of his art and with a general aspect of his personality . . . I knew Beardsley at Dieppe and can well understand what a loss it is as an artist and as a man . . . the article to be . . . not above the quantity of 35,000 letters . . . price . . . 12 pounds. . . .[1]

The very drawing on the letterhead, signed *L. Bakst*, was a tribute to Beardsley's influence. Later, when Diaghilev became a ballet impresario, he had sets designed from Beardsley, some of them done by Bakst (Lev Rosenberg).

The Beardsley influence in writing could be seen within years of his death, but generally in insubstantial products of insubstantial authors. By 1899, such an un-Beardsleyish figure as Harley Granville Barker, writing his first play, *The Marrying of Ann Leete*,

chose to write a pastiche, exquisite and artificial; a composition not too distantly related in manner to . . . Aubrey Beardsley's illustrations to *The Rape of the Lock*, or the famous contents page of the first number of *The Savoy*. Indeed, Carnaby Leete bears the marks of close relationship to Beardsley's disdainful, masterly and unexpectedly mercurial John Bull, armed with a pen, elegantly cloaked and garlanded.[2]

The young D. H. Lawrence, writing his idealized and autobiographical first novel, *The White Peacock* (1911), planted in it a sensitive youth's discovery:

It happened, the next day after the funeral, I came upon reproductions of Aubrey Beardsley's "Atalanta," and of the tail-piece to "Salome," and others. I sat and looked and my soul leaped out upon the new thing. I was bewildered, wondering, grudging, fascinated. I looked a long time, but my mind, or my soul, would come to no state of coherence. I was fascinated and overcome, but yet full of stubbornness and resistance . . . I went straight to Emily, who was leaning back in her chair, and put the "Salome" before her.

"Look," said I, "look here!"

She looked; she was short-sighted, and peered close. I was impatient for her to speak. She turned slowly at last and looked at me, shrinking, with questioning.

"Well?" I said.

"Isn't it—fearful?" she replied, softly.

"No!—why is it?"

"It makes you feel—Why have you brought it?"

"I wanted you to see it."

Already I felt relieved, seeing that she too was caught in the spell. . . .

"Give it [to] me, will you?" George asked, putting out his hand for the book. I gave it [to] him, and he sat down to look at the drawings. . . .

"I want her more than anything.—And the more I look at these naked lines, the more I want her. It's a sort of fine sharp feeling, like these curved lines. I don't know what I'm saying—but do you think she'd have me? Has she seen these pictures?"

"No."

"If she did perhaps she'd want me—I mean she'd feel it clear and sharp coming through her."

"I'll show her and see."[3]

As a painter Lawrence—a watercolorist—was an amateur, and was able to summon nothing of the Beardsley ambience; yet he knew what he admired in art. "Think of the malice, the sheer malice of a Beardsley drawing," he wrote in 1922, "the wit and venom of the mockery." But *alter ego* figures like Paul Morel and Will Brangwen paint more like an idealized D. H. Lawrence.

Even James Joyce, before his sight dimmed, had been attracted by Beardsley's brooding images. The floating head that Stephen Daedalus conjures up could not have come from elsewhere than the *Salome* drawings, for Joyce's language in describing Cranly in *A Portrait of the Artist as a Young Man* (1916) suggests only Beardsley: "Why was it that when he thought of Cranly he could never raise before his mind the entire image of his body but only the image of his head and face? Even now against the grey curtain of the morning he saw it before him like the phantom of a dream, the face of a severed head or deathmask, crowned on the brows by its stiff black upright hair as by an iron crown. It was a priestlike face, priestlike in its pallor, in the widewinged nose, in the shadowings below the eyes and along the jaws, priestlike in the lips that were long and bloodless and faintly smiling." The two drawings the description evokes are among the most familiar in *Salome.*

Later, some of the fiction of Carl Van Vechten and all of the fiction of Ronald Firbank echoed the artificial graces of *Under the Hill*. Firbank's early (but posthumously published) *The Artificial Princess* seems the most derivative,[*1] although Firbank first brought a different manuscript to his publisher. When Grant Richards refused *Vainglory*, unhappy with its "schoolboy naughtiness" and lighthearted perversity, Firbank made a trip to the publisher's office to protest:

What was the matter with his story? Surely it was better than most stories. He had attempted to do something like Beardsley had done in the illustrations to *The Rape of the Lock*. Was I an admirer of Beardsley? Did I like Felicien Rops' work? So I knew Beardsley . . . ! Surely I would bring his child into the world. I could not be so unkind as to turn it from my door. It was my impression that the book was so slight and so unusual that there was little chance of it selling more than a few copies. Well, he would of course like it to sell, but it wouldn't matter so very much if it didn't. But it would matter to me. Yes, he supposed that it would. Supposing he paid for the cost of production, would that make any difference? He was not rich; really he was

---

[*1] Ronald Firbank, Edmund Wilson wrote in 1923, "has gone to school with Beardsley."

very poor; besides he loved clothes. And he waved himself a little more sinuously. How much would it cost to produce his book in a small edition, but beautifully—yes, beautifully?[4]

Brilliant, precious, baroque, Firbank survives as a minor modern classic, a satirist who wrote elegant improvisations on a theme by Beardsley, whether he titled them *Caprice* or *Concerning the Eccentricities of Cardinal Pirelli.*

Few poets found any genuine inspiration in Beardsley's art or his verses, although Roy Campbell, comparing him to the literature which followed, called him "a peal of morning dew";[5] and Spanish poet Rubén Darío, in "Dream," wrote:

> Like an intractable sylph,
> Aubrey Beardsley is gliding away.
> With charcoal, snow and ashes
> He gives flesh and a soul to reverie.[*2]

Unpredictably, the thin Beardsley shadow fell also across the work of William Faulkner. In 1920, while a student at the University of Mississippi, he wrote and "published" (elaborately writing out and illustrating half a dozen copies for his friends) an artificial one-act play, *Marionettes*, in which a Pierrot seduces the heroine. In his "edition" Faulkner combined text with related illustrations, elaborately stylizing language, action and drawings. The stage directions recall the early Beardsley:

> The sky is a thin transparent blue, a very light blue merging into white with stars in regular order, and a full moon. At the back centre is a marble colonnade, small in distance, against a regular black band of trees; on either side of it is the slim graceful silhouette of a single poplar tree. Both wings are closed by sections of wall covered with roses, motionless on the left wall is a peacock silhouetted against the moon. . . .[6]

The facing illustration partly reflected the stage directions, and was "very much in the Beardsley manner, and it seems likely that one source of Faulkner's inspiration, both for the stylization and vague, *fin de siècle* sensuality of the play itself and for the manner of its 'publication,' may have been the

[*2]"Dream," in *El canto errante* (1907), trans. Gerald Moser.

> Aubrey Beardsley se desliza
> como un silfo zahareno.
> Con carbon, nieve y ceniza
> da carne y alma al ensueno.

edition of Wilde's *Salome*; with illustrations by Beardsley, which was in his library at the time of his death."[7]

For some reason the memory of Beardsley remained with Faulkner, part, perhaps, of the self-conscious aestheticism he adopted so early in his career and never completely discarded. When Margaret Powers makes her entrance in *Soldier's Pay* (1926), Faulkner writes of her, "Had Gilligan and Lowe ever seen an Aubrey Beardsley, they would have known that Beardsley would have sickened for her: he had drawn her so often dressed in peacock hues, white and slim and depraved among meretricious trees and impossible marble fountains"; while Januarius Jones in the novel seems to be a Beardsleyan satyr. In *Light in August* (1932), Joanna Burden's perversely erotic and grotesque postures are compared to Beardsley's females; and in *Absalom! Absalom!* (1936) Mr. Compson's effete disenchantment suggests *fin de siècle*, as much as Southern, decadence. The description of the octoroon's visit to Sutpen's grave in the novel makes two bows in Beardsley's direction:

. . . the magnolia-faced woman a little plumper now, a woman created of by and for darkness whom the artist Beardsley might have dressed, in a soft flowing gown designed not to infer bereavement or widowhood but to dress some interlude of slumbrous and fatal insatiation, of passionate and inexorable hunger of the flesh, walking beneath a lace parasol and followed by a bright gigantic negress carrying a silk cushion and leading by the hand the little boy whom Beardsley might not only have dressed but drawn . . . .

In one sense the Beardsley manner was inimitable, for probably no one else had his control of hand and pen. His hair-line technique exhausted the possibilities of the then new (and cheap) line-block method of reproduction. (Lineblock allowed no intermediate tones between black and white, but Beardsley's fine line could provide the illusion of any intermediate tone he wanted.) Often he left much of the surface virtually untouched, boldly, yet sensitively, striking in a line or a curve, and creating dramatic effects with masses of black and white. It was an approach to line and form which stripped away nonessentials and sometimes came perilously close to having nothing on the page—a technique satirically exaggerated in *The Green Carnation*:

"I will stay at home and read the last number of *The Yellow Disaster*. I want to see Mr. Aubrey Beardsley's idea of the Archbishop of Canterbury. He has drawn him sitting in a wheelbarrow in the gardens of Lambeth Palace. . . ."

Cul-de-lampe from *The Pierrot of the Minute*

"I have seen it; it is very clever. There are only three lines in the entire picture, two for the wheelbarrow and one for the Archbishop."

"What exquisite simplicity!"*

Simplicity was a key to Beardsley's appeal to a new generation of artists, for as important as were the details in his drawings, often one of their most striking features was the eschewing of every conventionally expected detail which did not contribute to the effect desired. As Kenneth Clark explained it,

I doubt if any artist with a conventional academic training [then] could have allowed himself such drastic elimination. . . . The same disregard of actualities which allowed him to eliminate anything which he could not absorb into his system left him free from all anxieties about period or probability. The result is to liberate Beardsley's sense of design. . . . The complete exclusion of anything, any conventions which do not contribute to the essence of the design, is startling. No wonder the young artists of the nineties who felt the need for abstraction—the Kandinskys and the Klees— looked with astonishment . . . at the precision with which Beardsley has extracted these shapes.[8]

In his linear economy or in his more opulent effects Beardsley was difficult to imitate; yet his techniques had numerous followers. And since his subject-matter attracted artists at least as often as his technique, and was easier to approach, the Beardsley manner was rapidly well-established. His influence came to art earlier than it came to writing, and pervaded it longer. By the mid-nineties, the aesthetic climate of cities as far away as Chicago was being affected, humorist George Ade writing that young Chicago artists were already drawing "shell-eyed women with worms in their hair" in imitation of Beardsley, but most of them he thought would get over it: "others will have to be cared for. We had something of the same trouble when Oscar Wilde came over here."[9]

The shadow of Beardsley "was far-reaching: it spread from the art of book-illustration to literature and even to the style of living."[10] It extended from Will Bradley's illustrations for The Chap-Book, in Chicago,* and Alla Nazimova's silent film of Salome (1922), with sets and costumes by Natasha

---

*Adapted from the fuller version quoted in Chapter 4.

---

*Bradley, later the art director for Collier's Magazine, Metropolitan and the Century, was profoundly influenced by Beardsley middle-period work, and in turn exerted considerable influence over poster, book and magazine art in America.

Rambova after Beardsley, to Léon Bakst's sets for the *Ballet Russe* in St. Petersburg. According to Robert Schmutzler's massive history-anthology, *Art Nouveau,*

In Germany, Marcus Behmer, Franz von Bayros, and Alastair [Hans Voight] gratefully acknowledged Beardsley's stimulus. Without him, Thomas Theodor Heine's style would not be imaginable, any more than the styles of Otto Eckmann or Heinrich Vogeler-Worpswede, and it has been proved that even Paul Klee was initially influenced by Beardsley. In Glasgow, Mackintosh and the Macdonald sisters were known to be Beardsley's followers. It is less easy to obtain evidence of the deep impression he made in Vienna, though Fritz Wärndorfer whose famous music room was decorated by Mackintosh . . . assembled a great number of Beardsley's drawings and autographs and translated some of his letters into German. In the poems that served as the text for Arnold Schönberg's *Pierrot Lunaire*, in the manner it was performed (the reciting lady standing before a Japanese screen), but most of all in its very music, we hear an echo of the hysterical Beardsley atmosphere. In Russia, extensive Beardsley monographs were published, and as late as 1914 a play was staged in Moscow entirely in the Beardsley manner, the sets, the costumes, and even the masks of the actors being in Beardsley's black and white.

Apart from Lautrec, Paris at first showed little interest in Beardsley, whose drawings were nevertheless shown at the World's Fair of 1900. . . . Subsequently in the styles of the couturier Paul Poiret and the sophisticated designers around him [such as Georges Barbier], as well as in the *Gazette du Bon Ton* (1915-1926), . . . Beardsley found many Parisian followers.[11]

At the 1900 exhibition Whistler's great friend Count Robert de Montesquiou had discovered Beardsley, and wrote an article ecstatically describing his work as characterized by

geometric lines and curves which, seeming to have been traced with a compass, suddenly take the place of an arm or drapery, with a baffling sense of ornamentation and without one's knowing whether the artist is making a reform in decoration, slurring over a difficulty or trying to astonish the world."[12]

In return a young novelist who had just published *Claudine* and called herself Colette wrote Montesquiou, "I have an almost guilty passion for Beardsley—so many drawings of this slightly mad young man speak to what lies hidden in me."[13]

By his clearing out of "representational clutter" Beardsley made way for the drawings of Matisse and Picasso.[14] Some of his line-blocks had appeared in the Barcelona journal *Joventut*, which also published early illustrations by Picasso, and he was aware of Beardsley even before he left Barcelona for

Paris. Also attracted was Alfred Kubin, who produced in Germany a powerfully macabre drawing, "The Death of Beardsley," and followed the Beardsley tradition in his early masterpieces. The precise fantasy of Kubin's turn-of-the-century drawings, inspired by writers for whom he felt an affinity—Poe, de Nerval, Hoffmann, Flaubert, Strindberg, Kleist, Wedekind, Hofmannsthal and Kafka—preceded his frenetic later responses to Expressionism.

The seemingly Russian-influenced stage designs and book-illustration work of London-based Charles Ricketts owed so much to Beardsley that he often felt his dead predecessor was his most serious competitor; and little more than a decade later Noel Coward's musical play *Bitter Sweet*, with an ironic and then-shocking "Green Carnation" number inspired by *The Yellow Book*, was a long-run success in New York and London in 1929-30. How extensive the Beardsley impact was in England was indicated by a sampling of it in the great Victoria and Albert Museum exhibition of 1966, in the art of Laurence Housman (whose writings also reflected the Beardsley influence), Alan Odle, Eric Gill, Edward Gordon Craig, and Arthur Rackham; and in the exhibition's aftermath, poster art, fashion- and fabric-design, and even the much-imitated visual style of Heinz Edelmann's psychedelic extensions of Beardsley for the Beatles' film *Yellow Submarine* (1968) continued to register an impact not afterwards undermined by its surge into a temporary vogue.

American artists at mid-century were no less immune to Beardsley than their European counterparts, Will Barnet, for example, demonstrating that devotion in the clean "Japonisque" lines of his woodcuts, lithographs and serigraphs from the late 1940s into the 1970s. (His well-known serigraph *The White Stairway* is quintessential Beardsley, and would not have been out of place in *The Savoy*.)

Spreading his net wide, Lord Clark suggested that the Beardsley *Volpone* designed for Smithers had "a cover like a Jackson Pollock," and that it was "not his intimations of immorality which accounted for Beardsley's influence on the pioneers of modern art—on Munch, Klee, Kandinsky, Diaghilev, Mackintosh and Picasso. . . ." His conclusion was no less sweeping:

Even those who do not care for it . . . must recognize that Beardsley is a small, hard, irreducible fact in the history of the modern spirit. In Meier-Graefe's *Modern Art*, that pioneer work which, for the first time, saw the movement as a whole and in relation to the past, there is an ardent appreciation of Beardsley which contains this surprising sentence: "Not until we have learnt to understand Beardsley or Dostoyevsky or Manet as we understand Bismarck shall we reach the stage of culture." Slightly obscure: but he adds, apropos of Beardsley, a sentence which throws light on it. "Our utilitarianism was never rebuked in stronger or haughtier terms." No doubt that this great critic . . . regarded him as one of the essential men of genius of his time.

Genius: almost everyone who met Beardsley committed himself to this questionable word and made claims for his art which seem to us extravagant. But genius it was, that immediate access to some world outside our own, that perfectly clear conviction, which creates its own skill, that a thing must be thus and thus and not otherwise.[15]

"If I am not grotesque I am nothing," Beardsley once said of himself, and one critic, Brian Reade, sees him primarily as a master of irony in his grotesques and his mockery of earlier styles. Others, such as the Dutch critic Cornelis Veth, have seen the staying power of Beardsley's art in his decoration and form. "Though part of Aubrey Beardsley's designs," he has written, "are simply the most accomplished and beautiful compositions in flat and toneless black-and-white ever invented, yet it is not in these calligraphic qualities (which have been not unsuccessfully imitated since) that his personality shows itself most. With him, it is the form that matters. . . ."[16]

Through the years, the slender Beardsley shadow has lengthened over the arts, even though ever since his work first appeared it has been characterized as derivative and diseased, "literary" and licentious, mannered and morbid, precious and perverse. Whatever the plausibility of the allegations, his work possessed the only passion he knew, the icy passion of the artist for his medium.

Ex Cathedra V

Mr. Beardsley's Fifty Drawings*

by Max Beerbohm

I do not suppose that I have ever written one honest word in praise or blame of anyone. I am, personally, capable of the strongest reverence and of the strongest contempt, and, when I am talking, I can give a quite straightforward expression to these feelings. But, when I sit down to write, lo! my honesty does desert me, leaving me a prey to irony and poses. Would I extol, all the defects of my subject stand out most suddenly in a scheme of lurid colour, and I must needs proclaim them till they become, at length, the basis of an ironic eulogy. Would I denounce, my harsh humour soon vanishes in sweet irony. Thus has my own temperament ever baulked itself of right expression. I have loaded my blunderbuss with incense, and dropped grains of gunpowder into my swaying censer. Insomuch that, all being over, my victim lives, my god is frowning, and I am in a very false position.

I, therefore, having a real admiration for Mr. Beardsley's genius, am rather loth to write of it. There is no knowing what may not happen before I have finished. But, possibly, the fact that I am a personal friend of Mr. Beardsley

*Tomorrow, January 1897, pp. 28-35.

may suffice to guide my pen in reverence and in truth. For do not imagine that friendship can generally discount the value of praise given! If it be (it should be) the critic's aim to appreciate all that is good in the work that he has selected, and if that work be (it is) the expression of the artist's own temperament, then has that critic, who is also the personal friend, a high advantage over the other critics, though they be, for the rest, his equals. Stevenson has said, admirably, in one of his dedications, that all his books contained that which none but his own friends could love fully. A very pregnant plea for log-rolling! The finest criticism is not that which lingers over blemishes, and friendship is the very touchstone of genius, for this reason, that I can ignore the blemishes and find fuller appreciation of the beauties. It is always "they of his own country and of his own people" who gain the prophet his tardy hearing. But why am I thus paltering on the threshold of Mr. Beardsley's temple? I suppose that I cannot quite trust myself to behave seemly under the dome. Moreover, I feel that I, not an initiated art-critic, am rather presumptuous in venturing there. Were I even a book-reviewer for a newspaper, I should feel no diffidence at all. I remember that the late Mr. Hamerton having called Beardsley a "young genius," was severely taken to task by a person who writes an article on Sport for a weekly paper. "Genius! A man who draws a woman with a neck like a giraffe! Oh fie, Mr. Hamerton!" Indeed, I think that every great artist should follow Mr. Whistler's example and publish an anthology of his press-cuttings, for the public good. Mr. Beardsley's anthology would be splendid reading. But I should advise him to wait still for a short time, till his critics have passed through the whole process of insult, doubt and servility. At present, these dull dogs are in the doubtful stage. They have taken their teeth out of Mr. Beardsley's calves, but they have not yet fastened them in his coat-tails. They soon will.

For Mr. Beardsley's genius is so swift that his critics' process must be strangely congested. At a time when most artists are still throwing about for ideals, and cursing their ineffectual fingers, he is—Aubrey Beardsley. What strikes one first in his book of drawings* is his unique exuberance. I had seen most of his drawings, as they were done in swift succession, but not until I read Mr. Vallance's iconography printed at the end of the book, did I realize how many, many hundreds he had achieved in the span of three

*Fifty Drawings by Aubrey Beardsley (Smithers).

short years. A mere few examples of his originality and technical accomplishment would have sufficed to make him the marvel of London and of Paris; the terror whose name has passed into every English household, and is used for frightening naughty children; the pervasive influence which has filled all the United States, from Frisco to N'York, with a horde of abominable imitators. But Mr. Beardsley's work is not the careful, slender outcome of a merely exquisite mind. It is a thing of utterly colossal bulk. Three short years! When we know that this artist hardly drew a line before he was fourteen years of age, that he has never had one tittle of instruction, and that he has been always the prey of physical delicacy, which prostrates him only too often and makes activity of any kind impossible, what can we do but throw up our hands and wonder at the miracles which Nature is still working in this flat world? Mr. Beardsley forces us to readjust all our ordinary scale of judgement. He is most comparable, perhaps, with the painter-children of the Renaissance. Like them, *in varias artes distulit ingenium*. At the age of nine, he was already a musician of great skill. He has written delicate prose and verses. He has read vastly and is most learned in all the French and English literature of the eighteenth century. Yet, for all this, he has ever gadded restless through all the drawing-rooms where young lions are asked to roar. None of his friends has ever seen him working. Five or six new pictures would always be evident on a side-table, but no one ever knew how they came there. He had none of the artist's paraphernalia, none of the artist's habits. He was always a preposterous mystery.

This book can but deepen that mystery. Through it, for the first time, I may form some synthetic notion of Mr. Beardsley's work. Of course, in this section of fifty from so many drawings, I am bound to miss some that especially delighted me. Perhaps Mr. Beardsley will make a fuller selection hereafter. For the present, this one is generally satisfying. I do not complain that nothing has been printed from the early "Scrap-Book," which is in the enviable possession of Mr. Robert Ross. That volume, curious and delightful though it is, must be regarded as a precedent, rather than a presage, of Mr. Beardsley's sudden genius. But I am sorry that we have not the "Birthday of Madame Cigale," a pretty drawing done under the direct influence of Japanese art. And I am inclined to think that there are too many of the illustrations to the *Morte Darthur*. True, each is a proof of versatility, technical accomplishment, a rich fancy. But Mr. Beardsley would never have undertaken, of his own bent, to illustrate this book, and his drawings are obviously not the outcome of his own peculiar being. Their plenteous inclusion is a compliment to Sir Edward Burne-Jones, but it robs us of many examples of Mr. Beardsley's later work. In the drawings of Salome, the first influences had been assimilated. Jones and Japan were there, but blent and metamorphosed. It was not until *The Yellow Book* was thrown at the heads of an angry public, that Beardsleyism was seen, for the first time, absolute. Can one wonder at the sensation made by those drawings, with their simple ordering of black blots and cobweb lines, so flawless in their accomplishment, so very decorative, so very strange? All the criticasters were furious. The word "ugly," which ever serves them for new things, came spouting from all their pens. To the work of new painters, this word is applied in virtue of *technique*. Corot's fields, and Turner's sea, and Whistler's ladies were not ugly subjects, but it was long before the criticasters were shamed even into a pretence of admiring the beauty of these things, as newly rendered. Even if Mr. Beardsley had drawn the prettiest subjects, the criticasters would have been very angry, and, as a matter of fact, his subjects were then far from pretty, for the most part. The criticasters like, above all, to be reminded of something they are fond of, in a manner that is easy for them to understand. If one of Mr. Beardsley's extraordinary women could be materialized, no criticaster would propose to her. Thus was there a twofold barrier between the artist and their praise. They will never realize that, in art, subject is the least important of all things. Even if they were really to like the "Lady Archibald Campbell" and the "Lady Meux," you could hardly explain to them the beauty of that canvas which Mr. Whistler has covered with a most venomous caricature of a certain art-pattern. Mr. Beardsley's "Fat Woman" is beautiful in draughtsmanship, in decoration; artistically a beautiful creature, though one might not care to meet her. "She is not like life!" cries the criticaster. She was not meant to be. Utamaro's women were not meant to be. "She is hideous!" cries the criticaster, running away to contemplate a paving-stone on which black eyelashes curl over carmine cheeks.

But, perhaps, the favourite charge against Mr. Beardsley's work was the charge of indecency. Some professed to see actual indecency in the drawings, others declared it was rather the spirit of them that was indecent. I have no wish to enter into a discussion on this point. I would merely have suggested to the indignant that they should not look at the drawings, nor talk about them. If they supposed that they could cure Mr. Beardsley by newspaper diatribes, they were much mistaken. An artist may alter his method, but the impulse is always within himself. Critical anger tends, if anything, to make him more strenuous in his own method. If he be not quite indifferent, he probably retaliates by a wilful exaggeration of what offends. I think there is some evidence, in *The Savoy* especially, that Mr. Beardsley tried, now and again, in a spirit of sheer mischief, to scandalize the public. An artist should not do that.

But there is, in *The Savoy*, and in all the later drawings, evidence of another kind. Mr. Beardsley's bent is no longer the bent to pure fantasy and curious conventions. The "Catalogue Cover" shows an agreeable faun, in a glade by a river, reading to a lady. There, as elsewhere, we have a straight tendency to realism. The trees, the reflections on the surface of the water, are all imitated from nature. In the "Fruit Bearers," we find a curiously real effect of light thrown by candles upon night air. And, even in the "Atalanta in Calydon," where the huntress wears a Gainsborough hat, and her hound, with his coronetted coat seems to be fresh from the Dogs' Toilet Club in Bond Street, we find a rather truthful rendering of limbs. Sometimes, too, Mr. Beardsley's art is positively human, now. Than the mourner in "Ave atque Vale," Catullus could not have craved a more finely emotional picture for his elegy.

Now, these new elements will secure for the artist less tardy homage from the public. To me, they are interesting as steps in the process of a unique mind. But, of course, the important thing in these drawings is their decorative value. Some of them, I think, suffer from an excessive elaboration. As, in his Japanese days, Mr. Beardsley, unable to restrain his abundance, did sometimes overfill his pictures from the cornucopia of his fancy; so, now that he loves the things of the eighteenth century, do a few of his pictures suffer from a plethora of exquisite inventions. The "Toilet of Helen" cries aloud for some blank spaces that would (not merely distinguish the many figures, but) make the page generally effective in design. Nothing could be much more exquisite than two of the drawings for *The Rape of the Lock*, "The Baron's Prayer," and "The Battle of the Beaux and the Belles." In them, the artist's love of fashioning elaborate furniture and costume has not been allowed to spoil the design with too much beauty. They are amazing and delightful. But, to my mind, "The Coiffing" is the supreme outcome of Mr. Beardsley's genius. It is a drawing of pure outline mostly, built up obliquely across the page; utterly simple; utterly exquisite; a decoration for which I have no words. Only this artist could have conceived and executed so marvellously so marvellous a thing.

It seems improbable that Mr. Beardsley could ever top this achievement. But we know not to what new powers new phases may bring him. This book of his is valuable as a monument of all that he has done hitherto in his bewildering progress. It lets us formulate our wonder. It is a cue for our congratulations. To dedicate the collection "to Joseph Pennell," was a singularly gracious impulse. It was Mr. Pennell who, in an article called "A New Illustrator," first introduced Aubrey Beardsley to the public. But young men, who have climbed on to the roof of fame, do not usually gild the ladder.

Max Beerbohm

Notes

Aubrey Beardsley's letters and other writings have been quoted and/or described from manuscript sources when accessible and otherwise (where noted) from published sources. Ms. letters and documents are from collections at Princeton University, The University of Texas, Harvard University, the William Andrews Clark Memorial Library (U.C.L.A.), the Huntington Library, Yale University, the Bodleian Library (Oxford) and The Pennsylvania State University. Where I have utilized manuscript originals of published texts, my transcription will sometimes differ from the regularized or edited text.

Preface

1. The incident is described in the first person as presumably witnessed by Haldane MacFall, in *Aubrey Beardsley* (New York and London, 1928), p. xiii; however, it is possible that it was inspired less by life than by a full-length portrait by Walter Sickert, painted from memory after the event. The portrait is now in the Tate Gallery, London.

Chapter 1

1. From an interview with Mrs. Beardsley by R. A. Walker in December 1920, published in Walker's *A Beardsley Miscellany* (London, 1949), p. 79.
2. Interview, ibid., p. 79.
3. A. W. King, *An Aubrey Beardsley Lecture* (London, 1924), p. 26.
4. Interview, op. cit., p. 79.

5. 1 October [1878], in the Gallatin Collection, Princeton University Library. Additional references to Beardsley's school letters are from this source.

6. "Aubrey Beardsley," a memoir by Ellen and Mabel Beardsley, published in *Miscellany*, p. 75.

7. The letter, dated "1 February," has been attributed to 1879, when Beardsley was six (eight, erroneously, using these dates, in the catalogue of the Victoria and Albert Museum Exhibition, 1966, nos. 97 and 98). The mature language of the letter, however, suggests a much later date, perhaps 1883, when A. B. was doing other work after Kate Greenaway. Sir Edmund Gosse, who was a friend of Lady Henrietta's nephew (who inherited the drawings) as well as of A. B., wrote of the drawings that the Beardsley family was "in destitute circumstances" at the time they were produced.

8. The letter is in the Rosenwald Collection of the National Gallery of Art, Washington, D.C., bound in with fifteen A. B. drawings.

9. Interview, op. cit., p. 80.

10. C. B. Cochran, *Secrets of a Showman* (London, 1925), p. 4.

11. R. Thurston Hopkins, "Aubrey Beardsley's School Days," the *Bookman*, March 1927, p. 306.

12. King, op. cit., p. 26.

13. Reproduced in J. Lewis May, ed., *The Uncollected Work of Aubrey Beardsley*. (A. B. wrote *he's* mistakenly for *his* in the last line.)

14. Hopkins, op. cit., p. 306.

15. "The Valiant" continues:

> Then up he called his goodly crew
> And unto them thus spake:
> "A musket and a cutlass sharp
> Each must directly take.
>
> "For yonder see a pirate ship,
> Behold her flag so dark;
> See now the gloomy vessel
> Makes straight for this our bark."
>
> Scarce had the Captain spoke those words
> Than a shot o'er his head did fly
> From the deck of the pirate ship which now
> To the *Valiant* was hard by.
>
> Approaching near, twelve desperate men
> On the *Valiant's* deck did leap,
> But some there were less brave and strong
> Who to their ship did keep.
>
> And then a moment afterwards
> Did a bloody fray ensue,
> And as the time sped onward
> Fiercer the fray it grew.
>
> "Come on!" the *Valiant's* captain cried,
> "Come on, my comrades brave,

> And if we die we shall not sink
>   Inglorious 'neath the wave."
>
> When the morning came, and the men arose,
>   The pirates, where were they?
> The ship had sunk and all its crew;
>   Dead 'neath the sea they lay.

16. The letters to Miss Felton are printed as well as reproduced in Henry Maas, J. L. Duncan and W. G. Good, eds., *The Letters of Aubrey Beardsley* (London, 1971), pp. 14-15, with an estimated date of "*circa* 1887." The drawings, however, have the appearance of Beardsley's 1886 work.
17. Hopkins, op. cit., p. 307.
18. "The Artist of 'The Yellow Book.'" The *Bookman*, I (April 1895), p. 159.
19. Cochran, op. cit., p. 4.
20. *Programme of the Brighton Grammar School Annual Entertainment at The Dome*, Tuesday 20 December 1887, pp. 9-10.
21. *Nineteen Early Drawings by Aubrey Beardsley from the Collection of Harold Hartley*, with an introduction by Georges Derry [R. A. Walker] (London, 1919). According to this volume the drawings were c. 1886, before A. B.'s fourteenth birthday.

Chapter 2

1. "The Artist of 'The Yellow Book,'" p. 159.
2. Letter to King, postmarked 12 July 1891; in King, op. cit., p. 63.
3. Ibid.
4. Letter to Scotson-Clark, n.d. (probably late July or early August 1891). Princeton.
5. Quoted in an undated letter to Scotson-Clark, c. summer 1891.
6. Later American millionaire Charles Lang Freer bought the Peacock Room and had it shipped to the U.S. to augment his huge collection of Whistler's work. It was, with the rest of Freer's collections, offered to the government, and became the chief ornament of the Freer Gallery of Art when it opened in Washington, D.C. in 1923, four years after its donor's death.
7. Letter to Scotson-Clark reproduced in May, ed., *Uncollected Work*, as c. 1891, but actually dated from Charlwood Street in Beardsley's minute hand as 2 September 1891.
8. From a letter, Huysmans to Théodore Hannon, quoted in Robert Baldick, *J.-K. Huysmans* (Oxford, 1955), p. 83.
9. Arthur Symons's phrase.
10. Last page of letter to Scotson-Clark, 2 September 1891.
11. Letter to Scotson-Clark, 12 September 1891.
12. Hind, Introduction to *Uncollected Work*, p. xiv, quoting Vallance's reminiscences in the *Magazine of Art*, May 1898.

Chapter 3

1. Hind, quoting a letter to him from Vallance, ibid., p. xiv; Shaw, ms. note on flyleaf of a copy of the *Morte*, as quoted by Dan H. Laurence and Daniel Leary in *The Bulletin of the New York Public Library*, Spring, 1976.

2. Robert Ross, *Aubrey Beardsley* (London, 1909), pp. 16-17. (The Balzac authority alluded to was probably More Adey.)

3. Letter to King, 9 December [1892], in King, op. cit., p. 72.

4. Letter to Scotson-Clark, undated.

5. J. M. Dent, *The Memoirs of J. M. Dent* (London, 1928), pp. 67-9; Haldane MacFall, op. cit., pp. 26-7; C. Lewis Hind, op. cit., pp. xv-xvi.

6. Letter to King, 9 December [1892], in King, op. cit., pp. 73-4.

7. Brian Reade, *Aubrey Beardsley* (London, 1966), p. 5. (The drawing referred to is "How King Arthur Saw the Questing Beast.")

8. The date has been in doubt, as Hind in 1921 recalled the time as the late summer of 1892, and in 1929 erroneously thought it had been in January 1893—the date generally accepted afterwards, perhaps because it appeared in a more accessible source. A Beardsley letter to King dated 9 December [1892] makes reference to Hind's new magazine, *The Studio*, while there are such obvious memory lapses in the 1929 piece as recollections of seeing illustrations for *Salome* which had not yet been drawn. ("Bookman's Memories: Aubrey Beardsley," *Christian Science Monitor*, 17 May 1921, p. 3; *Uncollected Work* [1929], p. xvi.)

9. "Bookman's Memories," ibid.

10. D. S. MacColl, "Aubrey Beardsley," originally in *Le Monde Artiste*, March-April 1900, but reprinted in an English version in *Miscellany*, pp. 21-2.

11. Joseph Pennell, *Aubrey Beardsley and Other Men of the Nineties* (Philadelphia, 1924), pp. 21-3.

12. Elizabeth Pennell, *Nights* (Philadelphia, 1916), pp. 138-9.

13. Letter to Scotson-Clark, undated.

14. Vallance to Hind, in *Uncollected Work*, p. xiv; MacFall, op. cit., pp. 30-1.

15. Letter to Scotson-Clark, undated.

16. *Uncollected Work*, p. xvi.

17. Jacques Blanche painted him in this costume that year, the portrait acquired by the National Portrait Gallery in London in 1923.

18. Joseph Pennell, op. cit., pp. 28-9.

19. The stories about this incident in various volumes by the Pennells, including their *James McNeill Whistler*, differ from each other slightly in details, and in Whistler's quoted remarks. The account here is a composite of the several versions, with inconsistencies eliminated.

Chapter 4

1. Arnold Bennett, *Journals*, I (New York, 1933), 169. Entry for 26 April 1904.

2. Facsimile of postcard dated 20 April 1893, in King, op. cit., p. 75.

3. Rupert Hart-Davis, ed., *The Letters of Oscar Wilde* (London, 1962), p. 348n. (From the inscription dated "March '93," in the copy in the Sterling Library, University of London.)

4. MacFall, op. cit., p. 49.

5. Letter to William Rothenstein, August 1893, in Rothenstein's *Men and Memories* (London, 1931), p. 183.

6. Holbrook Jackson, Introduction to the Limited Editions Club edition of *Salome* (London, 1938), pp. 13-14.

7. Quoted from Osbert Sitwell's *Laughter in the Next Room* in Leslie Frewin, ed., *Parnassus near Piccadilly. The Café Royal Centenary Book* (London, 1965), p. 23.

8. Rothenstein, op. cit., p. 231.

9. Frank Harris, *Oscar Wilde* (New York, 1960), p. 87.

10. Hesketh Pearson, *Oscar Wilde* (New York, 1946), p. 205.

11. Alfred Douglas, *Oscar Wilde and Myself* (New York, 1914), p. 197.

12. Harris, op. cit., p. 87.

13. Chapter xii of Book XIX.

14. Rothenstein, op. cit., p. 134.

15. Beerbohm to Reggie Turner, 19 August 1893, in Rupert Hart-Davis, ed., *Letters to Reggie Turner* (London, 1964), pp. 52-3.

16. Letter dated 5 September [1893], from 114 Cambridge Street; Margery Ross, ed., *Robert Ross*, p. 26.

17. Letter to King, postmarked 27 September 1893; in King, op. cit., pp. 76-8.

18. Letter to Ross, undated, in *Robert Ross*, p. 28.

19. Letter to William Rothenstein, c. 1893, in op. cit., pp. 181-2.

20. Ibid., pp. 29-30.

21. From the proof of the first-state drawing, then in the possession of Frank Harris, as quoted in Aymer Vallance's "List of the Drawings of Aubrey Beardsley," an appendix to Robert Ross's *Aubrey Beardsley* (London, n.d.), p. 88. Another proof with the same inscription exists, inscribed to the artist Alfred Lambart (Princeton University Library).

22. MacFall, op. cit., p. 44.

23. Wilde to Lane, c. December 1893, in *Letters of Oscar Wilde*, p. 348.

24. Wilde to Mrs. Campbell, prob. February 1894, in ibid., p. 353.

25. Max Beerbohm in a letter to Holbrook Jackson, Rapallo, 30 October 1913.

26. Wilde to Douglas, c. 16 April 1894, in *Letters of Oscar Wilde*, p. 354.

27. Pearson, op. cit., p. 205.

28. *The Green Carnation* (London, 1895), p. 71 (in the 1949 reprint).

29. Osbert Sitwell, *Noble Essences* (New York, 1950), p. 154.

30. Ibid., p. 154.

31. Fr. Brocard Sewell, *Two Friends* (London, 1963), quoting Ada Leverson's preface to her *Letters to the Sphinx from Oscar Wilde*.

32. Letter to Mrs. Leverson, undated, from the autograph ms. in the Houghton Library, Harvard University.

33. Quoted from the autograph note by Bernard Shaw on the flyleaf of a copy of the Beardsley-illustrated *Morte d'Arthur*, in the Sotheby catalogue for the sale of 25 July 1949, p. 18.

Chapter 5

1. Ellen Beardsley to Robert Ross, 29 September [1893], in *Robert Ross*, pp. 27-8.

2. Quoted from Vallance's article in the *Magazine of Art in the Academy*, 30 April 1898, p. 475.

3. Julius Meier-Graefe, *Entwicklungsgeschichte der modernen Kunst* II (Stuttgart, 1904), 605 ff., as quoted in Robert Schmutzler, *Art Nouveau* (New York, 1962), p. 183.

4. Rothenstein, op. cit., pp. 134-5.

5. Letter to Ross, undated [1893], in *Robert Ross*, p. 30.

6. Royal Cortissoz, "Art," *New York Herald Tribune*, 31 January 1928.

7. R. A. Walker, *Some Unknown Drawings of Aubrey Beardsley* (London, 1923), No. 17.

8. MacFall, op. cit., p. 54.

9. "The Art of the Hoarding," *New Review*, XI (July 1894), 53-5.

10. Letter to Florence Farr, undated (c. early March 1894), Huntington Library.

11. Shaw to Miss Alma Murray, 30 March 1894; entry in Shaw's diary for 30 March 1894, in Dan H. Laurence, ed., *Bernard Shaw: Collected Letters 1874-1897* (New York, 1965), pp. 422, 420.

12. Rothenstein, op. cit., pp. 179-80.

13. David Cecil, *Max* (London, 1964), pp. 95-6.

14. Ibid., p. 96.

15. Beerbohm to Reggie Turner, 21 September 1893, in *Letters to Reggie*, p. 66.

16. From a letter, Max Beerbohm to Mrs. K. L. Mix, c. 1930, in Mix, *A Study in Yellow* (Lawrence, Kansas, and London, 1960), p. 67.

17. Beerbohm to Turner, 1 January 1894, in *Letters to Reggie*, p. 88. The letter is dated only "Monday," but internal evidence makes it certain that the body of the letter was written on New Year's Day 1894. The postscript about *The Yellow Book* could have been added as late as the next day, but there is no postmark evidence.

18. Arthur Waugh, *One Man's Road* (London, 1931), pp. 250-51.

19. Letter to Ross, c. early 1894 (but printed under a suggested date of c. December 1893), in *Robert Ross*, pp. 30-31. (Actually, *The Yellow Book* was not registered at Stationer's Hall until 4 April, much later than this letter could have been written. Beardsley may have been substituting the intention for the fact.)

20. Henry James, Preface to vol. xv of the New York edition of the *Works*, reprinted in *The Art of the Novel* (New York, 1934), pp. 217-18.

21. J. Lewis May, *The Path Through the Wood* (New York, 1931), p. 141.

22. Suggested by Percy Muir in *Minding My Own Business* (London, 1956), p. 4.

23. Undated letter to Lane, c. March 1894, in J. Lewis May, *John Lane and the Nineties* (London, 1936), pp. 48-9.

Chapter 6

1. Mix, op. cit., 81-3 (quoting primarily from Waugh, op. cit., pp. 254-5).

2. Beerbohm to Turner, 16 March 1894, in *Letters to Reggie*, p. 92. (Ada Reeve, a music-hall comedienne, was twenty in 1894, and had been a child star.)

3. Mix, op. cit., p. 89, quoting the *Daily Chronicle*, 17 April 1894; *Punch*, 4 May 1894; *Granta*, 28 April 1894.

4. Dated 27 April [1894] from the Bodley Head, Vigo Street.

5. Heading illustration for Chapter XLVII of the Tenth Book. (Evans was a devotee of Blake, and once published a book of reproductions of Blake's engravings.)

6. Initial letter for Chapter XI of the Eleventh Book.

7. Jackson, *The Eighteen Nineties* (New York, 1927), pp. 99-100.

8. *The Letters of Henry James*, ed. Percy Lubbock, I, 222.

9. *Punch*, 9 March 1895, p. 118.

10. Quoted in Doris Langley Moore, *E. Nesbit* (Philadelphia, 1966), p. 133.

11. Letter to Henry James, 30 April 1894. Harvard.

12. Gosse to A. E. Gallatin, 19 June 1902, Princeton. (Beardsley also began a series of illustrations for *Volpone*, as Gosse had suggested, but by then it may have been an independent idea.)

13. Thomas Beer, *The Mauve Decade* (New York, 1926), p. 247.

14. *Critic*, 18 August 1894, p. 108.

15. Letter to Henry James, 30 April 1894.

16. MacFall, op. cit., p. 70.

17. Gertrude Atherton, *Adventures of a Novelist* (New York, 1932), pp. 248-9.

18. *Idler*, XIII (1898), 544.

19. Penrhyn Stanlaws, "Some Personal Recollections of Aubrey Beardsley," *Bookbuyer*, XVII (October 1898), 213-14.

20. Ibid., p. 212.

21. Ellen Beardsley to Robert Ross, 14 November 1894, in *The Letters of Aubrey Beardsley*, ed. Henry Maas, J. L. Duncan and W. G. Good (London, 1971).

22. May, op. cit., p. 79. The story is attributed to 1896, which is impossible, and it could only have happened (if it happened at all), given the people involved and the events which followed the Christmas of 1894, that year.

23. Quoted in MacFall, op. cit., 59. ("The Second Coming of Arthur" was first published in the *London World*.)

24. Quoted from the *Boston Evening Transcript*, 16 February 1895, in Mix, op. cit., p. 139.

25. Letter to Palmer, dated "2-3." Huntington Library.

26. *Life and Letters of Joseph Pennell*, I, 294.

27. *Boston Evening Transcript*, quoted in Mix, op. cit., p. 141.

28. D. S. MacColl, in a letter to the *Week-End Review*, 28 February 1931.

29. W. B. Yeats, *Memoirs* (New York, 1972), p. 90.

30. Lane to "George Egerton," Boston, 21 April 1895, in Terence de Vere White, *A Leaf from the Yellow Book* (London, 1958), p. 38.

Chapter 7

1. W. B. Yeats, *Autobiography* [*The Trembling of the Veil*, 1922](New York, 1958), p. 220. Further references to Yeats are to this edition unless otherwise identified.

2. MacFall, op. cit., pp. 66-8.

3. May, op. cit., p. 49.

4. Beardsley to André Raffalovich, c. May 1895. Oxford.

5. Edgar Jepson, *Memories of a Victorian* (London, 1933), pp. 282, 285.

6. Beardsley to Smithers, postmarked 22 December 1896. Huntington Library.

7. Beardsley to Smithers, c. March 1896, and letter XVII in *Letters to Leonard* Smithers (London, 1937), ed. R. A. Walker. Those letters not cited from ms. are from this edition, which

is generally accurate except for the censoring of statements unintelligible without Beardsley's obscenities.

8. Letter XI in *Letters to Leonard Smithers.*

9. The twin theses of Malcolm Easton's *Aubrey and the Dying Lady: A Beardsley Riddle* (London, 1972). Incest is also suggested by Brian Reade in his *Aubrey Beardsley* (London, 1967), citing confidential oral sources.

10. "Beardsley communes with Monk," in "The Times Diary," *The Times*, London, 20 September 1972.

11. Yeats, *Autobiography*, pp. 222-3.

12. E. T. Raymond, *Portraits of the Nineties* (London, 1921), p. 197.

13. *Letters of Oscar Wilde*, pp. 630-31.

14. "A European Critic," anon. review of the German edition of Beardsley's letters to Smithers, the *Literary Review*, New York, 5 March 1921, p. 5.

15. Beardsley to Mrs. Savile Clarke, "Tuesday" [c. July 1895]. Princeton.

16. References to Symons on Beardsley, unless otherwise noted, are to Symons's *Aubrey Beardsley* (London, 1898), the book form of Symons's obituary essay in the *Fortnightly Review* that year, with an additional preface.

17. Joseph Hone, *W. B. Yeats* (London, 1941), p. 121.

18. From a Beardsley holograph in the Rothenstein Papers, Harvard.

19. Rothenstein, op. cit., pp. 185-6. "The Three Musicians" was apparently begun that summer in London, but according to Arthur Symons's account was completed in Dieppe.

20. Jacques-Émile Blanche, *Portraits of a Lifetime* (New York, 1938), pp. 91-2.

21. Rothenstein, op. cit., p. 249.

22. John Rothenstein, *The Life and Death of Conder* (London, 1938), pp. 120-21.

23. Rothenstein, *Men and Memories*, p. 245.

24. Blanche, op. cit., pp. 92-5.

25. Rothenstein, *Men and Memories*, pp. 244-5, 245-6.

26. Blanche, op. cit., p. 96.

27. Jepson, op. cit., pp. 286-7; Grant Richards (quoting a letter to him from Shaw), *Author Hunting*, pp. 33-4n. (The accounts vary slightly but this description blends the compatible particulars. A copy of the belatedly suppressed prospectus is in the Rare Book Room of the Pattee Library, at the Pennsylvania State University.)

28. Shaw, ms. note on flyleaf of a copy of *The Morte*, as quoted by Dan H. Laurence and Daniel Leary in *The Bulletin of The New York Public Library*, Spring, 1976.

Chapter 8

1. Max Beerbohm, "First Meetings with W. B. Yeats," *Mainly on the Air* (New York, 1958), pp. 107-9. (The essay, written in 1914 and broadcast over the BBC in 1954, suggested Smithers's dinner as Yeats's first meeting with Beardsley, but this is unlikely, considering Yeats's autobiographical statements, and his having lived for a time during the pre-*Savoy* period in rooms with Symons.

2. Yeats, *Autobiography*, pp. 220-21.

3. Since neither Yeats nor Beerbohm supplied dates, it is possible that each referred to a different supper party; but it is unlikely that Smithers hosted two such events, and sufficient

data in the two accounts overlap to suggest that it was the same occasion, which—after all—was a two-part affair, from Yeats's description, a fact which helps account for seeming inconsistencies. Given the state of Beardsley's health, few later dates would have been possible, for his days in London were near an end.

4. Stephen Marcus, *The Other Victorians: A Study of Sexuality and Pornography in Mid-Victorian England* (New York, 1966), pp. 271-2.

5. "The Monstrous Orchid," *Time*, 27 May 1966, p. 72.

6. Marcus, op. cit., pp. 273-4.

7. Haldane MacFall's holograph note on the typescript of the reader's report submitted to the publisher of his biography of Beardsley. Beinecke Library, Yale University.

8. Annette Lavers, "Aubrey Beardsley, Man of Letters," in *Romantic Mythologies*, ed. Ian Fletcher (London, 1967), p. 256.

9. According to Mario Praz, "Very likely Beardsley read Poliphilus in Claudius Popelin's French version, *Le Songe de Poliphile*, Paris, 1883, vol. i, p. 141." (*The Romantic Agony*, London, 1951, p. 475.)

10. Jack Smithers, *The Early Life and Vicissitudes of Jack Smithers* (London, 1939), pp. 28, 39.

11. Ibid., p. 40.

12. Marcus, op. cit., p. 279.

13. Beardsley to Heinemann, c. 9 January 1896. Princeton.

14. Beardsley to Persse, undated but on *Savoy* letterhead and addressed from 10 St. James's Place, London. Private collection.

15. Dowson to Henry Davray, Pont-Aven, c. 15 March 1896, in *The Letters of Ernest Dowson*, ed. Desmond Flower and Henry Maas (London, 1967), p. 345.

16. Symons, *Aubrey Beardsley*, p. 15. (For a vision Beardsley actually claimed to have seen, consult the next chapter.)

17. *Letters to Leonard Smithers*, X (undated). The connection of *solotaire* with *solitaire* is made by John Russell in "Why Beardsley is Back," *New York Times Magazine*, 5 February 1967, p. 55.

18. Beardsley to Smithers, undated letter. Princeton.

19. Beardsley to Mabel, undated but probably March 1896, from Paris. Princeton.

20. Vincent O'Sullivan, *Aspects of Wilde* (London, 1936), pp. 111-12.

21. Ibid., p. 113.

22. Beardsley to Smithers, Brussels, c. April 1896. Princeton.

23. *The Savoy*, No. 3, July 1896.

24. Beardsley to Smithers, postmarked 8 April 1896.

25. Beardsley to Smithers, Brussels, c. April 1896. Princeton.

Chapter 9

1. Ada Leverson to More Adey, c. 1895. Huntington Library.

2. Beardsley to Smithers, postmarked 12 August 1896. Huntington Library.

3. Introduction to *Uncollected Work*, and "Bookman's Memories," *Christian Science Monitor*, 17 May 1921, p. 3.

4. Yeats, *Autobiography*, pp. 216-17.

5. "Anne Southampton Bliss" [Gelett Burgess], "Our Clubbing List," *Le Petit Journal des Refusées*, Summer 1896.

6. Yvette Guilbert to Symons. Quoted in Catalogue #4 (Summer 1962), Winifred A. Myers (Autographs) Ltd, p. 36, item 191.

7. Influenced by the Greek vases Beardsley saw in the British Museum, they may have been equally affected by *Greek Vase Painting* (1894), the striking cover for which was done by his friend D. S. MacColl.

8. "The spirit of the play has been caught with true insight by the artist. Ribald and bawdily impudent, the illustrations have none of the prurience to be found in some of the earlier works [*Salome*?]; there is about them an air of maturity. Drawn without background, they were influenced by the Greek vases in the British Museum. Technically, they are superb, showing all Beardsley's mastery of his medium and sense of design...." (W. G. Good, "Aubrey Beardsley: A Reappraisal," *The Saturday Book* [Boston and Toronto, 1965], p. 76.)

9. Beardsley to Smithers, postmarked 27 September 1896. Huntington Library.

10. Quoted in full in *Letters to Leonard Smithers*.

11. "It is," a critic has faint-praised, ". . . one of the few bits of Aubrey Beardsley's work which is not arch, mischievous, or downright salacious...." As far as the quality of the translation from Catullus went, it was "quite respectable...." (Wendell Harris, "The Poetry of "The Savoy," *PMLA*, 77 [December 1962], 631.)

12. "There is little need to insist that Beardsley's genius dominated each number. *The Savoy* was Beardsley. Nevertheless, many writers contributed to its success.... All of them together, plus the technique of the publisher, sent it on its merry way. Beardsley gave it life and Smithers nursed it." (Jack Smithers, op. cit., p. 31.)

Chapter 10

1. O'Sullivan, op. cit., p. 115.

2. Beardsley to Smithers, 27 November [1896] and c. 28 November 1896 (postmarked 29 November 1896), both Huntington Library; David R. Clark, "Aubrey Beardsley's Drawing of the 'Shadows' in W. B. Yeats's *The Shadowy Waters*," *Modern Drama*, VII (December 1964), 267-72; W. B. Yeats (ed. David R. Clark and George Mayhew), *A Tower of Polished Stones. Early Versions of "The Shadowy Waters"* (Dublin, 1972).

3. O'Sullivan, op. cit., pp. 116-17. (O'Sullivan, obviously, was reporting those periods of pique with Dowson. There had been times when Beardsley, in better health, had enjoyed Dowson's company; and Dowson remained loyal.)

4. Ellen Beardsley to Ross, quoted as a footnote in the *Collected Letters*, p. 224.

5. Beardsley to Smithers, postmarked 13 December 1896. Huntington Library.

6. Elizabeth Robins Pennell, *Life and Letters of Joseph Pennell*, II (Boston, 1929), 310; also the Pennells' *Life of Whistler*, p. 345.

7. Gosse to Beardsley, 29 December 1896. Princeton.

8. Arthur H. Lawrence, "Mr. Aubrey Beardsley and His Work," the *Idler*, XI (March 1897), 189-202.

9. Sewell, p. 28.

10. Beardsley to Smithers, from Boscombe, postmarked 31 December 1896. Huntington Library.

11. Beardsley to Raffalovich, from Boscombe, no date but just prior to Christmas 1896. Oxford.

12. Beardsley to Julian Sampson, 22 March 1897, on the flyleaf of a presentation copy of Dowson's *Pierrot of the Minute*; the letter quoted in full in Malcolm Easton, "Aubrey Beardsley and Julian Sampson: An Unrecorded Friendship," *Apollo*, 59 (January 1967), 66.

13. Ibid.

14. Letter to H. C. Pollitt, 14 February 1897. Princeton.

15. Letters to Pollitt, 24 March 1897 and 26 March 1896 (postmarks). Princeton.

16. Ms. of "The Celestial Lover," 2 pp. Princeton.

17. Beardsley to Smithers, postmarked 25 March 1897. Princeton.

18. Beardsley to Raffalovich, c. 1 April 1897. Oxford.

19. D. J. Gordon, "Aubrey Beardsley at the V & A," *Encounter*, XXVII (October 1966), 13.

20. Roger Fry, "Aubrey Beardsley's Drawings," *Vision and Design* (New York, 1924), p. 236. (The essay first appeared in 1904.)

21. Beardsley to Raffalovich, c. February 1897, from Bournemouth. Oxford.

22. Reade (catalogue), pp. 10-11.

Chapter 11

1. Beardsley to Smithers, c. 11 April 1897, from Paris. Huntington Library.

2. Beardsley to Mabel, c. 26 April 1897, from Paris. Princeton.

3. Rothenstein, *Men and Memories*, pp. 317-18.

4. Beardsley to Mabel, c. 26 April 1897.

5. Beardsley to Davray, c. 30 April 1897. Princeton.

6. Beardsley to Smithers, postmarked 31 May 1897. Huntington Library.

7. Beardsley to Raffalovich, late May 1897, from St. Germain. Oxford.

8. Beardsley to Raffalovich, 31 May [1897], from St. Germain. Oxford.

9. Beardsley to Smithers, postmarked 11 June 1897, from St. Germain. Huntington Library.

10. O'Sullivan, op. cit. p. 77.

11. Wilde to Ross, 26 July [1897], in *Letters of Oscar Wilde*, p. 627.

12. Reprinted from the Stuart Mason *Bibliography* of Wilde in *Letters of Oscar Wilde*, p. 635n.

13. Wilde to Smithers [4 September 1897], in *Letters of Oscar Wilde*, p. 637.

14. Shortly after Beardsley's death, Wilde wrote from Paris to Smithers, "I was greatly shocked to read of poor Aubrey's death. Superbly premature as the flowering of his genius was, still he had immense development, and had not sounded his last stop. There were great possibilities always in the cavern of his soul, and there is something macabre and tragic in the fact that one who added another terror to life should have died at the age of a flower." (*Letters of Oscar Wilde*, p. 719.)

15. Beardsley to Smithers, 19 December [1897], from Menton, in R. A. Walker, *Letters to Leonard Smithers*, CLXXXIV.

16. John Rothenstein, *Conder*, pp. 135-6.

17. Atherton, op. cit., pp. 261-2. (Her correspondent was Mrs. Trulow, an American artist.)

18. E. R. and J. Pennell, *Whistler*, p. 352. (Whistler's wife, Trixie, had died in 1896 after a long, agonizing, illness.)

19. Beardsley to John Lane, postmarked 29 July 1897, from Dieppe. Bodleian Library, Oxford.

20. Beardsley to Mabel, prob. late October 1897. Princeton.

21. Beardsley to Mabel, late October or early November 1897. Princeton.

22. Beardsley to Smithers, 2 November 1897. Princeton.

23. Blanche, op. cit., p. 97.

24. *Letters to Leonard Smithers*, CLXXIV (19 December [1897]).

25. Beardsley to Smithers, 26 December [1897]. Princeton.

26. Beardsley to Raffalovich, 29 December [1897]. Princeton.

27. Extracted from Beardsley's 4 January 1898 ms. as published by R. A. Walker in *Miscellany*, pp. 87-8.

Chapter 12

1. Beardsley to Raffalovich, 11 January [1898], from Menton. Oxford.

2. *Miscellany*, p. 116.

3. Beardsley to Mabel, c. February 1898, from Menton. Princeton.

4. Beardsley to H. C. Pollitt, 22 February 1898, from Menton. Princeton.

5. Ellen Beardsley to Robert U. Johnson, 15 May [1898], from London. Princeton.

6. Beardsley to Leonard Smithers, postmarked 7 March 1898, from Menton. Huntington Library.

7. Mabel Beardsley to Robert Ross, c. 16 March 1898, in *Collected Letters of Aubrey Beardsley*, p. 440.

8. Ellen Beardsley to Robert U. Johnson.

9. From an account by Mrs. Beardsley in the possession of Mr. Donald Weeks; cited in Reade, *Aubrey Beardsley* (New York and London, 1967), p. 14.

10. W. B. Yeats to Lady Augusta Gregory, 11 February [1913]. in Wade, ed., *Letters of W. B. Yeats* (London, 1954), p. 575.

Chapter 13

1. Diaghilev to MacColl, 21 September 1898, in Arnold Haskell and Walter Nouvel, *Diaghileff* (New York, 1935), pp. 72-3.

2. Margery Morgan, *A Drama of Political Man* (London, 1961), p. 66.

3. Crosscurrents Modern Fiction edition (Carbondale & Edwardsville, Illinois, 1966), pp. 174-6.

4. Grant Richards, *Author Hunting* (London, 1934), p. 200.

5. "Flowering Rifle," II, 156.

6. Reproduced in James B. Meriwether's *The Literary Career of William Faulkner*, and quoted in Michael Millgate, *The Achievement of William Faulkner* (New York, 1966), pp. 8-9.

7. Millgate, ibid., pp. 8-9. A later, more detailed appraisal of Faulkner's extensive indebtedness to Beardsley appears in Addison C. Gross's "*Soldier's Pay* and the Art of Aubrey Beardsley," *American Quarterly*, XIX (Spring 1967), 3-23.

8. Kenneth Clark, "Out of the Black Lake," *Sunday Times*, 8 May 1966, p. 43.

9. *Stories of the Streets and of the Town from the Chicago Record 1893-1900*, ed. Franklin J. Meine (Chicago, 1941), p. 152.

10. Quoted in *Art Nouveau*, p. 184.

11. Ibid., p. 184.

12. Philippe Jullian, *Prince of Aesthetes: Count Robert de Montesquiou*, trans. John Haylock and Francis King (New York, 1968), pp. 177-8.

13. Ibid., p. 249.

14. A. Hyatt Mayor, *Prints and People: a social history of printed pictures* (New York, 1971), text accompanying illustration 707 (unpaged).

15. Kenneth Clark in the London *Sunday Times*, 8 May 1966.

16. Quoted in A. E. Gallatin, preface to the catalogue of the Beardsley Collection, Princeton University Library, 1952, p. 1.

Index

Printed in the United States
29688LVS00001BA/129

9 780595 008087